Rick Stein's
Fruits of the Sea

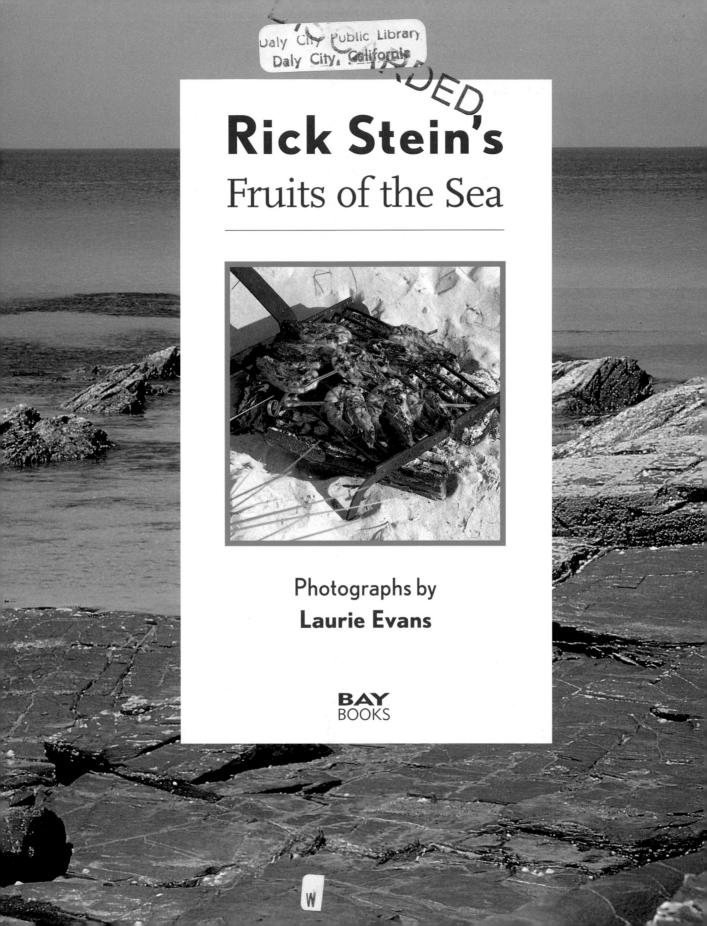

Rick Stein's
Fruits of the Sea

Photographs by
Laurie Evans

BAY
BOOKS

For my wife Jill and my boys Edward, Jack and Charles

First published in 1997 by BBC Books. North American Edition published 1998 by Bay Books & Tapes, Inc., by arrangement with BBC Books an imprint of BBC Worldwide Publishing.

This book is published to accompany the television series entitled *Fruits of the Sea*, which was first broadcast in 1997. The series is a production of BBC Television by Denham Productions and directed by David Pritchard.

Bay Books may be purchased for education, business, or sales promotional use at attractive quantity discounts.   For information, address: Bay Books & Tapes, Inc., 555 De Haro Street, No. 220, San Francisco, CA 94107.

Publisher: James Connolly
Art Director: Jeffrey O'Rourke
Design: David Albertson Design, San Francisco
Production: Ken Rackow
American Editor: Sharon Silva
Proofreader: Marianna Cherry

Library of Congress Cataloguing-in-Publication Data

Stein, Rick.
        Fruits of the Sea / Rick Stein: photographs by Graham Kirk.
            p.   cm.
        Reprint. Previously published: London: BBC Books.
        "Companion to the Public Television series."
        Includes index.
        ISBN 0-912333-48-0
        1. Cookery (Fish) 2. Cookery (Seafood) 3. Cookery,
International.   I. Taste of the Sea (Television program).
II. Title
        TX747.S664   1997   97-43584
        641.6'92–dc21   CIP

ISBN 0-912333-48-0

Printed in China

10 9 8 7 6 5 4 3 2 1

Distributed to the trade by Publishers Group West

Acknowledgements: Special thanks to Debbie Major for testing all the recipes, typing most of them, and generally being a great person to talk about food with. But also those long-suffering chefs at The Seafood Restaurant, particularly Paul Ripley and David Pope who had to stop what they were doing to provide us with fish, vegetables, and fruit for all the recipes. Thanks, yet again, to Heather Holden-Brown, Anna Ottewilol, Ippa Middleton, Isobel Gillian, and Frank Phillips at BBC Books for their serious professionalism and, again, sorry about the deadlines everyone! I'd also like to thank Laurie Evans who came down and took all the wonderful photographs in this book and put me thorough an extremely busy but fun two weeks all around Padstow.

Lastly thanks to David Pritchard, the best director of cookery programs in the business, and the rest of the crew, Julian, Tom, Maggin, Johnny and Phil, for being such fun to work with, even when we were bickering about things like those simple dishes, remember! And last, but not least, that small modest dog Chalk, who somehow doesn't realize he's famous.

Author's Note: Seven recipes in this book have been repeated from my first book *Taste of the Sea*. This is because I have demonstrated them in the new series *Fruits of the Sea*.

Contents

Introduction

"I wonder if you'd mind signing this book for my husband? He's gone out to the car at the moment and I know he'd be too embarrassed to ask you himself."

"Of course," I said. "But why didn't he want to ask me?"

"Well," she said, "he'd never cooked anything before I bought him your book (*Taste of the Sea*) but he saw your TV series and everything you cooked on the series he wanted to try himself, so I bought the book for him and he's never looked back."

"Gosh," I said. "You couldn't have said anything more complimentary if you'd really thought about it."

Her husband came back and I quickly signed his book and gave it to him.

"I hear you're quite interested in cooking," I said.

"Well, yes, sort of," he said shyly, almost looking the other way, obviously not wanting to make a fuss.

"Your wife says you quite liked the TV series."

"I did actually," he said, now becoming a little more animated. "I really did, I thought it was wonderful. I thought you cooked dishes that I would like to eat and you didn't make it all seem too difficult or too technical."

Then, even more enthusiastically, he began talking about how his love of fish had grown out of watching the series, and how he'd been given the book by his wife and had cooked well over half the recipes, and that he would never have believed that fish could taste so good.

After that, I felt I had to write another book. In fact, when I wrote my last book, *Taste of the Sea*, I got rather overenthusiastic and had to cut fifty recipes out of it. So, I wanted to write a second book to incorporate those fifty recipes and lots of other dishes that I've always wanted to get down on paper, particularly lots of easy dishes designed to persuade harassed people living in the twentieth century to cook fish. I've written this book and blow me if I haven't had to cut out another fifty recipes. →

Facing page: Stir-fried Salt and Pepper Shrimp (see p. 56).

I wanted to have a whole chapter about spicy fish. Actually, initially I wanted to write a whole book about fish with spice to include the exotic delights of prawn masala, Sichuan squid, seafood laksa, tom yam gung, a Thai fish stew (tasted in Australia, of all places, which was served a bit like bouillabaisse but blew the top of my head off), a deep-fried whole fish with chopped chili and garlic that I once had at Hua Hin in Thailand, some hot little Moroccan fish dishes with charmoula, and those wonderful fish tacos you get in the Baja California in Mexico. I certainly could have made a whole book out of my fascination with this area of fish cookery. But then, last time I was in Australia, I showed *Taste of the Sea* to some people who said how nostalgic it made them feel for good old northern European butter sauces, and I realized that to include a variety of recipes to cater for all tastes is probably a good thing after all.

I also wanted to include a selection of fish dishes from colder climates with warming, comforting buttery sauces, braised and baked dishes, the sort of food that makes you think of convivial eating on winter nights, perhaps in a rented house near a windswept, foam-splattered beach in Cornwall.

I then thought of a section on what I love to call handheld food—all those parcels, pasties, tacos and turnovers particularly well suited to cooking with fish. How lacking in joy are pasties served with a knife and fork; they're for fishermen and miners, and for sailors to take a satisfying bite between splicing the mainsail.

Then I thought of a section where I wouldn't make any bones about the fact that the recipes were hard to do, required a good deal of work in the kitchen but where the results would be elegant and deft and would impress and delight friends at a special dinner.

To balance this, I then put together a selection of light lunch dishes that would double up as simple first courses for a more elaborate evening meal and, last but not least, I included an area of cooking that is very dear to me but which I've never been able to put in a book before—puddings. Why not finish the book with a dozen or so of my favorite desserts, the sort of things that are so well loved at my restaurant? With both of my previous books, quite a few people have expressed their disappointment that they didn't include any of those wonderful sweet dishes, so, at last, here they are.

One of the criticisms of my first TV series, which I made in 1995, was that I used seafood of a quality very few people could get hold of. Therefore, in spite of the fact that the recipes were simple, they remained rather impracticable, rather exclusive. I appreciate the problem but I feel I must still use the best ingredients and encourage you to do so. At the risk of sounding flippant, I could hardly imagine introducing a recipe on television with, "This dish is ideal for making with stale cod."

Don't think, incidentally, that curry is the answer either. What is that old saying about silk purses and sows' ears? But while I'm on the subject, the recipe on p. 185 for *Deep-fried Shredded Fish Wrapped in Lettuce with Chili, Shrimp and Cilantro* just might fit the bill for not perfect, top-quality or well-flavored fish. Fish markets do not always offer the best-quality fish and it's not usually their fault but rather the lack of brisk turnover in their shops. The more I can interest you in the quality, the more fish will get sold, the more demanding customers will become and we'll all benefit.

For this book, wherever possible, I bought fish at shops that most of us use—supermarkets and fish markets—and I also made sure that the majority of the recipes use fish that are easily obtained. Having said that, however, I still like to include the occasional recipe using something quite special like *Spiny Lobster with Vanilla Sauce* on p. 140 or *Salad of Grilled Garfish with Fennel Seeds* on p. 93.

A further criticism of my last book was that many of the recipes are too complicated for ordinary cooks. I'd like to think this isn't really true, but nevertheless I've taken note and included a whole chapter of dishes that are quick and simple to prepare. And I've tried to simplify all the recipes in this book as much as possible by suggesting, for example, that you use ready-made pasta and puff pastry, or make mayonnaise and hollandaise in a blender. But, just to keep the serious cooks happy, I've also slipped in the long way round as well.

About twenty years ago, in the early days at my restaurant, I went through a bit of a crisis of confidence about what I was doing cooking in a small kitchen in a small fishing port miles from anywhere. We weren't very busy then and were only just making ends meet. Few people seemed particularly interested in eating fish. My wife, Jill, and I seriously considered moving back to Oxfordshire where I originally came from. We thought we'd carry on selling mostly fish dishes but some meat dishes too and make a living in a place where people really took an interest in food. I used to play rugby with the Cornish comedian Jethro and I asked him why he didn't come to the restaurant at all.

"I don't like fish," he said.
"Look, Jethro, we sell meat too," I retorted.
"It'd still taste of fish."

Well, I stuck it out. I suppose I always felt that there was something special and worth shouting about in freshly landed fish, simply cooked, and so it seems to have turned out.

I'll have to have another word with that Jethro.

Preparing Fish

I'm really pleased to be able to include some proper step-by-step photographs showing you how to prepare raw fish. I've always felt that filleting, gutting and scaling are much more straightforward operations than most people think, and I hope these simple steps will allay any fears you might have about these processes. The bold type refers to the actions in the photos. Don't forget that there are always plenty of trimmings left over that can be turned into wonderful stocks, particularly the shells from the prawns (see p. 18).

Cleaning Round Fish

1. Trim the fish by snipping off the fins with kitchen scissors. **Working over several sheets of newspaper or under cold running water, remove the scales by scraping the fish from tail to head with a blunt, thick-bladed knife or a fish scaler.** With some very delicate-skinned fish, such as sardines and small herrings, you can simply rub off the scales with your thumb.

2. To remove the guts, slit open the belly from the anal fin (two-thirds of the way down the fish from the head) up toward the head. **Pull out most of the guts with your hand,** cut away any pieces of the entrails left behind and then wash out the cavity with plenty of cold water.

3. To remove the gills, **pull open the gill flaps and cut them away from the two places where they join the fish, at the back of the head and under the mouth.**

Filleting Large Round Fish (such as sea bass and salmon)

1. Lay the fish on a chopping board and **cut closely around the head in a V-shape** so that you don't lose too much of the fillet.

2. Lay the fish with its back toward you. **Cut along the length of the back, keeping the blade of the knife above the horizontal back bones.**

3. Starting at the head, cut the fillet away from the bones, keeping the blade as close to them as you can. Once you have released some of the fillet, **lift it up with your fingers to make it easier to see where you are cutting.** When you near the rib bones that surround the intestines, if they are thick enough, cut as close to them as you can (with hake, for example); if very fine, cut through them and then remove the bones from the fillet with tweezers afterward.

Turn the fish over and repeat on the other side.

Filleting Small Round Fish (such as small sea bass, mackerel, herring and trout)

1. Lay the fish on a chopping board with its back toward you. **Cut around the back of the head, through the flesh of the fillet down to the backbone.**

2. Turn the knife toward the tail and, beginning just behind the head, carefully start to cut the fillet away from the bones, down toward the belly.

3. Once you have loosened enough flesh to enable you to get the whole blade of the knife underneath the fillet, **rest a hand on top of the fish and cut away the fillet in one clean sweep right down to the tail, keeping the blade close to the bones as you do so.** Remove any small bones left in the fillet with a pair of tweezers.

Turn the fish over and repeat on the other side.

Cleaning Flat Fish

1. To remove the guts, locate the gut cavity by pressing on the white side of the fish just below the head until you find an area that is much softer. Make a small incision across this area (if you wish to remove any roe at this stage, make a slightly longer incision) and pull out the guts (and roe if you wish) with your little finger. Trim the fish by snipping off the fins with kitchen scissors.

Dover sole and petrale sole are the only flat fish that need cleaning. **If you do need to scale them, follow the method for round fish on p. 11.**

Filleting Flat Fish

1. You will get 4 fillets from one flat fish. Lay the fish on a chopping board and cut around the back of the head and across the tail. **Then cut through the skin down the center of the fish, very slightly to one side of the raised backbone, working from the head down to the tail.**

2. Starting where the backbone meets the head, slide the blade of the knife under the corner of one of the fillets. **Carefully cut it away from the bones, folding the released fillet back as you do so.** Keep the blade of the knife almost flat and as close to the bones as possible. Remove the adjacent fillet in the same way.

Turn the fish over and repeat on the other side.

Skinning Fillets of Fish

1. Place the fillet skin-side down on a chopping board, with the narrowest (tail) end nearest to you. **Angling the blade of the knife down toward the skin, start to cut between the flesh and the skin until a little flap is released.**

2. Flip the flap of fish over. **Firmly take hold of the skin and, working away from you, continue to cut along its length, sawing with the knife from side to side and keeping the blade of the knife close against the skin.**

Filleting Monkfish

1. You may need to skin the monkfish tail before you start. **Hold the thick end of the tail in one hand and the skin in the other. Briskly tear off the skin, which should come away quite easily.**

2. Cut through the fish along either side of the thick backbone, keeping the blade of the knife as close to the bone as possible.

3. You now need to remove the membrane that encases the fillets of fish; otherwise it will shrink during cooking, causing the fish to twist unattractively. Pull away as much as possible with your fingers. Remove as much of the remainder as you can with a sharp knife by releasing a flap of the membrane with the knife and then **cutting it away by sawing from side to side** (as if you are skinning an ordinary fish fillet, see opposite), being careful not to cut away too much of the flesh.

Preparing Squid

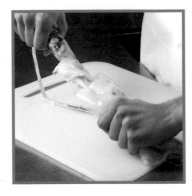

1. Grasp the head in one hand and the body in the other. Gently pull the head and it should come away easily, taking the milky white intestines with it. You may like to retain the ink sac, which will be in the intestines—it will be pearly-white in color with a slight blue tinge. You can also save the 2 pieces of muscle running down either side of the intestines. The rest of the intestines can be discarded.

2. Cut off the tentacles from the head, then discard the head. Squeeze out the beaklike mouth from the center of the tentacles, **cut it off** and discard. The tentacles can either be separated or left intact if very small.

3. Reach into the body and **pull out the plasticlike quill** and the soft white roe, if there is any.

4. Pull off the two fins from either side of the body pouch. Then **pull away the purple, semitransparent skin from both the body and the fins.** Wash the pouch out with water. If the pouch is too long and narrow for you to reach right down inside when cleaning (and you are not planning to stuff it), a trick for cleaning it out thoroughly is to cut off the very tip and then wash it out with running water, squeezing out any residue as you do so.

Cleaning Mussels

1. Wash the mussels in plenty of cold water and scrub the shells with a stiff brush. **Use a knife to scrape off any barnacles that are sticking to them.**

2. Discard any open mussels that do not close when lightly tapped on the work surface. **Pull out the tough, fibrous beards** protruding from the tightly closed shells.

Opening Oysters

1. Scrub any grit and sand off the oyster shells. Wrap one hand in a tea towel and hold the oyster in it, with the more bowl-shaped half of the shell underneath and the flatter shell on top. Take an oyster knife or small, thick-bladed knife in your other hand. **Push the point of the knife into the hinge of the oyster, located at the narrowest point.** Work the knife forward and backward between the two halves of the shell to break the hinge. As the hinge breaks, twist the point of the knife to lever the top shell upward.

2. Now slide the knife under the top shell to sever the ligament that joins the oyster to the shell. The ligament is slightly right of center in the shell. **Lift off the top shell,** trying not to let any fragments fall on to the oyster and keeping the bottom shell upright so as not to lose any of the juice. Pick out any little pieces of shell that might have broken off into the oyster.

Preparing Shrimp

1. Firmly twist the head away from the body and discard. or use for stock. Turn the shrimp over and **break open the soft shell along the belly, then carefully peel it away from the flesh.** For some recipes you may wish to leave the tail section in place.

2. With some large raw shrimp you may need to remove the intestinal tract, which looks like a thin black vein running down the back of the shrimp flesh. Run the tip of a small knife down the back of the shrimp and then **lift up and pull out the vein.**

Preparing Scallops

1. Wash the scallops in plenty of cold water. Hold the scallop flat shell uppermost and **slide the blade of a filleting knife between the shells.** Keeping the blade flat against the top shell, feel for the ligament that joins the shell to the muscle meat of the scallop and cut through it.

2. Lift off the top shell and **pull out the black stomach sac and the frilly "skirt,"" which surrounds the white scallop meat and bright orange coral.** Cut the scallop meat away from the bottom shell.

3. Pull off and discard the small white ligament that is attached to the side of the scallop meat.

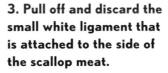

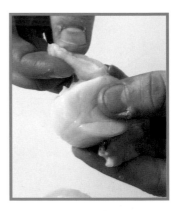

Removing the Meat from a Cooked Lobster

1. Twist off the larger claw arms and the legs. Cut away any bands binding the claws together. Break the claw arms apart at the joints and then **crack the shell with the back of a knife blade** or a hammer.

2. Remove the meat from each section of the claws in as large pieces as possible.

3. Now cut the lobster in half lengthwise. **Lift out the intestinal tract that runs down the center of the meat,** then remove the meat from the tail section.

4. Remove the soft, greenish tomalley (liver) and any red roe from the head and tail (these are edible). Use the rest of the head, all the shell pieces and the legs to make Shellfish Stock (see p. 214).

5. If you wish to remove the tail meat in one piece for slicing into discs, don't cut the lobster in half lengthwise; instead, detach the head from the tail and then cut the head in half and remove the tomalley and roe. Turn the tail section over and

cut along either side of the flat undershell with scissors. Lift back the flap and take out the meat. Slice as required and remove the intestinal tract from each slice with the point of a sharp knife.

Removing the Meat from a Cooked Crab

1. Break off the tail flap from the underside of the crab. **Twist off the 2 larger claw arms and the legs.**

2. Break the legs at the joints and, unless the crabs are large, discard all but the first largest joint. Crack the shells with the back of a knife blade or a hammer, then **use a crab pick to remove the meat.**

3. Break the claw arms apart at the joints and then crack the shells as before, trying not to shatter them completely. **Remove the meat from each section in as large pieces as possible.**

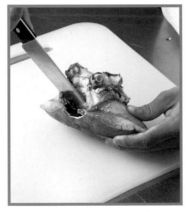

4. Remove the meat from the claws, discarding the very thin, flat bone from the center of the meat.

5. Detach the body of the crab from the back shell by inserting a sturdy knife between them and giving it a firm twist, then lifting out the body.

6. To remove the meat from the body, first **pull off and discard the inedible "dead men's fingers."** These are the feathery-looking gills attached to either side of the body and there will be about 12 of them, varying in size.

7. Now cut the body section into quarters with a large knife. **Using a crab pick, extract the white meat from the little channels in the body,** being careful not to let any small pieces of the wafer-thin shell get mixed in.

8. To remove the brown meat from the back shell, first remove the stomach sac by **pressing firmly on a little piece of shell located just behind the eyes. The bone and the stomach will come away together.**

9. Pour away any excess water from the back shell and then **scoop out the thin layer of brown meat.** If it is still firm, you will be able to lift it out in one piece; otherwise, scrape it out with a teaspoon. Cut it into small pieces if you wish.

Unusual Ingredients

Most of the ingredients used in this book, particularly the seafood, are easy to get hold of, but one of my real enthusiasms as a cook is borrowing ideas from cuisines all over the world, and inevitably there are some things that haven't quite made it to the main-street shops or supermarkets yet. However, I continue to be delighted by the speed with which supermarkets get new products onto their shelves these days. It is a competitive game from which we customers can only benefit. Just in case you might think that everything to do with food is better in France, I do think that our supermarkets have a much bigger range of food than those in France. Try buying a jar of fennel seeds or star anise there, and, as for wine, I wouldn't be surprised if the average Frenchman was unaware that wine is produced in Australia, California and South Africa. We still lag behind a bit with fresh food, and I keep hoping that one day I will sit down at a simple enamel table in an out-of-town shopping center and eat freshly opened oysters, mussels, just boiled conch and shrimp, all served up with mayonnaise, shallot vinegar and a cold bottle of white Côtes du Rhône – which was just what I did last time I was in France.

All of the ingredients mentioned here are now quite easy to get hold of, but for those of you who are unfamiliar with them the following advice and information might be useful.

Candle Nuts and Macadamia Nuts Candle nuts are originally from Indonesia, and macadamias from Australia. Both are round with exceptionally hard shells and are similar in flavor, being rich and creamy. Candle nuts are much used in Malaysian and Indonesian cookery for adding richness and as a thickener for curries. Either is pretty essential to the Malaysian *Laksa* (p. 40), but I find that cashew nuts, though different in flavor, have a similar rich, sweet creaminess.

Chilies In order to try to establish some sort of common heat factor, I mention just two types of chilies—finger and bird's-eye. The difference between red and green chilies is merely a question of ripeness. In Britain, our understanding of different types of chili is not yet advanced enough to be more specific. By finger chili I mean cayenne chilies, those most commonly available, which are thin, about as long as your finger and medium hot. There are also some slightly more snub-nosed chilies readily available that are less hot but can be used instead of finger chilies in the recipes. Bird's-eye chilies are those tiny red or green ones often found in Asian food shops that are always blindingly hot. The heat-producing substance in chilies is called capsaicin and is measured in Scoville units that have been simplified into a chart from 1 (very mild) to 10 (awfully hot). Finger chilies are about 3 and bird's-eye 9.

The hottest chilies I know are called habanero, which are a clear 10.

Pasilla chilies, from Mexico, are particularly good with seafood. They are a dried chili, usually 6 to 8 inches in length and an inch or so wide. Their dark, wrinkled forms carry a deep flavor reminiscent of cocoa. Look for them in Latin American markets.

Crabmeat There are many recipes using crabmeat in this book and, though I tend to say that freshly dressed crabmeat is best, I think that either chilled pasteurized crabmeat or frozen is a perfectly good substitute, since the task of dressing crabs is time-consuming. Personally, though, when time allows, I like jobs like picking crab. I get myself a couple of bowls and a bucket for the debris, pour myself a glass of wine, put on some Mozart, then sit outside next to the herb garden and relax.

Creamed Coconut and Coconut Milk Creamed coconut is sold in a small, hard block. Small pieces chipped straight off the block are ideal stirred into sauces and curries to thicken them toward the end of cooking. It can also be dissolved in an equal quantity of hot water to make coconut milk, also best added at the end of cooking as it has a tendency to separate quite quickly.

Coconut milk can be bought in cans and is used in most soupy Thai curries and a lot of southern Indian, Sri Lankan and Southeast Asian dishes. By not shaking the can before opening it, you can lift off the cream that forms on the top of the milk and use it separately as required. But, in most cases, just shake well before opening. If you want to make your own fresh coconut milk, simply remove the flesh from the coconut shell and peel off the brown skin. Finely grate the flesh, put it into a blender with 2 cups of very hot water to every 8 ounces (about 2 cups) of coconut and blend for a few seconds. Strain through a cheesecloth-lined sieve and then squeeze out all the liquid. The liquid can be left to settle for a while and the cream skimmed off the top to use separately.

Curry Leaves These lend a distinctive flavor to curries and other Indian dishes and fresh ones can often be found in Asian groceries and some of the larger supermarkets. They can be frozen in plastic bags for later use. There is no real substitute, so simply omit them if you can't find any.

Fennel Seeds I share a passion with Italians for fennel seeds. I love those dishes of pork and rabbit with garlic, white wine and fennel seeds that you get in parts of Umbria. Fennel seeds go exceptionally well with fish, too. Look for them in the spice section of your supermarket or specialty-food store. You might also try collecting them from wild fennel plants growing along roadsides.

Fish Sauce Fish sauce, or *nam pla,* as it is known in Thailand, is a salty fish liquid derived from the salting of anchovies. It is an essential ingredient in Thai and other Southeast Asian cuisines. It has a slightly fishy but not unpleasant salty taste and, when combined with lime, lemongrass, chili and cilantro, forms a basic flavoring alliance for many Thai, Vietnamese and Laotian dishes. Available in most supermarkets, it should be fairly clear and not too brown. If you can't get hold of it, the best alternative is a light soy sauce or anchovy paste.

Galangal Galangal, a rhizome root related to ginger, is available in most Asian food shops. You may find it a bit too unusual on the first few tries; all I can say is persevere. Ginger is a perfect substitute.

Kaffir Lime Leaves The leaves of a gnarled and thick-skinned lime that has almost juiceless fruit. You can buy dried kaffir lime leaves in jars quite easily now. Use the zest of lime as a substitute. If you can get the fruit of the kaffir lime, the zest is well worth adding to dishes such as the *Green Monkfish and Shrimp Curry* on p. 66.

Lemongrass I think this is the single most recognizable flavor in Thai cooking, the thick, moist stem of a tropical grass with a lovely lemony taste and smell. Incidentally, lemongrass does grow reasonably well in greenhouses over here and even outdoors in summer. Just buy a stem or two and put in moist potting compost. There is no real alternative to lemongrass but, in a pinch, you could use lemon zest.

Palm Sugar A moist, light, soft brown sugar made from the sap of the coconut palm, palm sugar is ideal for use in Thai dishes. Indeed, sugar is used to great effect in Thai savory cooking, as the dipping sauce for the *Thai Fish Cakes with Green Beans* on p. 57 will confirm. The secret lies in combining sugar with lime juice or vinegar, fish sauce and often chili. This pleasing combination of opposites—sweet and sour, salty and hot—is a system that underlies much Chinese cooking. It is an approach that I think Western cooking could use a lot more, though, funnily enough, this is what has made fish-and-chips with salt and malt vinegar such a winner. A good substitute would be soft dark brown sugar, which has a strong molasses flavor.

Preserved Lemon This is a North African way of keeping lemons. You just leave them in brine and in three or four weeks they soften and lose their bitterness. They are great in salads and finely chopped in sauces, as in the *Moroccan Fish Tagine* on p. 30. See p. 220 in the Basics chapter for my own recipe for preserved lemons.

Rices There are numerous types of rice available today from all around the world. Each one is very individual in both taste and texture.

Basmati Rice This is from the northern regions of India and has a distinctive flavor and delicate texture. It must be rinsed with water before cooking to remove the excess starch so that the grains remain separate and fluffy during cooking. You can soak the rice, too, if you wish. Some claim that it needs soaking for up to 20 minutes, but I find that the grains break up too much during cooking and that 5 minutes is sufficient.

Thai Jasmine Rice As the name suggests, this is a jasmine-scented rice from Thailand. It is similar in appearance to basmati rice but is more sticky and tends to cling together in small clumps during cooking. The perfect authentic accompaniment to all the Thai curries in this book.

Arborio Rice This is just one type of Italian medium-grain rice, essential for making risotto because it breaks down during cooking to produce the creamy texture required in the final dish. Other varieties include Carnaroli, Maratelli, Roma or Nano Vialone. There is no substitute for risotto rice, but happily it is now widely available.

Valencia Rice This is the classic Spanish rice used to make the authentic paella. Unfortunately, it is not widely available, unless, of course, you are lucky enough to live near a Spanish deli or specialty-food shop. However, through trial and error, I have found arborio rice is a very respectable alternative.

Rice Vinegar A clear vinegar called for in many Chinese dishes, especially the well-known sweet-and-sour sauces. It's not easily available, but a good substitute is to mix three parts white wine vinegar with one part water and a little superfine sugar.

Rice Wine This is used extensively in China and is made from glutinous rice, yeast and water. It is usually only available from Chinese markets but a dry/fino sherry makes a good substitute.

Salted Black Beans and Black Bean Sauce Salted black beans are available in Asian food shops and are much used in Chinese cooking—so much so that I would identify them as one of the definitive flavors. I haven't yet seen them in supermarkets but I wouldn't be surprised if they are on the shelves soon. They need to be rinsed to remove the excess salt and chopped before using. If you can't get them, use black bean sauce instead, but preferably the variety in which the beans are not totally puréed.

Sesame Oil I use both cold-pressed and Asian roasted sesame oil. The cold-pressed oil is light, delicate and fragrant and ideal for dishes such as the *Warm Crab Pancakes with Lemongrass and Cilantro* on p. 173, whereas roasted sesame oil, which is much stronger, is ideal for robust dishes full of spice.

Shrimp There are lots of recipes using shrimp in this book, largely because good-quality, large cooked and raw shrimp are now so easy to get hold of.

North Atlantic Shrimp Very good value, and the most commonly seen in fishmongers, these are sold both peeled and in the shell. The shells and the whole shrimp are ideal for making *Shellfish Stock* (p. 214).

Mediterranean Shrimp or Crevettes These are long, thin shrimp with very curly antennae, usually sold cooked. They are common throughout the Mediterranean but these days, although the small ones are still fished locally, the larger ones usually come from the waters of Madagascar. They are especially good served with an olive oil mayonnaise.

Raw Shrimp I have rather unceremoniously lumped together all the raw shrimp, which make up a number of different species. In Australia they have 13 different commercial species, all of which are probably represented in what you buy in fishmongers' and supermarkets both frozen and chilled. Generally I have specified headless unshelled shrimp in the recipes but occasionally the look of a whole shrimp will make all the difference, as with the *Tandoori Prawns* on p. 64.

Shrimp Paste, Blachan, Balachow, Dried Shrimp The process of salting and drying tiny shrimp is common all over the tropical and equatorial countries of the world. The result is sold as either a dry block or a paste, or simply loose as dried shrimp. The block and paste have a pretty unpalatable smell and taste but a little stir-fried with garlic and ginger gives a background flavor to many memorable dishes, like *Tom Yam Gung* from Thailand (p. 32) or *Laksa* from Malaysia and Indonesia (p. 40). With shrimp paste I'm always reminded of that phrase from the Bible: "the stone that the builders rejected has become the head of the corner." I feel much the same way about conch and the humble periwinkle. With a willingness not to waste what is, after all, good food, and a little adroitness, those seemingly unimportant raw materials can be transformed into the main attraction.

Soy Sauce Made from fermented and salted soy beans, soy sauce can be either dark or light and varies in flavor from salty to sweet. In most of my recipes I use dark soy sauce, and in my opinion the Japanese variety is the one to go for, as it has a superior, slightly sweeter flavor. Having said that, Chinese soy sauce does the job very well, too.

Spring Roll and Wonton Wrappers Both of these are available from Chinese markets and some well-stocked supermarkets. There is no real substitute for the characteristic texture of wonton wrappers, but for the recipe for *Deep-fried Shrimp Wontons with Chili Jam* (see p. 86) and for the *Spring Rolls with Squid, Crab, Bean Sprouts and Shiitake Mushrooms* (see p. 188), you could use filo pastry instead.

Star Anise This is a very useful spice for fish cookery. It is quite easy to get in good food shops and is always on sale in Asian food stores. I often sprinkle some in a fish stock for a subtle aniseed hint.

Sichuan Pepper A characteristic flavor of Chinese cookery that manages to be both peppery hot and yet slightly tart and has the effect of numbing the mouth a little. Also called anise pepper, it is not in fact a true pepper but comes from a type of ash tree.

Tamarind The pods of the tamarind tree, tamarind is usually sold in a rectangular block complete with seeds, which are as hard as small black stones. You normally mix the pulp with warm water and pick out the seeds. The paste can then be used in many types of curries, where its acid and scented flavor acts like the juice of citrus fruits, lime or lemon, both of which can be used as an alternative. Tamarind is now also available ready-prepared in jars.

Wasabi Paste This fiercely hot Japanese green horse-radish paste is fairly easy to get hold of now in larger supermarkets and Asian food stores. It is the essential accompaniment to the Japanese raw fish dish sashimi.

White Pepper In most of my recipes I use freshly ground black pepper, but in one or two instances I have called for white pepper. This is because it has a less assertive flavor than its black counterpart, and is better suited to some dishes made with delicately flavored fish. I also use it in butter sauces and in mayonnaise simply because it is less visible in the finished product.

Soups, Stews and Clear Broths

I've just come back from a week in Provence of *bouillabaisses* and *bourrides*. I've certainly never eaten so many robust fish stews in such a short time. After a particularly fierce *bourride* I woke up in the middle of the night thinking I was going to die of indigestion from the garlic. *Bourride* is not a dish for eating at night, and I think the Marseillais would regard it as very odd if you did, but then I was a foolish tourist.

At Restaurant Patalain near the Vieux Port of Marseilles I ate a *bouillabaisse* of such distinction that a nagging doubt I have about most fish stews was temporarily dispelled. Since then it has returned: fish stews usually involve boiling all the goodness out of the fish so that you are left with a well-flavored bouillon but a lot of dry and tasteless fish. It seems to me that, unless the fish is combined with overwhelming flavors, the only way to make fish stews successfully is to cook the fish and soup separately—or, if you do want to cook the fish in the bouillon, to add it at the very last minute. Most of the fish stews in this chapter have been made with this principle in mind, particularly the *bouillabaisse-* and *bourride*-inspired dishes, *Mediterranean Fish Soup* (see p. 28) and *A Small Stew of Bass, Squid, Mussels and Shrimp with a Warm Aïoli Sauce* (see p. 34). The *Moroccan Fish Tagine* on p. 30 was entirely changed from the original recipe because that just didn't work for me.

One of my favorite recipes in this chapter is *Seafood in a Crab and Ginger Broth* (see p. 36). It does require a great deal of work but the result is well worth it. When we were filming it, it occurred to me that cooking dishes like this is a bit like ballet dancing. The dancers look as light as feathers, their movements effortless, the pirouetting as if it were just an extension of walking, but then, if you saw them backstage afterward, sweating, their joints aching, you would realize the labor of love that has gone into their performance. And, in a way, it's the same cooking this dish. The broth seems to be an effortless, clear, clean, light creation but in fact a long process of boiling, clarifying, straining and neat cutting has gone into making it. I like that.

Facing page: Seafood in a Crab and Ginger Broth (see p. 36).

Mediterranean Fish Soup

Serves 8

1   small searobin or sea bass, weighing about 1 pound

1   goatfish, weighing about $^3/_4$ pound

1   small monkfish tail, weighing about 1 pound

$^1/_4$ pound prepared squid (see p. 16)

20   small mussels, cleaned (see p. 17)

$^2/_3$ cup white wine

1   fennel bulb, trimmed

1   red onion

1   leek

2   celery stalks

1   red bell pepper

5   plum tomatoes, peeled

6   small new potatoes, weighing about 6 ounces in total

$^1/_2$ cup olive oil

6   garlic cloves, thinly sliced

2   orange zest strips, cut into very thin shreds

•   A good pinch of red pepper flakes

2   teaspoons sun-dried tomato paste

20   turns of the black-pepper mill

2   young, fresh bay leaves, finely shredded

•   Leaves from 1 fresh thyme sprig, finely chopped

2   tablespoons chopped fresh fennel tops or dill

3   tablespoons Pernod or Ricard

This soup contains the type of fish you would normally associate with the Mediterranean and the flavors are those of a bouillabaisse: *saffron, orange, tomato, fennel, olive oil and a little Pernod. The vegetables are cut very neatly into small pieces, as is the fish, so that you are left with a sort of mini* bouillabaisse *to serve as a first course. The supreme advantage of this dish is that the fish is cut into such small pieces that it can be cooked very quickly at the last minute and tastes fresh and clean. The problem with most versions of* bouillabaisse *is that the fish often tastes as though all the flavor has been boiled out of it and while you get a very well-flavored soup the fish itself is rather dull.*

I like to serve some fresh baguettes with this that you dip into a little good olive oil and sea salt.

Fillet the searobin or sea bass, goatfish and monkfish (see p. 13 and p. 15). Make a fish stock with the bones (see p. 212), using about 2 quarts water.

Cut the squid lengthwise along one side of the pouch and open it out. Cut the squid and the fish fillets lengthwise into strips $^3/_4$ inch wide, then cut across each strip into slices $^1/_2$ inch wide. All the pieces of fish should be the same size and shape.

Put the mussels in a pan with a splash of the white wine, cover and cook over high heat for 3 to 4 minutes, until they have opened. Discard any that remain closed. Strain the mussel cooking liquor into the fish stock, then shell the mussels, discarding the shells.

Cut the fennel bulb and red onion into 6 to 8 wedges so that each wedge measures about $^3/_4$ inch at its thickest part. Cut the leek lengthwise into quarters and the celery stalks lengthwise in half. Cut the red pepper lengthwise into strips $^3/_4$ inch wide and the tomatoes and potatoes lengthwise into 4 wedges. Then cut each of the vegetables across into thin, arclike slices, making sure that they are all roughly the same size and shape—this is very important to the final look of the soup.

Heat the olive oil in a large pan—if you have a suitable oven-to-table one, this would be ideal. Otherwise just use a large saucepan and transfer the soup to a tureen to serve. Add the fennel, red onion, leek, celery, red pepper, garlic, orange zest and red pepper flakes. Cook over low heat for about 4 minutes, or until the vegetables are just softened. Add the sun-dried tomato paste, fish stock, remaining white wine, tomatoes, potatoes, salt and pepper. Bring to the boil and simmer for 5 minutes.

- Salt
- Extra-virgin olive oil, coarse sea salt and sliced ciabatta or French bread, to serve

Add the fish, plus the bay leaves, thyme, half the fennel tops or dill and the Pernod or Ricard. Simmer for 3 minutes only (otherwise you will overcook the fish), adding the mussels for the final 30 seconds.

Sprinkle the soup with the remaining fennel or dill and take to the table, together with little bowls of extra-virgin olive oil and coarse sea salt and the bread. Serve in large soup plates and instruct your guests to dip the bread in the oil and then the salt to eat with the soup.

Basque Squid Stew

Serves 4

1½	pounds squid
3	tablespoons olive oil
1	onion, chopped
3	garlic cloves, finely chopped
1	can (14 ounces) chopped tomatoes
⅔	cup red wine
1¼	cups water
1	teaspoon chopped fresh thyme
1	teaspoon salt
20	turns of the black-pepper mill

This recipe comes from a Basque girl, Rosie, who works a trawler with her husband Billy, fishing out of Padstow. She does all the same work—hauling nets, gutting, stowing fish and hosing down the decks—and still finds time to cook the sort of food that any fisherman would be completely happy with, even if they didn't like fish. I would call this the boeuf bourguignonne of fish stews—it is so deep and rich and the squid becomes very tender after long, slow cooking. This dish is great eaten on its own with crusty French bread, or it can be used as a base for a more substantial fish stew. Add extra seafood such as seasoned sliced scallops, halved small skinned fillets of flat fish, large shrimp or pieces of cooked lobster, bring back to a boil and simmer for another 2 minutes.

Clean the squid (see p. 16). Cut the pouches across into rings and separate the tentacles if large.

Heat the oil in a large, heavy-based pan. Add the squid and cook over a high heat, stirring from time to time, until lightly browned.

Add the onion and garlic to the pan and cook for about 5 minutes, or until softened. Stir in the tomatoes, red wine, water and thyme and bring to a boil. Cover and simmer very gently for 2 hours. Season with the salt and pepper and eat as it is or use as a base for a fish stew (see above).

Moroccan Fish Tagine

Serves 4 as a first course

2 tablespoons olive oil, plus extra for brushing

2 celery stalks, chopped

1 carrot, chopped

1 small onion, chopped

¼ preserved lemon, finely chopped (see p. 220)

4 plum tomatoes, sliced

2½ cups *Fish Stock* (see p. 212)

8 small new potatoes, cut lengthwise into quarters

2 goatfish, ocean perch or sea bass, weighing about 1 pound each, filleted (see p. 13), skin on

• Salt and freshly ground black pepper

8 black olives, halved

1 teaspoon chopped fresh cilantro

1 teaspoon chopped fresh mint

For the Charmoula

2 tablespoons roughly chopped fresh cilantro

3 garlic cloves, chopped

1½ teaspoons ground cumin

½ red finger chili, seeded and roughly chopped

½ teaspoon saffron threads

4 tablespoons extra-virgin olive oil

• Juice of 1 lemon

1½ teaspoons paprika

1 teaspoon salt

Andy West, one of the chefs at the Seafood Restaurant, described this dish to me after he had been to Essouria, a fishing port between Agadir and Casablanca9. He showed me an enchanting picture of Essouria—old white houses, fishing boats, nets, blue skies, blue sea—and told me a story about meeting Arab carpet dealers and sitting on rugs in their house eating this fantastic fish stew—just about the best he'd ever had. So enthusiastic was his description that I decided to cook the dish on television without ever having tried it before, just to see what happened. It didn't go according to plan but, in a way, I thought it was quite interesting that it didn't. First of all the recipe called for large chunks of fish and vegetables, so the tagine ended up looking very ungainly. The taste was fine but, like so many fish stews, all the goodness seemed to go into the sauce, leaving some rather tasteless bits of fish. When my son Edward saw the tagine he said it looked like python stew, and in fact some of the fish skin does look a bit like snake! My youngest son Charles just couldn't bear to eat any of it and Jill, my wife, got a large bone stuck in her teeth. I ended up saying to the camera, "Well, it hasn't quite worked—back to the drawing board!" So I turned it into what I would call restaurant food, by taking the basic elements of the dish, refining them and presenting everything in a neat and tidy package. The result is quite wonderful and, I think, reveals a great deal about how recipes evolve.

For the charmoula, put all the ingredients into a food processor and blend until smooth.

Heat the oil in a large pan, add the celery, carrot and onion and fry gently for 5 minutes, or until softened but not browned. Add half the chopped preserved lemon, 2 tablespoons of the charmoula, the tomatoes and the stock. Bring to a boil and simmer for 30 minutes, then add the potatoes. Simmer for 6 to 8 minutes until tender.

Preheat the broiler. Brush the fillets of fish with olive oil, season with salt and pepper and then cut each diagonally in half. Broil, skin-side up, for about 6 minutes.

Stir the olives, the rest of the charmoula and the remaining preserved lemon into the sauce and check the seasoning. Put the fish in 4 warmed soup bowls, spoon over the sauce and sprinkle with the chopped cilantro and mint.

Tom Yam Gung (Hot-and-Sour Shrimp Soup)

Serves 4

1   pound headless shrimp in their shells

1   tablespoon sunflower oil

1   small garlic clove, finely chopped

•   A pea-sized piece of *blachan* (shrimp paste)

2   lemongrass stalks

5   cups *Light Asian Chicken Stock* (see p. 213)

2   tablespoons Thai fish sauce (*nam pla*)

3   tablespoons freshly squeezed lime juice

1   red finger chili, thinly sliced into rings

½   teaspoon palm sugar or soft dark brown sugar

1   green finger chili, thinly sliced into rings

2   kaffir lime leaves or 1 lime zest strip, very thinly sliced

•   Fresh cilantro leaves, to garnish

This Thai soup is, I think, one of the world's great dishes. It's just a simple, clear chicken stock with shrimp, lemongrass, lime and chili, but the vital ingredient is the dried shrimp paste, or blachan, *which comes in blocks and smells perfectly revolting. However, a little bit fried in the oil—and I mean just a trace—adds the right Asian touch to this great soup.*

Peel the shrimp, leaving the tail section in place, then devein them (see p. 18).

Heat the oil in a large saucepan. Add the shrimp shells, plus the garlic and shrimp paste and fry over medium-high heat for 2 minutes. Cut each stalk of lemongrass in half and crush slightly with a rolling pin. This helps release the flavor. Add the lemongrass and chicken stock to the pan, bring to a boil and simmer for 10 minutes.

Strain the stock through a fine sieve, then return it to the cleaned pan and add the fish sauce, lime juice, red chili, sugar and shrimp. Bring back to a boil and simmer for 3 minutes. Add the green chili and the lime leaves or zest and simmer for just 30 seconds. Serve garnished with whole cilantro leaves.

Cullen Skink

Serves 4

2 medium onions
2 cloves
5 cups milk
1 fresh bay leaf
½ pound finnan smoked haddock fillet, or other good-quality undyed smoked haddock
4 tablespoons butter
¾ pound potatoes, cut into ½-inch cubes
6 tablespoons heavy cream
• Salt and freshly ground black pepper
2 tablespoons roughly chopped fresh parsley

When I was writing the recipe for this traditional Scottish smoked haddock soup, I was tempted to rename it Smoked Finnan Haddock Soup with Potato, Onions and Parsley, on the grounds that Cullen Skink sounds like something you wouldn't want to give to your pet Jack Russell. But it's a fine Scottish soup of great taste and simplicity. We're all a bit wet in Britain when it comes to naming dishes: if it sounds a bit offputting, we call it something else. On the restaurant menu we can never use words such as "boiled," as in boiled leg of lamb with caper sauce or boiled fish heads, but why not? If that's how you cook the thing, that's how it should be named.

This soup is very easy to prepare. Do make sure that you get the best undyed haddock possible, preferably Finnan haddock, and don't overcook it; the soup really is so much nicer if the flakes of haddock are moist and fresh. Overcooked smoked fish always has a slightly harsh aftertaste.

Serve with a chilled Alsace or Gewürztraminer wine.

Peel one of the onions, cut it in half and stud each half with one of the cloves. Put into a pan with the milk and bay leaf, bring just to a boil and simmer for 5 minutes. Add the fish and simmer for 4 to 5 minutes, or until just firm and opaque—a good guide is to allow 10 minutes per 1-inch thickness of the fillet. Lift the fish out on to a plate and strain the liquid through a fine sieve into a jug. When the fish is cool enough to handle, remove the skin and bones and discard. Flake the fish into large pieces and set aside.

Peel and finely chop the remaining onion. Melt the butter in a large pan, add the onion and cook over gentle heat for 5 minutes, or until softened but not browned. Add the reserved milk and the diced potatoes. Bring to a boil, then simmer gently for 10 minutes, until the potatoes are cooked but still just firm.

Blend half the soup in a blender until smooth. Return to the pan with the heavy cream and flaked haddock, season with a little salt and pepper and warm through for 1 to 2 minutes. Serve in a warmed soup tureen, scattered with the chopped parsley.

A Small Stew of Bass, Squid, Mussels and Shrimp with a Warm Aïoli Sauce

Serves 4

4 large cooked Mediterranean shrimp (*crevettes*)
· Scant 4 cups *Roasted Fish Stock* (see p. 212)
12 mussels, cleaned (see p. 17)
1 orange
1 teaspoon lemon juice
2 plum tomatoes, roughly chopped
6 tablespoons *Olive Oil Mayonnaise* (see p. 217)
3 garlic cloves, crushed with a little salt
2 tablespoons heavy cream
6 ounces sea bass fillet, skin on, cut into 8 thin slices
$1/4$ pound prepared squid (see p. 16), cut into rings
· Salt and freshly ground black pepper
1 teaspoon finely chopped fresh flat-leaf parsley

I have taken the flavorings of bourride, *the Provençal fish stew, to make this elegant starter. The seafood is cooked separately, grilled to produce some color. The sauce, flavored with garlic mayonnaise, surrounds a pile of seafood on the plate and is sprinkled with a little chopped parsley.*

Remove the shells from the shrimp and reserve. Cut the shrimp lengthwise in half. Make the fish stock, adding the shrimp shells to the other fish bones before roasting.

Put the mussels in a pan with a splash of the stock, then cover and cook over a high heat for 3 to 4 minutes until they have opened. Discard any that remain closed. Strain the mussel liquor into the stock. Cover the mussels and keep warm.

Remove a strip of zest from the orange with a potato peeler and then squeeze out the juice from the orange. Put the fish stock, orange zest, 2 tablespoons of the orange juice, the lemon juice and the tomatoes into a large saucepan. Bring to a boil and simmer for 15 minutes, until reduced to $2\frac{1}{2}$ cups. Strain into a jug and discard the residue.

Preheat the broiler. Put the mayonnaise, garlic and cream into a bowl, add a good splash of the warm stock and stir together until smooth. Gradually stir in the remaining stock. Return the mixture to the pan and heat gently to the temperature of an egg custard (hot enough to be just uncomfortable to your little finger), stirring all the time until slightly thickened. Remove from the heat, stir in $1/2$ teaspoon of salt and keep warm while you cook the rest of the fish.

Put the sea bass and squid on to the greased rack of a broiler pan and sprinkle with a little salt and pepper. Broil for 2 minutes, adding the shrimp toward the end to warm through. Arrange the squid, shrimp, sea bass and mussels in 4 warmed soup bowls and surround with the warm garlic cream sauce. Sprinkle with the chopped parsley and serve.

Seafood in a Crab and Ginger Broth

Serves 4

- 1-inch piece fresh ginger
- 2 limes
- 7 cups *Light Asian Chicken Stock* (see p. 213)
- 1 lemongrass stalk
- 1 red bird's-eye chili, cut in half lengthwise
- 1 tablespoon Thai fish sauce (*nam pla*)
- 1 tablespoon light soy sauce
- 8 headless shrimp in their shells
- 1 small cooked snow crab or Dungeness crab
- 1/2 ounce rice vermicelli
- 2 green onions
- 1 ounce fresh spinach or Chinese cabbage such as bok choi (about 1 cup)
- 1/4 pound monkfish fillet, cut across into very thin slices
- 1 ounce bean sprouts (about 1 cup)
- Fresh cilantro leaves, to garnish

To Clarify the Stock
- 1/4 pound white fish fillet, skinned and finely chopped
- 1 small leek, thinly sliced
- 2 egg whites

Shrimp, monkfish and crab are lightly cooked in a clear, Asian-flavored broth with some Chinese leaves, rice noodles and bean sprouts. I like to serve it with little side plates of chopped mint and cilantro and also some sliced red chili in rice vinegar, which you stir into the soup as you wish. A great deal of work goes into making this soup and the amazing thing is it looks so simple and clean that your guests will think it is just as simple to make. How wrong could they be!

Peel the ginger, reserving the peel, and cut into very thin slices. Remove a strip of zest from 1 lime with a potato peeler, then squeeze out the juice from both limes. Pour the chicken stock into a large pan and add three-quarters of the sliced ginger, the ginger peel, the strip of lime zest and juice, the outer leaves of the lemongrass, the bird's-eye chili and fish sauce. Gradually bring to a boil.

Meanwhile, peel and devein the shrimp (see p. 18), then cover and set aside in the refrigerator. Pull off the claws and legs of the crab and crack the shells with a rolling pin. Pull the body of the crab away from the shell and add to the boiling stock with the crab legs (but not the claws) and the shrimp shells. Bring back to a boil, cover and simmer very gently for 25 minutes.

Pour the stock through a large sieve into another pan, discarding all the solids except the crab. Leave the stock to cool slightly. Meanwhile, remove the white meat from the claws, legs and main body of the crab in as large pieces as possible.

Next you need to clarify the stock. This is worth doing because it is such a pleasure in the final dish to see the white fish, noodles and green vegetables through a sparkling-clear but deeply flavored liquid. Add the fish fillet, leek and egg whites to the pan and whisk steadily over medium heat until the mixture boils. Stop whisking immediately, lower the heat and leave to simmer very gently for 5 minutes. Line a fine sieve or conical strainer with a double thickness of cheesecloth and rest it over a clean pan. Carefully pour the stock into the sieve and leave until all the liquid has dripped through. The stock is now ready to use.

Bring a pan of lightly salted water to a boil. Turn off the heat, add the noodles, loosen with a fork and leave for 3 minutes. Cut the green onions into 2-inch pieces and then cut lengthwise into very thin shreds. Cut the spinach or Chinese cabbage into 1-inch pieces. Finely chop the remaining ginger and half the remaining lemongrass.

To Serve

1 tablespoon chopped fresh mint

1 tablespoon chopped fresh cilantro

2 bird's-eye chilies, thinly sliced

2 tablespoons rice vinegar or white wine vinegar

Bring the stock to a very gentle simmer, then add the shrimp, monkfish, ginger and lemongrass and cook gently for 1 minute. Drain the noodles and add to the pan with the crabmeat, green onions, spinach or Chinese cabbage and bean sprouts. Simmer for 30 seconds, then remove from the heat.

Mix the mint and cilantro together in one small bowl and the chilies and vinegar in another. Divide the noodles among 4 large soup plates and then ladle the soup over them. Garnish with whole cilantro leaves. Serve with the soup, instructing your guests to season their soup to their own taste.

Mussels with Turmeric, Cumin and Coriander

Serves 4

1/4 teaspoon cilantro seeds
1/4 teaspoon cumin seeds
2 1/4 pounds mussels, cleaned
    (see p. 17)
4 tablespoons dry white wine
4 tablespoons unsalted butter
2 shallots, finely chopped
1/4 teaspoon ground turmeric
3/4 teaspoon cayenne pepper
2 teaspoons softened unsalted butter
2 teaspoons all-purpose flour
2 1/2 cups *Fish Stock*
    (see p. 212)
1/2 cup heavy cream
• Salt and freshly ground black pepper

In France you often get mussel and other seafood dishes flavored with what the French call le curry, *and this is always a bland, boring powder bought, I expect, in vast quantities so it is completely old and tasteless by the time it is used. The French seem to have the same attitude toward Indian spicing that we had about 30 years ago, when a curry was flavored with a stale powder and lots of raisins and sliced onions. Today, thanks to the plethora of Indian, Pakistani and Bangladeshi restaurants, most people in Britain have a far more sophisticated idea of spicing than those in any other country in Europe. So this dish, although quite northern European in content, uses freshly roasted spices instead of some innocuous powder.*

Put the coriander and cumin seeds into a small dry frying pan and roast over high heat until they begin to smell aromatic. Tip into a pestle and mortar or a coffee grinder and grind to a fine powder.

Put the cleaned mussels in a pan, add the white wine, cover and cook over high heat for about 3 to 4 minutes, shaking the pan until the mussels have opened. Strain the liquor through a colander into a bowl, shaking the colander well to drain off the juice lodged in the shells. Shell about two-thirds of the mussels; set all the mussels aside.

Heat 2 tablespoons of the unsalted butter in a large pan. Add the shallots and fry for 2 minutes, until softened but not browned. Add the ground roasted spices together with the turmeric and cayenne and fry for 1 minute. Mix the softened 2 teaspoons butter and flour together to make a paste. Add the stock and the mussel cooking liquor to the pan with the cream, the remaining 2 tablespoons unsalted butter and the butter-flour paste. Simmer for 10 minutes. Add the mussels to the soup, warm through, and then serve with plenty of crusty French bread.

Laksa (Malaysian Seafood and Noodle Soup)

Serves 4

8 headless shrimp in their shells
5 tablespoons vegetable oil
Scant 4 cups *Light Asian Chicken Stock* (see p. 213)
$\frac{1}{2}$ pound medium egg noodles
$\frac{1}{4}$ pound rice vermicelli
$\frac{1}{4}$ pound bean sprouts
1 can (14 ounces) coconut milk
$\frac{1}{4}$ pound prepared squid (see p. 16)
2 teaspoons palm sugar or soft dark brown sugar
1 to 1½ teaspoons salt
1 lime, cut into wedges

For the Spice Paste
3 medium or large dried red chilies
1 ounce dried shrimp (optional)
2 lemongrass stalks, outer leaves removed and the remainder chopped
1 ounce candle nuts, macadamia nuts or cashew nuts (about ¼ cup)
2 garlic cloves, chopped
• 1-inch piece of fresh galangal or ginger, peeled and roughly chopped

A spice paste fragrant with lemongrass, chili, garlic and dried shrimp is fried in oil. Chicken stock and coconut milk are simmered with the paste, then seafood is cooked quickly in the soup. Precooked noodles are added and the whole dish is sprinkled with shredded cucumber, cilantro, mint, green onions and a bit of extra chili.

With a recipe like this, I always get a little bit anxious that nobody will ever cook it because of the enormous quantity of ingredients involved. I first had laksa in Australia and then discovered that you could buy jars of fantastic laksa paste made by a very well-known Sri Lankan now living in Australia, Charmaine Solomon. It is a pity that, as yet, small quantities of carefully made masalas and other spice pastes are not readily available in Britain. I doubt if any domestic cook in Malaysia would feel the need to make a laksa paste; they just go out and buy it from their favorite laksa paste shop. Once you have the paste, the rest is easy. The one in this recipe works extremely well and keeps for a couple of months in the refrigerator, so it is worth making a large quantity of it. Anyway, once you've made the dish you probably won't mind making the paste over and over again. It is so very good.

For the spice paste, put the dried red chilies and dried shrimp into a bowl, cover with warm water and leave to soak for 15 minutes. Drain and put into a food processor with all the remaining spice paste ingredients. Blend until smooth, then set aside.

Peel and devein the shrimp (see page 18). Heat 1 tablespoon of the oil in a pan, add the shrimp shells and fry for a few minutes until lightly browned. Add the stock, bring to a boil and simmer for 10 minutes. Meanwhile, cut along one side of the squid pouch and open it out flat. Score the inner side first one way and then the other to make a grid pattern (this not only looks attractive but tenderizes the squid). Cut into 1-inch squares and set aside.

Strain the stock and discard the shrimp shells. Heat the remaining 4 tablespoons oil in the cleaned pan, add the spice paste and fry gently for 5 to 6 minutes, until it smells very fragrant and the spices are separating from the oil. Add the stock, bring to a boil, then cover and simmer for 20 minutes.

1 teaspoon ground
turmeric

1 small onion, chopped

1 teaspoon ground
coriander

3 tablespoons water

For the Garnish

• 2-inch piece of
cucumber, cut into fine
matchsticks

1 tablespoon chopped
fresh cilantro

1 tablespoon chopped
fresh mint

4 green onions, thinly
sliced

1 red finger chili, thinly
sliced across into rings

Bring a pan of salted water to a boil, add the egg noodles, cover, then take off the heat and leave for 4 minutes. When they are tender but still have a bit of bite, drain and set aside. Bring another pan of water to a boil, drop in the vermicelli, then take the pan off the heat and leave for 2 minutes. Add the bean sprouts and leave for another minute, then drain and mix with the egg noodles.

Add the coconut milk to the stock and simmer for 3 minutes. Add the shrimp, squid, sugar and salt and simmer for 4 minutes.

Divide the noodles between 4 large warmed soup bowls. Spoon over the hot soup and garnish each bowl with the cucumber, cilantro, mint, green onions and red chili.

Light Lunch Dishes

When I am testing a new dish I always cook it for lunch first. I love lunch, particularly with a cold Loire wine. In the middle of the day you are at your most energetic and optimistic. Is it such a bad idea to enter into imaginative business deals over a long lunch, I wonder? I think that our senses are much more acute at lunchtime. One's whole system is ready to enjoy a good meal, tastes and smells are most appreciated and, as for wine, it never tastes as good at night. The fact that most people think of the evening as the right time to enjoy good cooking is more to do with the way we live; lunch may be better but not if you have to work in the afternoon. I believe that if you really want to understand all the thought or lack of thought that goes into a restaurant dish, you should eat it for lunch. So the dishes in this chapter are designed to be really enthused about when your tastebuds are at their most critical, and I suggest that you serve them on their own as a light lunch so they can be fully appreciated. But I also think that they make really great first courses in a more elaborate dinner menu.

When I thought up these recipes I had in mind a table I saw once in Deruta in Umbria, Italy. Deruta is a town near Perugia, where it seems that almost every other building is a ceramics shop or factory. The table would have seated about eight and the top consisted of eight segments of beautifully hand-painted tiles showing blue and yellow fruit and vines on a white background. The vendor wanted tons of money for it and almost more to send it to Britain, but I imagine these dishes on that table in a light, vine-fringed conservatory in the English summer.

Facing page: Thai Fish Cakes with Green Beans (see p. 57).

Escabèche of Sardines

Serves 4

12 sardines
⅓ cup all-purpose flour, seasoned with salt and pepper
⅔ cup olive oil
6 tablespoons red wine vinegar
1 medium onion, thinly sliced
• 2-inch strip orange zest
1 fresh thyme sprig
1 fresh rosemary sprig
1 fresh bay leaf
4 garlic cloves, crushed
2 dried red chilies
1 teaspoon salt
1 small bunch fresh flat-leaf parsley, roughly chopped

Although the word escabèche is of Spanish origin, this is a classic Provençal dish, reflecting the fact that fish is cooked in this way all around the Mediterranean. First the fish is fried in olive oil, then a hot marinade of red wine vinegar, chili, garlic, herbs and, in Provence, orange peel, is poured over it. I have added some roughly chopped flat-leaf parsley to produce a simple and delightful dish. I made this in Marseilles under the critical eye of Madame Forte, whose cabaño, *a charming old-fashioned beach chalet, I had borrowed while an episode of my television series, "Fruits of the Sea," was being filmed. Monsieur Forte assured me that his wife had made escabèche all her life and knew everything there was to know about it. She pronounced mine too vinegary and without enough olive oil. I have since made these essential adjustments and hope that when I send her the book she'll try it again and approve.*

Gut, scale and remove the heads from the sardines (see p. 11), then dust them in the seasoned flour. Fry them in half the olive oil for 1 minute on each side, then transfer to a shallow dish. Add everything except the parsley and the remaining oil to the pan, bring to a boil and simmer for about 15 minutes. Add the parsley and the rest of the olive oil, pour the hot marinade over the sardines and leave until cold.

Oysters with Beurre Blanc and Spinach

Serves 4

16   oysters in the shell, well scrubbed

16   fresh spinach leaves, washed and stems removed

$^1/_4$ cup finely chopped shallot or onion

1   tablespoon white wine vinegar

1   tablespoon dry white wine

4   tablespoons water

$^2/_3$ cup unsalted butter, cut into small pieces

I would normally only consider eating oysters raw, but I must say that in this dish, where the oysters are just "set" in a steamer and accompanied by that classic butter sauce, beurre blanc, *I'm more than happy to eat the lightly cooked ones.*

Pour a couple of inches of boiling water into a large saucepan and place some sort of rack in the bottom. Thoroughly wash the oysters, place them on a plate and rest it on the top of the rack. Cover the pan and steam for about 4 minutes. Remove the oysters from the pan and open, taking care to save all the juices that come out of them. Put the spinach leaves in the steamer and steam for 2 minutes. Remove and set aside.

Preheat the broiler. Meanwhile, to make the *beurre blanc*, put the shallot or onion, vinegar, wine and water into a small pan. Add the juice from the oysters and simmer until only 2 tablespoons of liquid are left. Take the pan off the heat and gradually whisk in the pieces of butter, a few at a time, to build up a light emulsion.

Remove the oyster meats from their shells and place a folded leaf of spinach into the base of each one. Place the shells onto a baking sheet and push very briefly under the broiler to warm the spinach. Remove and place the oysters on top. Pour a little beurre blanc over each one and slide back under the broiler for about 15 to 20 seconds to warm through. Serve immediately.

Scallops with Duck Livers and Spaghettini

Serves 4

12   large prepared scallops (see p. 18)

¼   pound duck livers

1¼   cups *Fish Stock* (see p. 212)

½   cup heavy cream

½   cup Muscat de Beaumes de Venise or a similar sweet white wine

6   ounces dried spaghettini or other thin pasta such as capellini

2   tablespoons unsalted butter

•   Salt and freshly ground black pepper

•   Fresh flat-leaf parsley sprigs, to garnish (optional)

This dish is designed to be cooked at the last minute, so you need to be well prepared beforehand. It is most successful if you can use fresh duck livers. These are hard to get hold of, however, and you will probably have to make do with frozen ones. You need to be careful with frozen livers because if they've been frozen for too long they tend to go soft and don't plump up nicely during cooking. Freshly frozen ones should be bright red—the older they are, the grayer they become.

A perfect wine to go with this would be a chilled Gewürztraminer or a Tokay Pinot Gris from Alsace.

Bring 2 quarts of water and 1 tablespoon salt to a boil in a large pan. Meanwhile, slice the scallops in half and cut the duck livers into similar-sized pieces, being sure to remove any traces of the greeny-yellow gall bladder. Put the stock, 6 tablespoons of the cream and the wine into a wide-based pan and boil rapidly until reduced to $^2/_3$ cup.

Add the pasta to the pan of boiling water and cook for 4 minutes or until al dente. Drain, then cover and keep warm.

Melt a small knob of the butter in a frying pan over a high heat. Add the scallop slices and fry for 1 minute, turning them over after about 30 seconds. Transfer to a plate and keep warm. Add the rest of the butter to the pan with the duck livers and fry for just 1 minute, turning them over as they color. Set aside with the scallops. Add the reduced stock and wine mixture to the pan and bring to a boil, scraping up all the bits from the bottom of the pan. Strain through a sieve into a small pan. Stir in the rest of the cream, adjust with salt and pepper and heat through.

To serve, pile the pasta on to 4 warmed plates and arrange the scallops and duck livers on top. Pour the sauce around the pasta and serve garnished with sprigs of flat-leaf parsley if you wish.

Crab and Spinach Cannelloni with Basil and Tomato Sauce

Serves 4

¼ pound fresh spinach
2 tablespoons unsalted butter
10 ounces crabmeat
· A pinch of freshly grated nutmeg
· A pinch of cayenne pepper
· Salt and freshly ground black pepper
8 sheets of fresh lasagne
3 tablespoons grated Parmesan cheese

For the Tomato Sauce
1 medium onion, finely chopped
1 garlic clove, finely chopped
2 tablespoons olive oil
1 can (14 ounces) chopped tomatoes
¼ cup red wine vinegar
2 teaspoons superfine sugar
· Salt and freshly ground black pepper
10 fresh basil leaves, thinly shredded

Rolls of pasta stuffed with flaked white crabmeat and spinach, topped with a rich tomato sauce with plenty of basil, then sprinkled with grated Parmesan cheese and browned under the broiler—what could be nicer? I can't claim that this is an authentic Italian recipe; it's one of mine, but all I've done is substitute crab for meat in a classic cannelloni and added some basil to the sauce. I think it is almost better than the traditional version. You can use fresh, pasteurized or frozen crabmeat.

For the sauce, fry the onion and garlic in the olive oil for 5 minutes, or until softened. Add the chopped tomatoes and simmer for 15 to 20 minutes. Meanwhile, put the vinegar and sugar in a separate pan and boil down until reduced to about 1 teaspoon. Stir into the tomato sauce and season with salt and pepper. Add the basil and set aside.

Preheat the oven to 375°F.

Remove any large stems from the spinach and wash the leaves well in cold water. Shake off the excess water, put the leaves into a pan and cook over high heat for 2 minutes, or until wilted. Drain well, chop finely and return to the pan with the butter. Cook for 1 minute, or until all the excess moisture has evaporated, then stir in the crabmeat and season with the nutmeg, cayenne and some salt and pepper.

Bring 2 quarts of water and 1 tablespoon salt to a boil in a large pan. Add the lasagne, take the pan off the heat, cover and leave for 5 minutes. Drain the pasta and lay out flat on a sheet of plastic wrap. Spoon some of the crab mixture along one short end of each sheet and roll up. Lay the rolls side by side, seam-side down, in a lightly greased shallow baking dish. Spoon over the sauce, sprinkle over the Parmesan cheese and bake for 20 minutes, or until golden.

Salad of Harbour Shrimp with Roasted Tomatoes and Fennel

Serves 4

1½ pounds tiger prawns or other large shrimp in their shells with heads intact

2 tablespoons olive oil

1 garlic clove, crushed
Salt and freshly ground black pepper

For the Roasted Vegetables

5 tablespoons olive oil

2 small fennel bulbs

2 leeks, trimmed

4 beefsteak tomatoes

8 garlic cloves, halved

½ teaspoon fennel seeds, lightly crushed

For the Salad Dressing

1 tablespoon olive oil

1 teaspoon lime juice

• Salt and freshly ground white pepper

2 ounces curly endive (chicory)

2 ounces baby sorrel leaves or mâche

I got this recipe from Leigh Stone-Herbert, a chef friend of mine in Australia. The roasting of large tomatoes with aromatic vegetables, which are left to go cold and then made into a salad, is exciting and unusual and tastes fantastic. This dish was originally made with Sydney harbor shrimp. Nothing quite beats the intensely sweet taste of these shellfish, but it is really well worth making with tiger shrimp.

Preheat the oven to 450°F.

Peel the shrimp (see p. 18). For the roasted vegetables, heat the oil in a large pan. Add the shrimp heads and shells and fry over high heat for 1 to 2 minutes, or until they are quite crisp. Tip into a sieve resting over a bowl and press out all of the oil. Discard the shells. Cut the fennel bulbs lengthwise into quarters. Cut the leeks in half. Place the fennel and the leeks in a roasting pan with the tomatoes. Mix the halved garlic and fennel seeds into the shrimp-flavored oil and pour over the vegetables, making sure that they are all wellcoated. Season well with salt and pepper and roast for 25 minutes, until the tomatoes blacken. Remove, peel and leave to go cold.

To cook the shrimp, mix the oil with the crushed garlic in a bowl. Add the shrimp and some seasoning and toss together well. Heat a large, heavy-bottomed pan until very hot. Add the shrimp and toss over a high heat for 2 minutes. Leave to cool.

To serve, cut a deep cross into the top of each tomato, almost down to the base. Open out each one and place into the center of 4 large plates so that they look like the petals of a flower. Arrange the pieces of roasted fennel in between the "petals."

For the salad dressing, squeeze the liquid out of the roasted leeks, strain all the juices into a small bowl and whisk in the oil, lime juice and salt and pepper to taste. Put the curly endive into a bowl and toss with a little of the dressing. Pile this into the center of the tomatoes and arrange the shrimp on top.

Drizzle the rest of the dressing around the edge of the plate and then garnish with a few sprigs of the sorrel and mâche.

Skate Persillé with Sauce Gribiche

Serves 10–12

1 skate wing, weighing about 2 pounds
4 tablespoons chopped fresh parsley
2 shallots, finely chopped
• Salt and freshly ground black pepper
3 tablespoons cold water
4 teaspoons unflamed gelatin
• Salad leaves, to garnish

For the Court Bouillon
1 bottle dry white wine
5 cups water
2 fresh bay leaves
12 black peppercorns
1 onion, chopped
2 carrots, chopped
2 celery stalks, chopped
1 teaspoon salt
2 lemon slices
2 star anise
1 fennel bulb, chopped

For the Sauce Gribiche
3 eggs
1 tablespoon white wine vinegar
1 teaspoon Dijon mustard
½ cup olive oil
3 small gherkins, very finely chopped
1 tablespoon capers, very finely chopped
1 tablespoon chopped fresh tarragon
1 tablespoon chopped fresh parsley

Skate is particularly suited to serving cold because it has lots of flavor and an attractive soft texture. This dish is based on a real favorite of mine, jambon persillé, *and uses similar flavoring. The skate stock has a naturally gelatinous quality and needs only a little extra gelatin to set everything. The stock calls for a whole bottle of wine. It needn't be expensive but you do need this much to achieve the necessary concentration of flavor.*

The sauce gribiche is a mayonnaise made with gherkins, capers and a little chopped egg and makes a very pleasant accompaniment to the dish. I would suggest serving a cool white wine from the Languedoc or elsewhere with it.

Put all the ingredients for the court bouillon into a pan and bring to a boil. Simmer for 15 minutes. Put the skate into the pan and simmer for 12 minutes, then lift out and leave to cool. Strain the court bouillon, return it to a clean pan and boil vigorously until reduced to 2½ cups. Leave to cool.

Lift the skate flesh off the bones and pull it apart a little. Put it into a bowl and mix with the parsley, shallots and a little salt and pepper.

Put the cold water into a small pan, sprinkle over the gelatin and leave for 5 minutes. Heat gently until clear, then stir into the cool stock.

Line a 9-by-5-inch loaf pan with plastic wrap. Spread one-third of the skate mixture over the bottom and pour over enough cooled stock just to cover it. Chill until almost set. Add another third of the skate and stock and chill again. Repeat once more. Cover and chill for 4 hours or overnight, until really firm.

You can make the sauce in advance. Boil the eggs for 5 minutes, then drain and leave in cold water to cool. Peel the eggs, cut them in half and scoop the still-runny yolks into a bowl. Reserve one egg white (discard the rest). Whisk the yolks until pale and creamy. Whisk in the vinegar and mustard and then gradually whisk in the oil to give a mayonnaiselike consistency. Very finely chop the reserved egg white and stir into the sauce with the gherkins, capers, tarragon, parsley and salt and pepper.

To serve, turn the terrine out on to a board and remove the plastic wrap. Cut into slices with a serrated knife or electric carving knife. Put a slice on each plate, spoon a little of the sauce to one side and serve with a few salad leaves.

Hot-smoked Salmon Sandwich with Crème Fraîche and Capers

Serves 4

$\frac{1}{2}$ pound hot-smoked
     salmon

6 tablespoons crème
   frâiche

2 tablespoons capers,
   drained and chopped

1 tablespoon chopped
   fresh chives

4 large or 8 small slices
   of sourdough or other
   crusty white bread

2 ounces mixed salad
   leaves, such as arugula,
   curly endive (chicory),
   radicchio, watercress
   and oakleaf lettuce
   (about 2 cups)

• Salt and freshly ground
   black pepper

This recipe and the three variations that follow it are served in our coffee shop in Padstow and are all based on the same principle. You take some good bread such as sourdough, whole-grain or ciabatta and toast it lightly, preferably on a cast-iron ribbed pan to give that slightly chargrilled flavor. Then you build up salad leaves on top of it with the main components of the dish and a flavored mayonnaise or dressing and serve the sandwich with a knife and fork. This formula has proved immensely successful for us and I think it's because it's the sort of light dish that everybody wants to eat these days. The salmon version is fantastic, particularly if you can get hold of hot-smoked salmon. This is salmon cured in the same way as smoked mackerel—in other words, it is actually smoked and cooked at the same time but then served cold. It is becoming more readily available but if you cannot get hold of it use cold-smoked salmon instead.

Remove the skin and bones from the salmon and break the fish into large flakes. Mix the crème frâiche with the capers, chives and a little salt and pepper. Put a cast-iron ribbed pan over a high heat and, when hot, broil the slices of bread for 1 minute on each side. Cut each one diagonally into 3 and fan out slightly on 4 plates. Arrange the salmon, crème frâiche and salad leaves at random on top of the bread and serve immediately.

Hot-Smoked Mackerel with Mustard Dressing

Substitute smoked mackerel for the smoked salmon, whole-grain bread for the sourdough and baby dandelion leaves and curly endive for the mixed salad leaves. Mix 2 teaspoons Dijon mustard with 2 teaspoons white wine vinegar and 4 tablespoons extra-virgin olive oil. Stir in 1 finely chopped shallot, $\frac{1}{2}$ crushed garlic clove and some salt and pepper. Toss the leaves with this dressing and arrange over the grilled bread with the flaked mackerel, 4 hard-boiled eggs, quartered, and $\frac{1}{4}$ pound cherry tomatoes, quartered.

Smoked Eel with Horseradish Mayonnaise

Substitute smoked eel fillet, broken into small pieces, for the smoked salmon and replace the sourdough bread with whole-wheat bread—I like to use walnut bread from our bakery (see p. 219). Mix 6 tablespoons mayonnaise (see p. 217) with 2 tablespoons of horseradish sauce and some salt and freshly ground black pepper. Arrange the smoked eel and horseradish mayonnaise over the grilled bread with some slices of cucumber and mixed salad leaves.

Shrimp and Avocado in Mary Rose Sauce

This is a variation on the theme of shrimp cocktail. Replace the salmon with good-quality cooked peeled shrimp mixed with 1 teaspoon lemon juice and some salt and pepper. Substitute ciabatta for the sourdough bread and use butter lettuce and watercress sprigs for the salad. Mix together 3 tablespoons each of mayonnaise (see p. 217) and plain yogurt, 1 tablespoon tomato ketchup, a few drops of Tabasco sauce, the finely grated zest of $1/2$ lemon, 2 teaspoons lemon juice and some salt and cayenne pepper. Arrange the shrimp, sauce, salad leaves and 1 peeled, pitted and sliced avocado on top of the grilled bread.

Oysters Charentais

Serves 4

20   Pacific oysters

For the Sausages
$3/4$ pound belly pork
      (uncured bacon)
$1/2$ teaspoon salt
$1/2$ teaspoon paprika
$1/2$ teaspoon black pepper
$1/2$ teaspoon thyme
$1/2$ teaspoon cayenne
      pepper
3   ounces *chorizo*
      sausages, skin removed
$1/4$ pound caul fat or pork
      back fat for wrapping
      the sausages

This classic dish from the southwest coast of France combines oysters with hot spicy sausages and is wonderful with a cold glass of Sauvignon.

Put all the sausage ingredients (except the caul fat) into a food processor and blend until the mixture is coarse. Remove, portion the mixture into 12 balls each about the size of a golf ball and mold into rough sausage shapes. Wrap them in 4 inch squares of caul fat.

Twenty minutes before serving, open the oysters (see p. 17) but keep them flat, taking care not to spill too much of the salty liquor. Divide the oysters among four plates.

Preheat the broiler and grill the sausages. Place 3 sausages beside each serving of oysters.

Crab and Gruyère Tartlets

Serves 4

10	ounces crabmeat
2	egg yolks
6	tablespoons heavy cream
•	A pinch of cayenne pepper
$^1/_2$	cup finely shredded Gruyère cheese
•	Salt and freshly ground black pepper

For the Pastry

$1^2/_3$	cups all-purpose flour
$^1/_2$	teaspoon salt
5	tablespoons butter
5	tablespoons lard
$1^1/_2$	tablespoons cold water
1	egg white

Made with the freshest crabmeat, some Gruyère cheese and the shortest of short-crust pastry, this dish needs no accompaniment except perhaps a single sprig of parsley—and a chilled glass of premier cru Chablis.

For the pastry, sift the flour and salt into a food processor, add the butter and lard cut into small pieces and process until the mixture looks like fine bread crumbs. Tip into a large mixing bowl and stir in the water with a round-bladed knife until everything starts to stick together. Bring together into a ball, turn out on to a work surface lightly dusted with flour and knead once or twice until smooth. Roll out the pastry thinly and use to line 4 shallow $4^1/_2$-inch tartlet tins with removable bottoms. Chill for 20 minutes.

Preheat the oven to 425°F.

Line the pastry shells with parchment paper, cover the base with a generous layer of pie weights and bake blind for 15 minutes. Remove the weights and paper, brush the inside of each pastry shell with a little unbeaten egg white and return to the oven for 2 minutes. Remove from the oven and lower the temperature to 400°F.

Mix the crabmeat with the egg yolks, cream, cayenne and some salt and pepper. Spoon the mixture into the tartlet shells and sprinkle with the Gruyère cheese. Bake at the top of the oven for 15 to 20 minutes, or until lightly golden. Serve warm.

Stir-fried Salt and Pepper Shrimp

Serves 4 as a first course

2 tablespoons salt
1 teaspoon Chinese
five-spice powder
1 teaspoon ground
Sichuan peppercorns
1 teaspoon ground black
pepper
• Sunflower oil for
deep-frying
2 pounds headless shrimp
in their shells

The idea for this recipe came from a dish I had on Lamma Island, Hong Kong, where I was struck by the starkness of the accompaniments—just salt and pepper. Actually, there is a bit more to it than that. I finally tracked down a recipe in Yan-Kit So's Classic Chinese Cookbook, so here it is.

Heat a dry wok over a medium heat. Add the salt and stir constantly for about 4 minutes, or until it has turned a slightly grayish color. Transfer to a small bowl and mix with the five-spice powder, Sichuan pepper and black pepper.

Pour some oil into a large pan until it is about one-third full and heat to 350°F, or until a small piece of white bread dropped into the oil browns and rises to the surface in 1$\frac{1}{2}$ minutes. Add half the shrimp and fry for 30 seconds, or until they have curled up and turned pink. Remove and repeat with the remaining shrimp.

Reheat the dry wok, add 2 tablespoons of the spiced salt and the cooked shrimp, then flip the shrimp over in the salt for 30 seconds so that it can permeate them. Tip on to warm serving plates and serve the remaining salt separately.

Shrimp Fried with Garlic Butter

Serves 4

2 large garlic cloves
• Salt
$\frac{1}{2}$ cup unsalted butter,
softened
1 teaspoon lemon juice
1 teaspoon brandy
24 large, cooked, shrimp
in their shells
• Freshly ground black
pepper
$\frac{1}{2}$ cup chopped fresh
parsley

There is really very little to this recipe except a first-rate set of ingredients, but it's just one of those dishes that is totally irresistible and can be turned out in, let us say, 5 minutes flat.

For the garlic butter, roughly chop the garlic cloves, then add a good pinch of salt and crush to a paste with the back of a knife. Mix with the butter, lemon juice and brandy.

Melt 2 tablespoons of the garlic butter in a large frying pan. Add the shrimp and gently fry for 2 minutes, or until heated through. Season with salt and pepper. Stir the chopped parsley into the remaining garlic butter, add to the pan and, when it has melted and is hot and foaming, spoon the shrimp into 4 warmed gratin dishes. Serve immediately, with lots of freshly baked French bread to mop up the garlic butter.

Thai Fish Cakes with Green Beans (Tod Man Pla)

Serves 4

1 pound ling or other firm, white fish fillets, skinned

1 tablespoon Thai fish sauce (*nam pla*)

1 tablespoon *Red Curry Paste* (see p. 219)

1 kaffir lime leaf or 1 lime zest strip, very finely shredded

1 tablespoon chopped fresh cilantro (leaves and stems)

1 egg

1 teaspoon palm sugar or soft dark brown sugar

½ teaspoon salt

1½ ounces French beans, thinly sliced into rounds

⅔ cup peanut or sunflower oil

For the Sweet-and-Sour Cucumber Sauce

4 tablespoons white wine vinegar

⅔ cup superfine sugar

1½ tablespoons water

2 teaspoons Thai fish sauce (*nam pla*)

⅓ cup very finely diced cucumber

3 tablespoons very finely diced carrot

3 tablespoons very finely chopped onion

2 red chilies, thinly sliced

I think this is a pretty authentic recipe for those delightful little flat fish cakes that are served as a starter in Thai restaurants, always quite spicy but not terribly hot. However, the sauce that accompanies them is usually hot and this one is no exception. I have put two bird's-eye chilies in it. In all my recipes using chili, I tend to include the amount you might expect to get in a dish made by Thais or Indians, not an English chef worried about customers overdosing on chilies. If you are at all unsure about the heat in this dish, remove the seeds from the chilies (see notes on chilies on p. 22).

For the sauce, gently heat the vinegar, sugar and water in a small pan until the sugar has dissolved. Bring to a boil and boil for 1 minute, then remove from the heat and leave to cool. Stir in the fish sauce, cucumber, carrot, onion and chilies. Pour into 4 small dipping saucers or ramekins and set aside.

For the fish cakes, cut the fish into chunks and put into a food processor with the fish sauce, curry paste, kaffir lime leaf or lime zest, chopped cilantro, egg, sugar and salt. Process until smooth, then stir in the sliced green beans.

Divide the mixture into 16 pieces. Roll each one into a ball and then flatten into a 2½-inch cake. Heat the oil in a large frying pan and fry the fish cakes in batches for 1 minute on each side, or until golden brown. Lift out and drain on kitchen paper, then serve with the sweet-and-sour cucumber sauce.

Serves 4

12 sardines
• Salt and freshly ground black pepper
$\frac{1}{3}$ cup grated Parmesan cheese
$1\frac{1}{2}$ tablespoons chopped fresh parsley
1 cup fresh white bread crumbs
$\frac{1}{3}$ cup all-purpose flour
2 eggs, beaten
• Sunflower oil for deep-frying
• Sprigs of fresh flat-leaf parsley sprigs, to garnish (optional)
• Lemon wedges, to serve

Fried Butterflied Sardine Fillets with Parmesan Crumbs

The heads are removed from whole sardines and most of the backbone is taken out, leaving an inch or so at the tail end, which gives the deep-fried fish a very pretty shape. The process of removing the bones is easier if the sardines are fresh, but this is not a recipe where frozen fish need be ruled out. The delight is the remarkably pleasant, crisp Parmesan and parsley crust sandwiching a moist but thin sheet of sardine fillet—served with nothing more than lemon wedges.

First butterfly the sardines (see below). Season the fish on both sides with a little salt and pepper.

Preheat the oven to 300°F. Line a baking sheet with plenty of paper towels.

Mix together the Parmesan cheese, parsley, bread crumbs and some seasoning. Dip the butterflied sardines into the flour, then into the beaten egg and finally into the bread crumb mixture, pressing it on well to give an even coating.

Butterflying Sardines

1. Trim the fins off the sardines with kitchen scissors. Cut off the heads and then cut along the belly from the gut cavity right down to the tail and pull out the guts with your fingers.

2. Open out each fish and place belly-side down on a chopping board. Gently but firmly, press along the backbone with your thumb or the palm of your hand, so that you gradually flatten out the fish.

3. Turn the fish over and carefully pull out the backbone, snipping it off at the tail end with scissors. Remove any small bones that are left behind with a pair of tweezers or pliers.

Pour the oil into a large pan and heat to 350°F, or until a small piece of bread dropped into the oil browns and rises to the surface in about 1½ minutes. Deep-fry the sardines one or two at a time for 1 minute, flipping them over halfway through so that they brown on both sides. Lift out with a slotted spoon on to the paper-lined baking sheet and keep hot in the oven while you cook the rest. Garnish with parsley, if liked, and serve with lemon wedges.

Salmon Rillettes

Serves 4

1/2 cup unsalted butter
1 1/4 cups water
1 teaspoon salt
2 lemon slices
2 bay leaves
10 black peppercorns
3/4 pound salmon
1/4 teaspoon ground mace
- A good pinch of ground allspice
- Freshly ground white pepper
- *Walnut Bread* (see p. 219) or whole-wheat bread, to serve

For the Green Chutney
2 teaspoons English mustard powder
1 tablespoon finely chopped capers
1 small gherkin, cut into fine matchsticks (about 1 tablespoon)
1 tablespoon chopped fresh *herbs fines*, (parsley, chervil, chives and tarragon)
2 tablespoons extra-virgin olive oil
1 teaspoon white wine vinegar
1/2 teaspoon salt

I first came across this dish in a restaurant near the rather unfortunately named town of Condom in southwest France. I suppose in Britain you might call it potted salmon, but rillettes seems more appropriate because the idea is to try and shred the salmon rather like duck or goose rillettes. Like its poultry counterpart, it is designed to use valuable trimmings, such as the heads and tails, which would normally be thrown away but actually contain plenty of good-tasting fillet. It is flavored with the sort of spices you would find in something like potted shrimp and served with a simple, fresh, green chutney made with capers, gherkins and herbs.

Leave the butter somewhere warm until it is really soft but not melted. Meanwhile, put the water, salt, lemon, bay leaves and peppercorns in a small pan, bring to a boil and simmer for 10 minutes. Add the salmon and simmer for 8 to 10 minutes. Leave to cool in the cooking water. Remove the skin and bones from the fish, place the flesh in a bowl and shred by pulling apart with 2 forks.

Add the butter to the salmon with the mace, allspice and 3 twists of freshly ground white pepper. Mix together gently with a fork, then cover and chill for 2 hours, or until just firm. If it gets too hard, leave to soften at room temperature for about 30 minutes before serving.

For the green chutney just mix together all the ingredients in a small bowl and season with freshly ground white pepper, then cover and chill. Serve the rillettes and chutney with lightly toasted walnut or whole-wheat bread.

Plaice with Leeks, Mint and Beaujolais

Serves 4

1/4 pound leeks
1/2 cup unsalted butter
1 bacon slice, cut into thin strips
1 teaspoon chopped fresh mint
• Salt and freshly ground white pepper
3/4 cup Beaujolais
1/4 cup port
1 1/4 cups *Fish Stock* (see p. 212)
1/4 teaspoon superfine sugar
4 plaice, flounder or sand dab fillets, weighing about 3 ounces each, skinned
• Fresh mint sprigs, to garnish

This is one of the most successful dishes for plaice—we've had it on the menu in my restaurant for twelve years.

I think its success lies in the almost indefinable satisfaction of the three components—the watery fragrance of the plaice, the tartness of the Beaujolais sauce and the freshness of mint with the leeks, with the slight taste of smoke from the bacon.

Cut the leeks in half lengthwise and once more into quarters if they are quite large. Cut across these strips into 1/2-inch pieces.

Bring a small pan of salted water to a boil, add the leeks and simmer for a few minutes until tender but still al dente. Drain them well. Melt 1 tablespoon butter in a small pan, add the bacon and leeks and cook gently until all the excess water has evaporated. Stir in the mint and season with some salt and pepper. Set aside and keep warm.

Preheat the broiler.

Put the Beaujolais, port, stock and sugar into a large pan and boil rapidly until reduced by three-quarters.

Melt another 1 tablespoon butter and brush over both sides of each fish fillet. Season with salt and pepper and lay them on the lightly oiled rack of the broiler pan. Broil for 2 minutes.

Dice the remaining butter. Bring the reduced wine and stock back to a boil and then whisk in the butter, a few small pieces at a time. Adjust the seasoning if necessary.

To serve, spoon the leeks on to 4 warmed plates. Put the fish fillets on the plates, and pour the sauce around. Garnish with sprigs of fresh mint.

Hot and Spicy Fish

One of the mystifying questions about Great Britain is why, for a country surrounded by some of the richest fishing waters in the world, are we so relatively uninterested in fish cookery? I find it terribly difficult to answer that one. If you ask Cornish people why they don't like fish, many of them reply that they were brought up on it and so it isn't a great delicacy to them. Then you argue that the people of Brittany, with a similar coastline and similar fish, have made much more of what's on offer, as have virtually all the people on the coastline from Brittany to Finland, and you come up with no real reason why.

But suppose that in Britain we were used to eating the sort of seafood dishes they cook in Goa, would our attitude be the same? I think not, because most of us love spicy food. One only has to observe the enormous popularity of Indian and Thai restaurants in this country to realize how different the case would be if we were much more relaxed about using plenty of heat and spice in our cooking, and that's why I think this is such an important chapter. I believe that fish cookery in this country will more and more feature ingredients such as chili, turmeric, cardamom, ginger, kaffir lime leaves, coriander, *nam pla* and everything else that still seems so exotic to us.

So what dishes would I particularly like to bring to your attention in this chapter? I think above all the Thai Red Seafood (see p. 70). If you want a fish stew that you'll never forget, this is it. I cooked it for the annual staff barbecue on Harlyn Beach near Padstow and I honestly think it was the best fish dish for large numbers I have ever cooked. We invited about 150 people and 200 came. We asked a band to play on the beach. We bought three barrels of beer and about 100 bottles of wine, plus a stack of soft drinks for the kids. We had shrimp tandoori and chicken tandoori, sparerib teriyaki and the Rice-Shaped Pasta on p. 104. We always make a salad of fusilli and pesto, plus a tomato, onion and cilantro salad with cumin and chili like the one served with Tandoori Shrimp on p. 64, some couscous salad with mint, a potato salad with lots of green onions chopped into it, and loads of freshly baked baguettes. The weather helped; it was one of those still, balmy summer evenings that make me think there is nowhere else in the world I would rather be than Cornwall.

Facing page: Tandoori Shrimp (see p. 64).

Tandoori Shrimp

Serves 4

32   large shrimp in their shells

³⁄₄   cup plain yogurt

For the Lemon Chili Marinade

1   teaspoon cayenne pepper

1   teaspoon salt

•   Juice of 1 lemon

For the Tandoori Masala Paste

¹⁄₃   cup fennel seeds

1   tablespoon coriander seeds

1   tablespoon cumin seeds

¹⁄₄   cup roughly chopped fresh ginger

6   garlic cloves, chopped

4   red finger chilies, seeded and roughly chopped

2   teaspoons paprika

1   teaspoon ground turmeric

•   Juice of 1 lemon

1   to 2 tablespoons cold water

For the Kachumber Salad

3   tomatoes

1   medium onion

2   tablespoons roughly chopped fresh cilantro

¹⁄₄   teaspoon ground cumin

•   A large pinch of cayenne pepper

1   tablespoon white wine vinegar

¹⁄₂   teaspoon salt

The tandoori spice mix that I use for my shrimp is quite unconventional. Although it includes all the standard tandoori marinade ingredients, such as yogurt, lemon juice, chili and curry spices, I also put in a great deal of pounded fennel seed,which I find gives the marinated shrimp an incomparable texture and aromatic flavor. Do use the best-possible whole uncooked shrimp for this dish; it is well worth it.

Mix together all the ingredients for the lemon chili marinade. Make 3 small slits in either side of each shrimp between the shell segments to allow the marinade to penetrate. Put the shrimp and marinade in a bowl, turning the shrimp to coat them, and set aside for 20 minutes.

For the tandoori masala paste, grind the fennel, coriander and cumin seeds in a spice grinder or in a mortar with a pestle. Put the spices in a food processor with all the rest of the ingredients, including the cold water, and blend until smooth. Stir the paste into the yogurt. Add the shrimp, stir together well and leave for 20 minutes.

Thread the shrimp onto metal skewers or bamboo skewers that have been soaked in water, piercing them just behind the head and through the tail. Cook them over a charcoal fire or under a very hot broiler for 4 minutes, turning them over halfway through.

While the shrimp are cooking, prepare the salad. Halve and thinly slice the tomatoes and onion, then mix with all the remaining salad ingredients. Serve with the shrimp, together with some warm naan bread.

Mild Potato Curry Topped with Smoked Haddock and a Poached Egg

Serves 4

3/4 pound undyed smoked haddock, cut into 4 pieces

2 teaspoons white wine vinegar

4 eggs

• Fresh cilantro sprigs, to garnish

For the Potato Curry

3/4 pound waxy new potatoes, peeled and cut into 1/2 inch cubes

2 tablespoons sunflower oil

1/2 teaspoon yellow mustard seeds

1/4 teaspoon ground turmeric

3/4 cup finely chopped onions

2 tomatoes, peeled and chopped

1 teaspoon roughly chopped fresh cilantro

• Salt and freshly ground black pepper

This dish must be made! The idea of putting spiced potatoes underneath smoked haddock with a poached egg turns a homely, well-known English dish into something much more elevated. It is not hard to do and it has a sort of joyous sophistication to it which, to me, is what good cooking is all about.

Poaching eggs carries the same sort of fear of failure as making omelets. The restaurant way is to use plenty of water and a fairly deep pan. Once the water is boiling, the pan is pulled slightly to one side to create a rolling boil and the eggs are then broken into the middle and roll up into a pleasing oval shape. But to avoid any possibility of failure in this recipe, I have suggested using a shallow pan and a small amount of water, which should be heated to the merest tremble of a boil. I always add vinegar to the poaching water, not because it helps the eggs to set but because I like the faint flavor that lingers in the eggs.

For the potato curry, cook the potatoes in a pan of boiling water for 6 to 7 minutes, or until tender, then drain. Meanwhile, heat the oil in a pan, add the mustard seeds and, when they begin to pop, add the turmeric and onions. Fry for 5 minutes, or until the onions are soft and lightly browned. Add the potatoes and some salt and pepper and fry for 1 to 2 minutes. Add the tomatoes and cook for 1 minute. Stir in the chopped cilantro, then set aside and keep warm.

Bring a pan of water to a boil, add the pieces of smoked haddock and simmer gently for 3 to 4 minutes, or until cooked. Lift out with a slotted spoon, cover and keep warm.

Pour about 1 1/2 inches water into a frying pan and bring to a very gentle simmer; the water should be just trembling and there should be a few bubbles rising up from the bottom of the pan. Add the vinegar, break in the eggs and poach for 3 minutes, basting the top of the eggs with a little of the hot water as they cook. Lift out with a slotted spoon and drain briefly on paper towels.

To serve, put the potato curry on 4 warmed plates, lay a piece of smoked haddock on top and a poached egg on top of that. Serve garnished with sprigs of cilantro.

Green Monkfish and Shrimp Curry

Serves 4

3 tablespoons sunflower oil
1 quantity of *Green Curry Paste* (see p. 215)
1 can (14 fl ounces) coconut milk
3/4 cup water
2 tablespoons Thai fish sauce (*nam pla*)
2 teaspoons palm sugar or soft dark brown sugar
4 kaffir lime leaves or 1 lime zest strip, cut into very fine shreds
• Juice of 1 lime
1/4 pound very small new potatoes, cut in half if large
2 ounces baby eggplants, quartered, or snow peas
12 headless shrimp in their shells
3/4 pound monkfish fillet, cut crosswise into slices 1/2 inch thick
1/2 cup sliced canned bamboo shoots
2 tablespoons finely shredded fresh basil
1 green finger chili, thinly sliced crosswise into rings

If you put the maximum amount of green chilies in this recipe that I've suggested, you will create a curry of such heat and intensity that you could be sitting in Bangkok. If you like your curries a little milder, use only two chilies. Either way, I hope you'll agree that this is probably the best recipe for green fish curry you have ever tasted. It is fragrant and blindingly hot but also sweet and delicious with the background flavor of coconut.

Heat the oil in a large pan, add the green curry paste and fry for 5 to 6 minutes, or until the ingredients begin to separate from the oil and it starts to smell aromatic. Add the coconut milk, water, fish sauce, sugar, lime leaves or zest, lime juice, potatoes and the eggplants, if using. Simmer for about 10 minutes, until the potatoes and eggplants are tender. Meanwhile, peel the shrimp and devein them (see p. 18). Cut each one in half lengthwise.

Add the shrimp to the pan with the monkfish, bamboo shoots and the snow peas, if using. Simmer for another 2 minutes. Stir in the shredded basil and serve sprinkled with the sliced green chili.

Goan Shrimp Balchao

Serves 4

6 tablespoons vegetable
oil

2 medium onions, finely
chopped

6 garlic cloves, finely
chopped

2 tablespoons red wine
vinegar

1 tablespoon palm sugar
or soft dark brown
sugar

1 pound cooked peeled
shrimp

4 fresh curry leaves or
2 young fresh bay
leaves, very finely
shredded

• Goan Masala Paste

1 teaspoon cumin seeds

2 teaspoons cilantro
seeds

2 teaspoons black
peppercorns

2 teaspoons cloves

1 teaspoon turmeric
powder

1/4 pound red finger
chilies, roughly
chopped

1 teaspoon salt

6 garlic cloves

1 teaspoon palm sugar or
soft dark brown sugar

2 tablespoons prepared
fresh tamarind
(see p. 25)

• 2-inch piece fresh
ginger, peeled and
roughly chopped

2 tablespoons red wine
vinegar

This Goan dish comes in two forms: either as a curry made with small shrimp or as a preserve, where more vinegar is added and the curry is cooked longer. The preserve is served with such great Goan dishes as pork vindaloo. In this recipe the shrimp are served freshly cooked as a curry. It makes a very pleasant dish that needs only plain steamed rice and, perhaps, a tomato and cilantro salad to accompany it.

For the Goan masala paste, grind the cumin seeds, cilantro seeds, peppercorns and cloves in a spice grinder or in a mortar with a pestle. Transfer to a food processor with all the remaining paste ingredients and process until smooth. Spoon into a sterilized glass jar, seal and store in the refrigerator.

Heat the oil in a medium-sized pan, add the onions and garlic and fry for 8 minutes, until golden. Add the masala paste and fry for 2 minutes, or until the spices start to separate from the oil. Mix the red wine vinegar and sugar together, add to the pan and simmer for 1 minute. Add the shrimp and the shredded curry or bay leaves and turn the mixture over gently for about 2 to 3 minutes, or until the shrimp are hot.

Goan Fish Curry

Serves 4

- 4 conger eel or shark steaks, weighing about 6 ounces each
- • Salt and freshly ground black pepper
- 6 tablespoons sunflower oil
- 1 medium onion, sliced
- 2 tomatoes, peeled and chopped
- 1 cup canned coconut milk
- 4 green or red chilies, split open
- 2 tablespoons chopped fresh cilantro

For the Curry Paste
- 6 red finger chilies, seeded and roughly chopped (leave the seeds in if you want extra heat)
- 2 tablespoons ground cilantro
- 2 teaspoons ground cumin
- 1 teaspoon ground turmeric
- 3 garlic cloves, roughly chopped
- • 2-inch piece fresh ginger, peeled and roughly chopped
- 2 tablespoons prepared fresh tamarind (see p. 25)

I have chosen steaks of cheap and readily available fish for this popular curry from Goa to either conger eel or shark. Very easy to make, it is what I would call a wet curry because there is plenty of sauce, rich in coconut milk and flavored with garlic, ginger and cilantro.

For the curry paste, blend all the ingredients in a food processor or until smooth.

Season the fish steaks well with salt and pepper. Heat the oil in a deep frying pan, add the onion and fry for about 10 minutes, or until richly golden. Add the curry paste and fry for 2 minutes. Stir in the tomatoes and fry for 1 minute, then add the coconut milk and bring to a boil. Add the fish and chilies to the pan, cover and simmer for 10 to 12 minutes, turning the fish over halfway through.

Lift the fish steaks out of the pan, put them in a serving dish and keep warm. Season the sauce with salt and pepper, add the cilantro and boil for a minute or two to reduce a little. Return the fish to the sauce and serve with steamed rice.

Thai Red Seafood

Serves 6

1 lobster, weighing about 1 pound, cooked

1 crab, weighing about 1½ pounds, cooked

½ pound prepared squid (see p. 16)

1 goatfish, weighing about ¾ pound, filleted (see p. 13)

3 tablespoons sunflower oil

1 quantity of *Red Curry Paste* (see p. 219)

5 cups *Chicken Stock* (see p. 213)

¼ pound creamed coconut (see p. 23)

3 tablespoons Thai fish sauce (*nam pla*)

2 limes

3 fresh or dried kaffir lime leaves (optional)

12 large shrimp in their shells

24 large mussels, cleaned (see p. 17)

1 small bunch fresh basil, finely shredded

For the Garnishes

4 red bird's-eye chilies, thinly sliced

6 tablespoons rice vinegar or white wine vinegar

1¼ cups sunflower oil

4 shallots, thinly sliced

6 garlic cloves, thinly sliced

½ cup cashew nuts, split in half

There was a bit of a toss-up whether I was going to put this recipe in this chapter or the one on soups and stews. But because it is particularly hot and deliciously full of Thai spices and coconut milk, I decided it belonged here. It is an expensive dish to make but well worth it, as it has so much of interest in it: pieces of lobster, crab, shrimp, a delicious sauce, and accompaniments of deep-fried garlic, shallots and nuts, chili-flavored vinegar and fresh basil.

Pull the claws off the lobster, break them into 3 and lightly crack the shells with a rolling pin (see p. 19). Detach the head and legs from the tail section and discard (or save for Shellfish Stock, see p. 214). Cut the tail into 3 sections through the shell. Detach the legs and claws from the crab, break them into 3 and lightly crack the shells. Remove the body from the back shell (see pp. 20 to 21). Scoop the meat out of the back shell and set aside, discarding the shell. Remove the dead man's fingers from the body (see p. 20) and then cut the body section into quarters. Slice the squid across into rings and each fish fillet into 3 pieces.

For the garnishes, mix the chilies with the vinegar in a small bowl. Heat the oil in a frying pan, add the shallots, garlic and cashew nuts and fry for about 3 minutes, or until crisp and golden. Lift out with a slotted spoon, drain on paper towels and then spoon into another small bowl. Set aside.

Heat the oil in a large pan, add the red curry paste and fry for 2 minutes, or until the paste starts to separate from the oil. Add the stock, coconut and fish sauce and heat gently until the coconut dissolves.

Meanwhile, pare 2 strips of zest from 1 lime and cut them across into very fine shreds. Squeeze out the juice from both limes. Add the zest and juice to the pan with the dried kaffir lime leaves, if using, and simmer everything together for 2 minutes.

Add the lobster and crab pieces to the pan and simmer for 2 minutes. Add the shrimp and simmer for 1 minute. Add the squid and fish fillets and simmer for 2 minutes. Add the mussels, cover and simmer for 2 minutes until they have opened. Discard any that remain closed.

Stir in the basil and the fresh kaffir lime leaves, if using, then transfer everything to a large shallow serving platter and serve with the little bowls of prepared garnishes and Baked Rice (see p. 218) made with Thai jasmine rice.

Malaysian Fried Lemon Sole

Serves 4

3 lemon sole or flounder, weighing about 1 pound each, filleted and skinned (see pp. 14 to 15)

1½ cups cornstarch

• Sunflower oil for deep-frying

• Salt and freshly ground black pepper

For the Chili Sauce

6 red finger chilies, roughly chopped

4 garlic cloves, roughly chopped

1 teaspoon ground turmeric

• 2-inch piece fresh ginger, peeled and roughly chopped

4 tablespoons sunflower oil

1 teaspoon salt

2 tablespoons vinegar

4 to 6 tablespoons cold water

Here, lemon sole is dipped in a sauce made with red chili, garlic, ginger and turmeric, then dusted with cornstarch and deep-fried. It is a simple and delightfully spicy way of serving up any fillets of flat fish, such as sand dab or flounder, and can be accompanied by a simple green salad and maybe some plain rice (see p. 218). However, I've added a couple of satellite recipes to the main one which I suggest you try after you have done the deep-fried fish a few times. I think that the total idea comprising three separate recipes is too much to attempt straight away. In addition to the deep-fried fish there is a Roasted Tomato and Chili Sambal, which is a hot Indonesian salsa made with dried chilies, and Nasi Goreng, which is egg-fried rice with shrimp.

Put all the ingredients for the chili sauce into a blender and blend until smooth. Pour into a pan and simmer gently for 10 minutes or so, or until the mixture begins to separate.

Pour the sunflower oil into a large pan until it is about a third full. Heat to 375°F, or until a small piece of white bread dropped into the oil browns and rises to the surface in 1 minute. Put the chili sauce in one shallow dish and the cornstarch in another. Season the fish fillets and dip them first into the chili sauce and then into the cornstarch, making sure that it coats the fish evenly. Cook the fillets in the hot oil, 2 or 3 at a time, for about 2 minutes, or until crisp and golden. Lift out with a slotted spoon and drain on paper towels.

Roasted Tomato and Chili Sambal

Serves 4

2   dried pasilla chilies
     (optional)
³⁄₄ pound tomatoes, cut
     in half
6   red finger chilies
3   shallots, peeled
2   tablespoons lime juice
2   tablespoons Thai fish
     sauce (*nam pla*)

Ideally, this should include dried pasilla chilies, which are available from larger supermarkets and Mexican markets. Pasilla is a fruity chili with overtones of smoke and licorice (I sound a bit like a wine writer!) and is fantastic with seafood. See p. 22 for a more general discussion on types of chili.

If using the dried chilies, cover them with boiling water and leave to soak for 15 minutes, or until soft. Preheat broiler to high. Put the tomatoes, whole red chilies and shallots on a broiler pan and broil for 5 to 10 minutes, turning now and then, until well blackened. Cool slightly, then chop roughly by hand. Drain the soaked chilies and chop them finely, then mix with the roasted vegetables and the lime juice and fish sauce.

Nasi Goreng

Serves 4

2   eggs
2   teaspoons sesame oil
¹⁄₂ teaspoon salt
2   tablespoons sunflower
     oil
2   garlic cloves, very
     finely chopped
•   1-inch piece fresh
     ginger, peeled and very
     finely chopped
6   green onions, thinly
     sliced
¹⁄₂ quantity of *Baked Rice*
     (see p. 218)
¹⁄₄ pound cooked peeled
     shrimp
1   tablespoon chopped
     fresh cilantro

Beat the eggs with the sesame oil and salt. Heat the oil in a wok or a large frying pan, add the garlic, ginger and the white part of the green onions and stir-fry for about 3 minutes, or until golden. Add the beaten eggs and stir-fry for 1 minute. Add the cooked rice and stir until it is thoroughly heated through, then add the shrimp and heat through. Finally, sprinkle over the green tops of the onions and the cilantro, then serve.

Deep-fried Fish

One day I'm going to open a fish-and-chips shop. I think that the satisfaction of serving good fish-and-chips would be as great as serving up a plate of Helford oysters in my restaurant with a bottle of *premier cru* Chablis, followed by a thick fillet of bass with some *beurre blanc*. It's got to be done with a bit of style, though. Of course I would serve cod, haddock and flounder but also searobin, skate in batter, and marinated and deep-fried monkfish. There would be whole shrimp, mackerel and fennel fish cakes, salmon and tarragon fish cakes and a variety of batters— not just the yeast and beer batter I enjoy so much (see p. 80) but also tempura batter for deep-frying scallops and fish wrapped in wonton or spring roll wrappers and, while we're at it, we'd sell some cold fried fish in matzo meal, to be eaten with horseradish and beetroot.

Most of us feel just a shade guilty about enjoying deep-fried food because it's not held to be too healthy. Lightly cooked fish and salads, Mediterranean fish cooked in olive oil, and Indian or Chinese fish dishes containing almost no oil are the sort of thing people feel safest eating because they taste good and don't do you any harm either, but oh the charm of deep-fried fish. Who cares if it is high in fat? Just don't eat it very often.

Fish and shellfish are the perfect foods for deep-frying. Their white delicacy and tenderness make the perfect contrast to crisp batter or bread crumbs. But there is one essential point about deep-frying that makes all the difference: be extravagant with the oil. Change it regularly. The charm of deep-fried food is seeing it dipped into a bubbling inferno of clear, sparkling oil and then emerge cloaked in bright, crisp batter. The alternative is a bit like cooking new potatoes fresh from the garden in water that you have used ten times already. I'm not being totally purist about this and suggesting that you discard oil after one frying, but go and look at your oil now and throw it out!

Facing page: Salmon Fish Cakes with Sorrel and Watercress Salad in a Caper and Lemon Dressing (see p. 77).

Fritto Misto of Scallops, Shrimp and Squid with Lemon

Serves 4

8   prepared scallops (see p. 18)

$^1/_4$ pound prepared squid (see p. 16)

12   large headless shrimp, peeled and deveined (see p. 18)

4   cups olive oil

$^2/_3$ cup all-purpose flour, seasoned with salt and black pepper

2   lemons

•   Salt

This is my version of the classic Italian dish, fritto misto di mare, *where small pieces of seafood are tossed in seasoned flour and then deep-fried in olive oil. Much as I've enjoyed this dish on many occasions, I've always balked at putting it in a recipe book because of the high price of olive oil— there's no point in writing recipes if you have a suspicion that nobody is ever going to cook them. However, I spent some time trying to work out the minimum amount of oil you'd need to deep-fry 4 portions of this superb dish successfully and I now present my own version of fritto misto, specially adapted to use just one bottle of olive oil.*

Preheat the oven to 300°F. Line a large baking tray with plenty of paper towels.

Detach the coral from each scallop and slice it in half lengthwise (this prevents them exploding during cooking). Then slice the scallop meat horizontally in half as well. Cut the squid across into thick rings. Season all the seafood with a little salt.

Pour the oil into a large saucepan and heat to 375°F, or until a small piece of white bread dropped into the oil browns and rises to the surface in 1 minute. Toss the fish in the seasoned flour and deep-fry in batches for 30 seconds to 1 minute, or until the floury coating is just beginning to be tinged with brown. Lift out with a slotted spoon, arrange on the baking tray and keep hot in the oven while you cook the rest. Slice each lemon across into chunky halves and serve with the seafood.

Salmon Fish Cakes with Sorrel and Water-cress Salad in a Caper and Lemon Dressing

Serves 4

- 2 pounds potatoes, peeled and cut into chunks
- 1½ pounds salmon, cooked
- 2 tablespoons butter, melted
- 1 tablespoon chopped fresh dill
- ⅓ cup chopped fresh parsley
- 1 teaspoon salt
- • Freshly ground black pepper
- ¼ cup all-purpose flour, seasoned with salt and pepper
- 2 eggs, beaten
- 2½ cups fresh white bread crumbs
- • Small handful of sorrel leaves, torn into small pieces
- • Small handful of watercress sprigs
- • Sunflower oil for deep-frying

For the Caper and Lemon Dressing
- • Juice of 1 small lemon
- 6 tablespoons olive oil
- 2 tablespoons capers, well drained, rinsed and finely chopped
- 1 small garlic clove, crushed
- 1 tablespoon chopped fresh chives
- 1 tablespoon chopped fresh dill or fennel tops

These fish cakes have plenty of fresh tarragon in them, which goes very well with salmon I always think, and they're served with a simple salad and quite a sharp dressing to cut the richness of the deep-frying. If you can't get sorrel leaves, don't worry; just use some other small salad leaves. Sorrel does, however, add a slightly tart accent that is most pleasing with the fish cakes.

Cook the potatoes in boiling salted water until tender. Drain well, tip back into the pan and mash until smooth. Leave to cool slightly.

Break the salmon into small flakes, removing any bones and skin. Put into a bowl with the mashed potatoes, melted butter, herbs, salt and some black pepper. Mix together well. Shape the mixture into 8 rounds about 1 inch thick, cover with plastic wrap and chill for 20 minutes.

Meanwhile, whisk all the ingredients for the dressing together and season to taste.

Pour the oil into a pan until it is no more than half full and heat to 350°F, or until a small piece of bread dropped into it browns and rises to the surface in 1½ minutes. Dip the fish cakes into the seasoned flour, then the beaten eggs and finally the bread crumbs, pressing them on well to give an even coating. Deep-fry them in batches for about 4 minutes, or until crisp and golden. Lift out and drain briefly on paper towels. Keep warm in a low oven while you cook the rest.

Toss the sorrel and watercress with 1 tablespoon of the dressing. Put the fish cakes on 4 warmed plates, pile the dressed salad leaves to one side and spoon a little more dressing over the remainder of the plate.

Deep-fried Sea Bass with Chili Sauce

Serves 4

4   sea bass weighing
      about $^3/_4$ pound each,
      cleaned (see p. 11)
$^1/_3$ cup all-purpose flour,
      seasoned with salt and
      pepper
•   Sunflower oil for
      deep-frying

For the Chili Sauce
2   tablespoons finely
      chopped garlic
2   large red chilies, finely
      chopped
2   tablespoons sunflower
      oil
2   tablespoons palm sugar
      or soft dark brown
      sugar
3   tablespoons Thai fish
      sauce (*nam pla*)
1   tablespoon tamarind
      mixed with 1 tablespoon
      water, or 2 tablespoons
      lemon juice

For the Garnishes
4   shallots, sliced
2   garlic cloves, thinly
      sliced
$^1/_3$ cup cashew nuts,
      halved
2   kaffir lime leaves, finely
      shredded (optional)
1   cup fresh basil leaves

I ate a whole fish served this way a few years ago at Hua Hin, in Thailand. The interesting thing about it is that I can't quite remember what the dish was like, so I keep on coming up with approximations, and each one seems almost nicer than the last. That reveals quite a lot about how one thinks up new recipes: little scraps of information bob around in one's mind and gradually build up into a firm idea. This dish is rather good. The fish is just dusted in seasoned flour, deep-fried, then served with deep-fried sliced garlic, shallots, lime leaves, cashew nuts and basil, and a hot-and-sweet chili sauce.

For the sauce, pound together the garlic and chilies in a mortar with a pestle until they form a coarse paste. Heat the oil in a small saucepan, add the garlic-and-chili paste and fry for 1 minute. Stir in the sugar, fish sauce and tamarind water or lemon juice, bring to a simmer and keep warm.

Next prepare the garnishes. Fill a pan large enough to accommodate the fish about one-third full with sunflower oil. Heat to 375°F, or until a small piece of white bread dropped into it browns and rises to the surface in 1 minute. Add the sliced shallots, garlic and cashew nuts and fry for 2 minutes. Lift out with a slotted spoon and drain on paper towels. Add the shredded lime leaves, if using, and the basil leaves and fry for about 30 seconds. Drain and set aside.

Rinse the fish and pat dry. Coat in the seasoned flour and deep-fry, one at a time, for 5 to 6 minutes, or until crisp and golden. Lift out, drain briefly on paper towels and keep warm while you cook the remaining fish.

Put the fish on 4 warmed plates and spoon over the sauce. Scatter with the garnishes and serve.

Deep-fried Cod in a Yeast and Beer Batter with Tartare Sauce and Chips

Serves 4

2 pounds Maris Piper potatoes, peeled and cut lengthwise into chips $\frac{1}{2}$ inch thick

4 thick pieces of cod fillet from the loin end, not the tail, weighing about 6 ounces each

• Sunflower oil for deep-frying

• Fresh flat-leaf parsley sprigs, to garnish (optional)

• Salt and freshly ground black pepper

For the Yeast and Beer Batter

1 tablespoon active dry yeast

$1\frac{1}{4}$ cups beer

$1\frac{2}{3}$ cups all-purpose flour

1 teaspoon salt

For the Tartare Sauce

$\frac{1}{2}$ quantity of Mustard Mayonnaise (see p. 216)

1 teaspoon finely chopped green olives

1 teaspoon finely chopped gherkins

1 teaspoon finely chopped capers

2 teaspoons chopped fresh chives

2 teaspoons chopped fresh parsley

The best ever! I used to think that the only decent chips were the thin and crispy French-style frites because, on the whole, my experiences of chips in British fish-and-chip shops have been rather limp and soggy, greasy and unappetizing. But the other day, while walking down London's Kings Road, I nipped into a place called Ed's Easy Diner because it looked so friendly in an American chrome-and-formica sort of way. I had a burger and a side order of American fries, which were big, thick chips but, as the current saying goes, these chips were "to die for." They were crisp and fat but also slightly grainy and sandy on the outside, like the best roast potatoes. I hope I've managed to re-create them here. I always use one type of potato, Maris Piper, a floury variety that I have found makes consistently the best chips. In summer most recently dug potatoes make great chips, but for the rest of the year potatoes tend to absorb the oil and look greasy. I don't find that the floury varieties normally recommended for chips work very well, and sometimes even Maris Piper potatoes fry up greasy and soggy, too. A good chip potato fries dry and crisp. When we get a good one, we buy a ton or so, but every time we buy in a new batch we have to test them.

I think you will very much enjoy the batter, which is lightened by yeast and beer. It has a taste and smell almost of fresh bread and remains perfectly crisp. Guinness gives it a pleasing dark appearance, but any beer will do.

For the batter, dissolve the yeast in a little of the beer. When it foams, gradually stir in the rest of the beer. Sift the flour and salt into a bowl, make a well in the center and pour in the beer mixture. Gradually whisk the liquid into the flour to make a smooth batter. Cover and leave at room temperature for 1 hour.

Preheat the oven to 300°F. Line a baking sheet with plenty of paper towels and set aside. Mix together all the ingredients for the tartare sauce and set aside.

If you don't have a thermostatically controlled chip fryer you will need to use a fairly good-sized friture, a pan that will take about $4\frac{1}{2}$ quarts with a frying basket to fit. Use about $2\frac{1}{2}$ quarts of oil; it is never sensible to fill a deep-frying pan more than that.

Cooking chips in 2 stages makes them crisp on the outside and fluffy inside. First you blanch them. Heat the oil to 275°F and fry the chips in 2 batches for about 5 minutes, emptying them into a roasting pan afterward. The object is to cook the potatoes through without color.

To fry the fish, heat the oil to 325°F, season the pieces of fish with salt and pepper and then dip them into the batter. Fry 2 pieces at a time for 7 to 8 minutes, or until crisp and deep golden brown. Lift out and drain on the prepared baking sheet, then keep hot in the oven while you cook the other 2 pieces.

Raise the temperature to 375°F and fry the chips, again in 2 batches, until crisp and deep golden brown. Serve immediately, with the tartare sauce. At the restaurant we finish the frying by dropping sprigs of parsley into the fryer for a few seconds, which we serve as a garnish.

Deep-fried Cod Stuffed with Pesto Butter

Serves 4

For the Pesto Butter

½   cup fresh basil leaves
2   large garlic cloves,
     roughly chopped
2   tablespoons grated
     Parmesan cheese
2   tablespoons pine nuts
3   tablespoons olive oil
½   teaspoon salt

The contrast between a crisp, golden bread crumb coating, delicate flakes of moist white fish and a just-melted center of fragrant basil, garlic and pine nut pesto is a delight. It is important to get the right cut of fish for this dish. A good thick fillet of cod cut from just behind the head of a large fish is ideal.

First make the pesto butter. Put all the ingredients except the butter into a food processor and blend until smooth. Scrape the mixture into a bowl and beat in the softened butter. Spoon the pesto butter onto a sheet of plastic wrap in a line about 4 inches long, then roll it up in the plastic wrap into a sausage shape, twisting the ends of the plastic wrap to secure it. Put in the freezer until hard. When the butter is firm, use to stuff the fish (see below).

Stuffing the Cod with Pesto Butter

1. Trim away the thinner belly flap from the fillet and cut the rest into four 6-ounce pieces, each about 5 inches long.

2. To make a pocket in the pieces of cod, make a deep cut, 3 inches long, in the side of each piece of fish with a small, sharp knife, taking care not to cut right through to the other side.

3. Remove the butter from the freezer, unwrap and cut into slices ½ inch thick. Gently poke 2 pieces of butter into the pocket of each piece of fish and then close up the pocket so that no butter is visible.

2   tablespoons butter, softened

1   thick fillet of cod, 2$\frac{1}{2}$ pounds, skinned

4   tablespoons all-purpose flour, seasoned with salt and pepper

1   egg, beaten

1$\frac{1}{2}$ cups fresh white bread crumbs

•   Sunflower oil for deep-frying

Pour the oil into a large pan so that it is about one-third full. Heat to 350°F, or until a small piece of white bread dropped into the oil browns and rises to the surface in 1$\frac{1}{2}$ minutes. Dip the pieces of fish in the seasoned flour, making sure that they are all well coated. Then dip them into the beaten egg and lastly the bread crumbs, pressing them on well to give a thick, even coating. Deep-fry the fish, 2 pieces at a time, for 5 minutes or until crisp and golden. Lift out and drain on paper towels, then serve straight away.

Sun-dried Tomato, Roasted Red Pepper and Chili Butter

Finely chop $\frac{1}{2}$ roasted red pepper, 2 sun-dried tomatoes and $\frac{1}{2}$ red finger chili, then mix together with a little salt. Beat in 2 tablespoons softened butter, then continue as for the main recipe.

Tempura

Serves 4

12	headless shrimp in their shells
6	ounces flounder fillets, skinned
1/4	pound prepared squid (see p. 16), sliced into rings
•	Salt
4	fresh shiitake mushrooms, cut in half
8	chrysanthemum leaves (optional)
1	small zucchini, cut lengthwise into slices 1/8 inch thick
12	sugar snap peas
6	green onions, cut into 3-inch lengths
8	asparagus tips
1/4	cup cornstarch
•	Peanut or sunflower oil for deep-frying

For the Dashi

6	cups water
1/2	ounce dried kelp (kombu)
1/2	ounce shaved dried bonito fillet (katsuobushi)

For the Dipping Sauce

3	tablespoons mirin (rice cooking wine) or dry sherry

Small pieces of fish and vegetables are dipped in the lightest batter imaginable and cooked in sparkling-fresh hot oil. The secret of making good tempura is to prepare the batter at the very last minute, keep the oil at the right temperature, and serve and eat the pieces as quickly as possible. For this reason I have specified cooking in a small pan with a small amount of oil and only frying a few pieces at a time. These are bought to the table and eaten by your guests while you, unfortunately, have to go back and deep-fry the next batch. But it is this sort of communal cooking and eating that is what relaxed and informal meals with friends are all about. You really should eat this dish with chopsticks and the idea is that you pick up a deep-fried morsel and dip it into the sauce.

Dashi, used to make the dipping sauce, is a Japanese stock, but if you cannot get the ingredients you can substitute chicken stock. You may wonder at the inclusion of chrysanthemum leaves in the tempura, but the Japanese use a number of different leaves of the chrysanthemum family in their cooking. They have a slightly bitter, scented flavor.

Peel the shrimp, leaving the last tail segment in place, and devein them (see p. 18). Sprinkle the shrimp, flounder and squid with a little salt.

For the dipping sauce, first make the dashi. Bring the water to a boil, add the dried kelp and stir around for 3 to 4 minutes to release the flavor. Remove the kelp with a slotted spoon and add the shaved bonito. Bring to a boil, then remove from the heat and leave for a few minutes until the flakes settle to the bottom. Strain through a cheesecloth-lined sieve and set aside 1 cup to use in the dipping sauce (the remainder can be frozen for later use).

Pour the mirin or dry sherry, soy sauce and dashi into a small pan, add a pinch of salt and bring to a boil. Keep warm over low heat while you fry the fish and vegetables. Mix together the daikon and ginger and set aside.

Pour some oil into a medium-sized saucepan until one-third full and heat to 375°F. Meanwhile, make the tempura batter. Put the egg and ice water into a bowl and stir together until well mixed. Sift over the flour and cornstarch and mix very briefly until just combined—there should be a few little lumps of flour still remaining. The batter should be as thin as light cream; if it is any thicker, add a little more ice water.

3 tablespoons Japanese soy sauce

• 6-inch piece of daikon (white radish), coarsely grated

2 tablespoons finely grated fresh ginger

For the Tempura Batter

1 egg

½ cup ice water

3 tablespoons all-purpose flour

1 tablespoon cornstarch

To test the temperature of the oil, drizzle a little batter into the pan; it should sink slightly, then rise to the surface and brown in 45 seconds. If the oil is too hot the batter will stay on the surface, while if it is too cool it will sink to the bottom and rise to the top only very slowly.

The seafood, mushrooms and chrysanthemum leaves can be dipped directly into the cornstarch and then the batter; the other vegetables need to be dipped into cold water before the cornstarch and batter to help the coating stick. Coat 6 pieces of fish and vegetables at a time, drop into the hot oil and fry for 1 to 1½ minutes, or until crisp and golden. Lift out with a slotted spoon and drain briefly on paper towels. As soon as a small selection of tempura is cooked, arrange on a large plate. Pour the warm dipping sauce into 4 shallow dishes or ramekins and pile the grated daikon and ginger into the center of each dish. Take the tempura and dipping sauce to the table and top up the plate with the remaining batches of tempura as you cook them.

Deep-fried Prawn Wontons with Chili Jam

Serves 4

20 headless shrimp in their shells
20 Chinese wonton wrappers
• Oil for deep-frying
• Salt

For the Chili Jam
1/4 cup sunflower or vegetable oil
2 tablespoons very finely chopped garlic
2 tablespoons very finely chopped ginger
1/2 pound onions, very finely chopped
5 large red finger chilies, seeded and very finely chopped
7 tablespoons red wine vinegar
2 tablespoons Japanese soy sauce
1/2 teaspoon ground star anise
1 tablespoon palm sugar or soft dark brown sugar
• Salt

Here, the shrimp are enclosed in wonton wrappers, but the tails are left on and, to highlight the appearance, are not wrapped, otherwise they look a bit like Egyptian mummies. They are served with a dark chili and onion relish flavored with garlic, ginger and soy sauce. Large raw shrimp in the shell are now available at most supermarkets, and wonton wrappers can be bought in Asian food shops. Try to use Chinese rather than Japanese wrappers, as they puff up nicely during frying.

Peel the shrimp, leaving the last tail segment in place (see p. 18), and reserve the shells. Heat the sunflower or vegetable oil for the chili jam in a medium-sized pan, add the shrimp shells and fry over high heat for 1 to 2 minutes, or until they are quite crisp. Tip everything into a sieve resting over a small pan and press really well to remove all the oil. The oil will now be pleasantly flavored with shrimp.

To make the jam, reheat the oil, add the garlic and ginger and fry quickly until both are beginning to color. Add the onions and chilies and fry fiercely for 3 to 4 minutes. Stir in the vinegar, soy sauce, star anise, sugar and some salt to taste. Bring to a boil and simmer gently for 20 to 30 minutes, or until the onions are very soft and the jam is well reduced and thick. Leave to cool, then spoon into 4 small dipping bowls or ramekins.

Wrap each shrimp in one of the wonton wrappers, leaving the tail end uncovered, and seal with a little water. Pour the oil into a pan until it is about one-third full. Heat to 375°F, or until a small piece of white bread dropped in the oil browns and rises to the surface in 1 minute. Fry the shrimp in batches for about 1 to 1 1/2 minutes, or until crisp and golden. Lift out and drain briefly on paper towels. Serve hot with the chili jam.

Mackerel Fish Cakes with Fennel

Serves 4

1   pound floury potatoes, peeled and cut into chunks

1   mackerel, about 2 pounds

2   tablespoons chopped fresh fennel tops or dill

2   tablespoons butter, melted

1   teaspoon salt

10 turns of the black pepper mill

1   tablespoon Pernod or Ricard (optional)

⅓ cup all-purpose flour, seasoned with salt and pepper

2   eggs, beaten

2½ cups fresh white bread crumbs

• Sunflower oil for deep-frying

• Salt and freshly ground black pepper

I'm very fond of mackerel in fish cakes. The taste takes me right back to my childhood in Cornwall, when we used to go out for mackerel around Padstow or the Scilly Isles. Couple it with some fresh fennel and a simple fish cake becomes something much more special. Except that the only sauce to go with this is tomato ketchup!

Cook the potatoes in boiling salted water until tender, drain well and then mash.

Preheat the broiler. Make 2 or 3 shallow cuts in either side of each mackerel—this helps the heat penetrate the fish—and season well with salt and pepper. Broil for about 5 minutes on each side, then cool slightly. When the mackerel are cool enough to handle, flake the flesh, discarding the skin and bones.

Mix the mashed potato and flaked mackerel with the chopped fennel herb or dill, melted butter, salt, pepper and the Pernod or Ricard, if using. Divide the mixture into eighths and shape into rounds 1 inch thick. Chill for about 20 minutes, or until firm.

Pour the oil into a large pan so that it is no more than half full and heat to 350°F, or until a small piece of bread dropped into it browns and rises to the surface in 1½ minutes.

Dip the fish cakes first in the seasoned flour, then in the beaten eggs and finally in the bread crumbs, pressing them on well to give an even coating. Deep-fry for about 4 minutes, or until crisp and golden, then lift out and drain briefly on paper towels before serving.

Deep-fried Fish Pies

Serves 4

2½ cups *Fish Stock*
(see p. 212)

6 ounces undyed smoked haddock

6 ounces haddock fillet or cod fillet

5 tablespoons butter

⅔ cup all-purpose flour

¼ cup heavy cream

⅓ cup finely chopped button mushrooms

2 tablespoons very finely grated Cheddar cheese

2 hard-boiled eggs, peeled and chopped

2 tablespoons roughly chopped fresh parsley

1 egg, beaten

1½ cups fresh white bread crumbs

• Salt and freshly ground black pepper

• Sunflower oil for deep-frying

• *Tartare Sauce* (see p. 80), to serve

I'm really pleased with this dish. What I did was take the filling for a good fish pie—a creamy velouté sauce, flaked white fish, parsley and hard-boiled egg—pour it into round molds lined with plastic wrap and chill it. When I took them out, the mixture had formed fish-cake shapes. I floured, egged and bread-crumbed them, then deep-fried them.

Bring the stock to a boil in a deep frying pan or a saucepan. Add the smoked haddock and the fresh fish, bring back to a simmer and cook for 5 to 7 minutes, or until firm and opaque. Lift the fish out of the stock and, when cool enough to handle, flake the flesh, discarding any bones and skin.

Melt 4 tablespoons of the butter in a clean pan, add 6 tablespoons of the flour and cook, stirring, for 1 minute. Remove from the heat and gradually stir in the stock. Return to the heat, bring to a boil, then add the cream and leave to simmer over very low heat for 15 minutes, stirring now and then, until you have a very thick sauce.

Melt the remaining butter in a small pan, add the mushrooms and fry briskly over high heat for 1 minute. Stir into the sauce with the grated cheese, hard-boiled eggs, parsley and flaked fish, then season to taste.

Put four 4-inch plain pastry cutters or egg poaching rings on a baking sheet and line each one with a sheet of plastic wrap, leaving the edges overhanging. Divide the fish mixture among the rings, level the tops and then cover with the overhanging plastic wrap. Chill for at least 6 hours, or until very firm.

To cook, lift off the rings from each "pie" and remove the plastic wrap. Pour the oil for deep-frying into a large pan until it is about one-third full. Heat to 325°F. Meanwhile, carefully dip each pie into the remaining flour, then the beaten egg and finally the bread crumbs, pressing them on well to give an even coating. Deep-fry for about 9 minutes, or until crisp and golden. Serve immediately, with Tartare Sauce and a crisp green salad.

Summer Fish and Salads

I was sitting on the lawn the other evening, drinking a glass of chilled Chenin Blanc, and eating some lobster with salad and mayonnaise that had been made with a divinely smoky Italian olive oil. I ruminated—as one does at tranquil times such as this, when all that is needed to set off the most perfect evening is the occasional firefly in the gathering dusk, flitting by with little bursts of yellow light—on barbecues and how the smell of barbecues on a summer's evening is quite often pretty repulsive.

A typical barbecue in many a garden involves flavoring pieces of meat and fish with the exhaust fumes from igniting oil coupled with the burning effect of sheets of flame. The smell is of burnt oil and fire lighters. The barbecue is lit but there are never enough coals on it in the first place, nor does anyone wait long enough for them to burn down and produce intense heat. Then the grid is loaded with far too much heavily oiled food. The oil drops into the coals, bursts into flame, and everything acquires that all-too-familiar blackened flavor. Charred lumps of meat and fish are then served up with little else but a green salad and everyone thinks they're having a great time. Plenty of beer and Chardonnay and the world is a fine and sunny place. This chapter is designed to take a slightly fresher look at outdoor eating. Not all the recipes are cooked on a barbecue, but they are all the sort of food that you can imagine eating outdoors and that tastes all the better for it. So I've got a fantastic monkfish dish, which is started off on a charcoal grill and then finished on the stove on a bed of ratatouille. I've got raw salmon and smoked salmon made into a neat shape with slices of avocado, a little chopped onion and olive oil and served with a basil and tomato dressing. I've got a beautiful salad that I first ate on Christmas day overlooking a beach in Australia, made with rice-shaped pasta, sun-dried tomatoes, grilled vegetables and lots of seafood. I've got fried squid served with a simple Greek salad, all cut very small. I've got grilled shark steaks with a simple tomato and cumin chutney but best of all, I've got paella, that superb, much messed-about dish from Valencia. I've made it as simple as I can, with the minimum of ingredients—just really good rice, the finest saffron and the best-quality seafood.

Facing page: Rice-Shaped Pasta with Seafood, Arugula and Roasted Vegetables (see p. 104).

Serves 4

4   tuna steaks, each
    weighing 7 ounces
6   tablespoons dark soy
    sauce
4   tablespoons balsamic
    vinegar

For the Salad

1   tablespoon sesame
    seeds
1   bunch fresh cilantro,
    2 ounces
6   green onions, trimmed
·   Coarsely grated zest
    and juice of 1 lime
2   tablespoons Thai fish
    sauce *(nam pla)*
6   tablespoons water
2   teaspoons Asian
    sesame oil
2   tablespoons sunflower
    oil
3   ounces rice vermicelli
    noodles
3   green finger chilies,
    seeded and finely
    chopped
2   tablespoons Japanese
    pickled ginger, peeled
    and cut into shreds
·   Small bunch fresh
    garlic chives (optional),
    chopped
1   bunch watercress,
    larger stems removed
    and broken into sprigs

Seared Tuna with Rice Noodle and Cilantro Salad

I cooked this on my last trip to Australia after we'd been out on a yellowfin tuna boat off Ulludulla—can you think of a more Australian sounding name than Ulludulla! This recipe sums up how I feel about Australian cooking at its best. The tuna is served very rare and the accompanying salad is designed to be served warm, not hot. I have suggested that you use three green chilies for this recipe because it needs to be quite punchy, but it will depend on how hot they are and how much you like chili, so feel free to adjust this to your own taste.

For the salad, preheat the broiler. Spread the sesame seeds onto a baking sheet and toast, shaking the pan now and then, until golden. Pick the leaves off the cilantro and discard the stems—if they are quite large, very roughly chop them. You will need about 6 tablespoons in all. Very thinly slice the green onions on the diagonal. Mix together the lime juice, fish sauce, water, and sesame and sunflower oils.

Bring a pan of water to a boil, drop in the noodles and take it off the heat. Leave for 3 minutes, drain well and tip back into the pan. Cover and keep warm. Heat a heavy-bottomed frying pan until very hot. Brush with a little oil, add the tuna steaks and cook for 2 minutes on each side. Add the soy sauce and balsamic vinegar to the pan and boil vigorously, turning the steaks once, until they become coated in a rich brown glaze. Remove from the heat and keep warm while you finish the salad.

Add the sesame seeds, cilantro, green onions, lime zest, green chili, pickled ginger, the garlic chives, if using, and the watercress to the noodles. Add the dressing ingredients and toss everything together.

Pile some of the salad into the center of 4 warmed plates, slice each tuna steak into 3 on the angle and rest them on top of the salad. Serve the rest of the salad separately.

Salad of Grilled Garfish with Fennel Seeds

Serves 4

4   garfish, weighing about
    10 to 12 ounces each,
    filleted (see p. 13)
2   tablespoons olive oil
·   Juice of $^1/_4$ lemon
1   teaspoon chopped
    fresh thyme
1   teaspoon fennel seeds
·   A good pinch of dried
    red pepper flakes
$^1/_2$ teaspoon salt
·   A few twists of freshly
    ground black pepper
4   to 6 sun-dried tomatoes
    in oil, drained and thinly
    sliced

For the Salad
4   tablespoons extra-
    virgin olive oil
1   fresh oregano sprig,
    finely chopped
1   tablespoon sherry
    vinegar
1   ounce arugula
1   ounce curly endive
$^1/_2$ ounce fresh flat-leaf
    parsley (about $^1/_2$ cup)
$^1/_2$ ounce fresh chervil
    (about $^1/_2$ cup)

The idea for this recipe came from Australia, where garfish are available from most fishmongers. The same species swims in British waters but is not so easy to buy—I suspect that people are put off by the bright turquoise bones. However, it's a delicious fish, firm in texture and eminently suitable for grilling. Should you ever see it on sale, snap it up; otherwise use searobin, mullet, sole or even mackerel.

It is important to arrange the components of the salad on the plates without flattening the delicate leaves too much, gradually building up the dressed salad leaves, tomato strips and grilled fish in layers. It should be served with a big bowl of chips (see p. 80) in the center of the table, so you can eat the salad while dipping in and out of the chips with your fingers.

Cut the fish fillets diagonally into 3-inch pieces. Mix together the olive oil, lemon juice, thyme, fennel seeds, red pepper flakes, salt and pepper. Brush a little of this mixture over both sides of the fish and leave for 5 minutes to allow the flavors to permeate it.

Put the arugula and curly endive in a large bowl. Break the parsley and chervil into small sprigs and add to the bowl.

Put a lightly oiled cast-iron ribbed pan over high heat until really hot. Add the pieces of fish, skin-side down, and cook for 1 to $1^1/_2$ minutes, turning them over halfway through. Transfer to a plate and keep warm. Add the olive oil/fennel seed mixture and sherry vinegar to the hot pan and swirl around. Remove from the heat.

Arrange the leaves, sun-dried tomato strips and fish in layers on 4 serving plates, poking in the pieces of the fish so that they don't flatten the salad leaves. Pour the warm dressing all around the salads and a little over the top. Serve immediately.

Stir-fried Crab with Black Beans, Ginger and Green Onions

Serves 4

1	cooked Dungeness crab, weighing about 3 pounds
$1/4$	pound rice noodles
3	tablespoons sunflower oil
•	2-inch piece fresh ginger, peeled and cut into fine matchsticks 1 inch long
8	green onions, sliced
1	tablespoon salted black beans or black bean sauce
4	garlic cloves, finely chopped
2	tablespoons Chinese rice wine or 1 tablespoon dry sherry
1	tablespoon dark soy sauce
6	tablespoons water
$1/2$	teaspoon salt

Serve this with the Chinese Cabbage with Oyster Sauce *below. Some people hate the idea of fiddling around with crab in the shell but if, like me, you find it a pleasure, do try this recipe, where pieces of crab in the shell are served with a pile of steaming fresh noodles with ginger and green onions. I have used a cooked Dungeness crab, but if by any chance you can get hold of a live crab, the flavor will be incomparably better. Kill it first by inserting a screwdriver or skewer between the eyes, then follow the method below, but increase the cooking time to 5 minutes.*

Put the crab upside down on a chopping board and twist off the claws and legs. Break the claws in half at the joint and lightly crack the shells with a rolling pin. Twist and remove the bony tail flap and discard. Pry the body away from the back shell, remove the dead man's fingers (see pp. 20–21) and cut the body into quarters. Remove the meat from the shell and reserve; discard the shell.

Cook the rice noodles in boiling water for 3 minutes, or until just tender, then drain and keep warm. Heat the oil in a wok or a large, deep frying pan. Add the ginger, the white part of the green onions, the black beans and garlic and stir-fry over high heat for 1 minute. Add all the crab pieces and the crabmeat, the rice wine or sherry, soy sauce, water and salt and stir-fry for $1^1/2$ to 2 minutes, or until the crab is heated through. Add the green onion tops and the warm noodles, toss quickly and serve with the Chinese Cabbage with Oyster Sauce (below).

Chinese Cabbage with Oyster Sauce

Serves 4

2	teaspoons salt
4	tablespoons peanut oil
2	pounds Chinese cabbage such as choy sum or bok choy, peeled and cut into 6-inch pieces
3	tablespoons oyster sauce

This can also be made with very long, thick Chinese chives.

Bring 2 quarts of water to a boil in a large pan. Add the salt, 2 tablespoons of the oil and the cabbage, bring back to a boil and boil for 1 minute, or until the cabbage is tender but still retains a bit of bite. Drain well, return to the pan with the remaining oil and 2 tablespoons of the oyster sauce and toss lightly. Spoon on to a serving dish and drizzle with the remaining oyster sauce.

Warm Salad of New Potatoes with Matjes Herring, Chives and Sour Cream Vinaigrette

Serves 4

- 1 pound Pink Fir Apple potatoes or other waxy new potatoes
- 6 tablespoons sour cream
- 1 large shallot, very finely chopped
- 1 teaspoon English mustard
- 1 tablespoon white wine vinegar
- 1/2 tablespoon chopped fresh chives, plus a few whole chives to garnish
- 1 small garlic clove, crushed
- 1/2 pound matjes herring fillets, cut into slices 1 inch wide
- Salt and freshly ground black pepper

Pink Fir Apple potatoes, a beautiful waxy salad variety, are in the shops from late summer until the end of the year. If you can't find them, any waxy salad potato will do just fine. Cured with sugar, salt and saltpeter, matjes herrings are the most delicious cured herrings on earth, popular in Holland, Belgium and Germany. The word matjes means "virgin," and the herrings are young, with the roe not fully developed. These days they are only very lightly salted and normally sold presoaked, filleted and ready to eat. If you cannot get matjes herrings, any cured but not smoked herring fillets will do instead.

Cook the potatoes in boiling water until tender, then drain and leave to cool slightly. Meanwhile, mix together the sour cream, shallot, mustard, vinegar, chives and garlic. Cut the potatoes into thick slices and put them into a bowl with the herrings and the sour cream dressing. Season with a little salt and pepper and stir together gently. Spoon the mixture on to 4 plates and garnish with a few chive stems.

Stuffed Squid

Serves 4

8   squid

·   Salt

⅓   cup pine nuts

1   medium onion, finely chopped

2   garlic cloves, finely chopped

4   tablespoons olive oil

½   cup long-grain rice

3   tablespoons raisins

2   tablespoons chopped fresh flat-leaf parsley

·   Freshly ground black pepper

1   can (14 ounces) chopped tomatoes

2   sun-dried tomatoes in oil, drained and finely chopped

½   cup dry white wine

This is the classic Greek recipe for stuffing the bodies of squid or cuttlefish. You will need to use medium-sized squid with a body section measuring about 5 to 6 inches in length.

Preheat the oven to 350°F.

Clean the squid (see p. 16), taking care not to split the pouches. Rub the outside of the pouches liberally with 1 teaspoon of salt, leave for 5 minutes and then rinse well with cold water. Chop the tentacles into small pieces.

Spread the pine nuts on a baking sheet and toast in the oven for about 7 minutes, or until lightly browned. Remove from the oven and set aside.

Fry the onion and garlic in 2 tablespoons of the olive oil for 5 minutes, or until softened and lightly browned. Add the chopped squid tentacles and fry for 3 minutes. Stir in the rice, pine nuts, raisins and parsley and season with salt and pepper. Leave to cool slightly and then spoon into the squid pouches, making sure they are only two-thirds full to allow room for the rice to swell up. Secure each one with a sturdy toothpick, if you wish.

Heat the remaining oil in a large dutch oven. Add the squid and fry for a few minutes on all sides until lightly browned. Add the canned tomatoes, sun-dried tomatoes, wine, and salt and pepper to taste. Cover and bake in the oven for 1 hour. Serve hot or cold.

Grillade of Tuna with Olive Oil Mashed Potatoes

Serves 4

½ quantity of *Tomato Sauce* (see p. 48), made without the basil

3 tablespoons olive oil

• Leaves from 2 fresh thyme sprigs

4 tuna steaks, weighing about 6 ounces each

• Sea salt and freshly ground black pepper

For the Dressing

½ cup extra-virgin olive oil

2 tablespoons red wine vinegar

3 tablespoons chopped mixed fresh herbs, such as dill, young bay leaf, thyme, rosemary, oregano, savory

1 teaspoon salt

• Freshly ground black pepper

For the Potatoes

2 pounds floury potatoes, peeled and cut into chunks

2 tablespoons heavy cream

6 tablespoons olive oil

4 tablespoons *Chicken Stock* (see p. 213)

2 garlic cloves, crushed

½ teaspoon salt

I cooked this when we were filming the third program in the second television series, in Sormiou, an idyllic beach just outside Marseilles in the Calanques. We arrived in Marseilles, typically, with no cooking equipment and nowhere to cook, but we managed to borrow a cabano, a terra-cotta–tiled holiday cabin, just up from the beach, with a tiny kitchen to film in and a nice big terrace that had a glorious view over the limestone hills behind, dotted with wild thyme, mallow and great clumps of daisies. The fish in that case were sea bass and daurade royale, also known as gilt-head bream, but tuna works well too, as do swordfish and shark.

The dressing for the grillade is a difficult concept to grasp. I start with a simple, well-reduced, sharp tomato sauce and add lots of chopped aromatic herbs—what I loosely call Provençal herbs—to a dressing of olive oil and wine vinegar. The idea is that the finished dressing should look split, i.e., the tomato should appear to have separated from the dressing. It just looks much more fresh and appetizing than a smooth tomato sauce. Texture is very important visually as well as for the taste in my cooking.

Make the tomato sauce and then pass it through a sieve into a clean pan. If necessary, simmer for a few minutes until the sauce is thick enough to coat the back of a spoon. Adjust the seasoning and keep warm.

Put all the ingredients for the dressing into a bowl, season with black pepper and whisk together. Stir into the tomato sauce and keep warm.

For the olive oil mashed potatoes, cook the potatoes in boiling salted water until tender, then drain. Add the cream, olive oil, stock, garlic and salt and mash until smooth. Set aside and keep warm.

Place a lightly oiled cast-iron ribbed pan over high heat. Mix the olive oil with the thyme leaves. Brush the tuna with the thyme oil and season well with sea salt and black pepper. When the pan is very hot, put the tuna on it and cook for about 4 to 5 minutes on each side, pressing down firmly with the back of a spatula to help mark the fish with the lines from the griddle.

To serve, put the tuna on 4 warmed plates and spoon the potatoes to one side. Using a teaspoon, spoon little pools of the sauce to the other side of the fish.

Monkfish Roasted over Charcoal with Ratatouille

Serves 4

2¼ pounds monkfish tail
1 head of garlic, cloves peeled and thinly sliced
1 teaspoon ground fennel seeds
2 red and 2 green bell peppers
⅔ cup olive oil, plus extra for brushing
• Salt
2 eggplants, sliced into rounds ¼ inch thick
2 large onions, sliced
1 pound zucchini, sliced
• Freshly ground black pepper
3 beefsteak tomatoes, peeled and cut into quarters
• Leaves from 1 fresh thyme sprig
2 fresh bay leaves, very thinly sliced

This dish is far better cooked on a charcoal or gas-fired grill because not only does the monkfish get that wonderful grilled flavor but you can also barbecue the peppers and eggplants for the ratatouille, which lends it a marvelously smoky taste. However, if you don't have a grill, you can do all the cooking indoors and the dish will still taste good.

The secret of making a great ratatouille is to cook the vegetables thoroughly so that the flavors are concentrated and you end up with something full of flavor rather than everyone's weak and watery nightmare vegetarian dish! Although this ratatouille is made with grilled vegetables, you can also serve the monkfish with a more conventional ratatouille. Try following the recipe in the poem called "Ratatouille" on p. 154. I've done it and it works perfectly.

Remove the skin from the monkfish and cut off most of the membrane (see p. 15), otherwise the tail will curl up rather unattractively while it cooks. Make 10 small incisions all over it with the point of a small knife. Take 10 slices of the garlic and turn them over in the ground fennel to coat. Slide them down the blade of the knife into the monkfish.

For the ratatouille, brush the peppers with some of the oil and cook on a grill, turning them as they blacken and blister. Put the sliced eggplants in a shallow dish with 4 tablespoons of the olive oil, sprinkle with salt and turn them over in the oil until well coated. Cook on the grill for a few minutes on both sides until soft. If you don't have a barbecue, you can cook the vegetables on a cast-iron ribbed pan or cook the peppers under a broiler and fry the eggplants in the same amount of oil.

Heat half the remaining oil in a dutch oven, add the onions and cook very gently for about 30 minutes, stirring occasionally. Add the remaining garlic and the zucchini, season with salt and pepper and cook for another 5 minutes.

Pour the rest of the oil into a frying pan and fry the tomatoes over high heat until just beginning to fall apart. Add the tomatoes and oil to the dutch oven.

Remove the blistered skin from the peppers, cut them in half and remove the seeds, taking care not to pour away the delicious juice that will have accumulated inside. Pour this into the dutch oven. Slice the peppers and add them, too, with the eggplants. Stir in more salt and pepper and the thyme and bay leaves, then cook the ratatouille, uncovered, over very gentle heat for about 1 hour, by which time the excess moisture in the vegetables will have evaporated and the vegetables should shine with oil.

Meanwhile, brush the monkfish with oil and season well with salt and pepper. Cook over the grill for 5 minutes on each side until lightly browned. Alternatively, broil it for 5 minutes on each side. Now put it on top of the ratatouille, cover with a lid and simmer for the last 20 minutes of the ratatouille cooking time. Check that the monkfish is cooked by making a small incision in the thickest part right into the center. The fillet should be white right through. If it still looks a bit translucent in the middle, give it another 5 minutes.

To serve, lift out the monkfish and cut it into slices. Spoon the ratatouille on to 4 warmed plates, place the sliced monkfish on top and serve with a green salad and a bottle of ice-cold Bandol rosé wine.

Seared Scallop Salad with Prosciutto and Croutons

Serves 4

12 prepared scallops or 24 bay scallops (see p. 18)
· Salt and freshly ground black pepper
$2\frac{1}{2}$ tablespoons unsalted butter
3 slices whole-wheat bread, $\frac{1}{2}$ inch thick, crusts removed, cut into $\frac{1}{2}$-inch cubes
$\frac{1}{4}$ pound mixed young salad greens
8 slices of prosciutto, cut into strips $\frac{3}{4}$ inch wide
1 quantity of *Mustard Dressing* (see p. 216)
1 teaspoon walnut oil
$\frac{1}{2}$ tablespoon snipped fresh chives

A simple salad of young leaves with scallops, strips of prosciutto and croutons, finished with a few snipped chives. The scallops are sautéed in a hot frying pan in which a very small amount of butter has been melted, giving them a really sweet, caramelized exterior. But they are only cooked briefly so that they remain succulent.

Slice the large scallops horizontally into 2 disks. If using bay scallops, leave whole. Season with a little salt and pepper and set aside.

To make the croutons, melt 2 tablespoons of the butter in a frying pan, add the cubes of bread and fry for a few minutes, turning them over as they brown. Lift out and drain on paper towels.

Arrange the salad leaves on 4 plates. Heat the frying pan until very hot and melt the remaining butter in it, then add the scallops and fry for just 30 seconds on each side. Remove from the pan and tuck them in among the salad leaves. Add the strips of prosciutto and the croutons to the pan and fry briskly over high heat for just a few seconds to warm through. Sprinkle them over the salad. Now add the dressing and the walnut oil to the pan. Bring to a boil, stir in the chives and taste for seasoning. Drizzle over the salads and serve immediately.

Sautéed Squid with Greek Salad

Serves 4

$^3/_4$ pound prepared small squid (see p. 16)

2   tablespoons olive oil

2   fresh thyme sprigs

1   garlic clove, finely chopped

•   A pinch of red pepper flakes

•   A good pinch of sea salt

10   turns of the black pepper mill

For the Greek Salad

2   salad tomatoes, peeled, seeded and cut into $^1/_2$-inch pieces

3   ounces cucumber, cut into $^1/_2$-inch pieces

2   ounces feta cheese, cut into $^1/_2$-inch pieces

1   small red onion, finely chopped

8   unpitted black olives

$^1/_2$ tablespoon chopped fresh fennel tops or dill

For the Dressing

2   tablespoons extra-virgin olive oil

$^1/_2$ tablespoon red wine vinegar

1   teaspoon retsina (optional)

The squid is cooked very simply with a little thyme, garlic and dried chili and then is served with one of my favorite salads—Greek salad, made with feta cheese, cucumber, tomato, olives and onion in a good olive oil dressing. Greek salad is usually fairly rustic, with the ingredients in rough chunks, but here they are cut very small so that the salad looks neat on the plate next to the squid.

For the salad, put all the ingredients in a bowl and mix together gently. Whisk together all the ingredients for the dressing and season to taste. Stir it into the salad and set aside.

Cut the body of the squid into rings, the fins into strips and the tentacles into 3. Heat the olive oil and thyme in a frying pan. When hot, add the squid and fry for about 2$^1/_2$ minutes. Add the garlic, red pepper flakes, salt and pepper and toss for 1 minute. Serve immediately, with the Greek salad.

Tians of Lightly Cured Salmon and Avocado with a Fresh Tomato and Basil Dressing

Serves 4

14	ounces salmon fillet, skinned
$1/4$	pound smoked salmon
1	large garlic clove, very finely chopped
3	shallots, very finely chopped
$1^1/2$	tablespoons lemon juice
$1/2$	teaspoon salt
12	turns of the black pepper mill
•	A pinch of cayenne pepper
•	A few drops of Worcestershire sauce
2	small avocados
•	Mixed young salad greens, to garnish

For the Dressing

4	tablespoons extra-virgin olive oil
1	tablespoon lemon juice
2	tomatoes, peeled, seeded and finely diced
$1/2$	teaspoon coarse sea salt
8	fresh basil leaves, very finely shredded
•	A few turns of the black pepper mill

Smoked and raw salmon are shaped into small disks that sandwich slices of avocado. The salmon is flavored with lemon juice, garlic and shallots and accompanied by a sauce of lemon juice, tomato, basil and virgin olive oil. Since the salmon is not cooked, it is essential that it is absolutely fresh. This is not a recipe for making in advance. Everything is just mixed together, molded and then served so that it all tastes of itself. Serve as a first course or maybe as something exceptional to eat outdoors with that special glass of white wine from the Loire.

Thinly slice the salmon fillet and smoked salmon, then cut them into strips about $1/4$ inch wide. Put them in a bowl with the garlic, shallots, 1 tablespoon of the lemon juice, salt, black pepper, cayenne pepper and Worcestershire sauce and mix together well. Halve the avocados and remove the pit and peel. Cut each half into thin slices, then mix with the remaining lemon juice and a pinch of salt.

Place a $3^1/2$-inch poaching ring or plain pastry cutter in the center of each of 4 large plates. Divide half the salmon mixture between the rings and lightly level the top; don't press the mixture down—you want it to be loosely packed. Cover each one with avocado slices and then with the remaining salmon mixture, lightly leveling the top once more. Carefully remove the rings.

Lightly stir the dressing ingredients together in a bowl. Arrange 4 small piles of the salad leaves around each tian. Using a teaspoon, spoon little pools of the dressing in among the leaves and then serve.

Rice-Shaped Pasta with Seafood, Arugula and Roasted Vegetables

Serves 4

$^3/_4$	pound rice-shaped pasta
1	small eggplant, cut into 1-inch cubes
1	red onion, cut into thin wedges
1	red bell pepper, cut into 1-inch pieces
1	plum tomato, cut into thin wedges
2	garlic cloves, finely chopped
6	tablespoons extra-virgin olive oil
$^1/_2$	teaspoon coarse sea salt
3	to 4 tablespoons wine or water
1	pound mussels, cleaned (see p. 17)
$^1/_4$	pound prepared squid (see p. 16), cut into rings
•	Salt and freshly ground black pepper
$^1/_4$	pound best-quality cooked, peeled shrimp
3	sun-dried tomatoes in oil, thinly sliced
1	red finger chili, seeded and finely chopped
$^1/_4$	cup grated Parmesan cheese
1	tablespoon white wine vinegar
5	tablespoons chopped fresh parsley
2	ounces arugula

I've seen rice-shaped pasta sold as puntalette, puntine and orzo. Made to look like rice, it provides a bit of a culinary joke, if you like, because a lot of people will think they're eating a rice salad and then be surprised to find they're not. I dreamed up this dish last Christmas in Sydney, where I ate a salad using rice pasta with sun-dried tomatoes and olive oil. I thought, what a great base for a seafood salad. We spent Christmas day out at Newport, one of Sydney's beaches, and were asked to bring along a salad. Besides the seafood, rice and sun-dried tomatoes, I put in roasted vegetables, garlic, Parmesan cheese and, lastly, fresh arugula, torn into pieces and folded into the salad at the last minute to give it a nice, peppery bite.

Actually this dish serves as a memory of a very good friend of mine, Ed Ifould, and that Christmas lunch in the hot sun with him and his family. He died a few months ago of a heart attack when he was out in his boat on the sea. Ed was the same age as me and I'd known him ever since I was 19. Every time I went over to Australia we ate lots of good food and drank lots of great Australian wine, and he promised to come over to Cornwall one day but he never made it. His life was a sort of mirror image of mine on the other side of the world. He had similar enthusiasms but he was, unlike me, the most competitive sportsman imaginable, and exceptional at everything he did. I think he would have liked Padstow. He certainly would have liked May Day, 'Obby 'Oss Day in Padstow, when the rebirth of the year and the coming of summer are celebrated with a pagan fertility rite of immense antiquity and a complete lack of whimsical folk-music chumminess. Like many Australians, he liked things that were lacking in pretension, and was practical and full of enthusiasm. He probably would have realized after his visit that although Australia is the finest country in the world, England is not all grayness and drizzle.

Unite and unite and let us all unite
For summer is acome unto day
And whither we are going we shall all unite
In the merry morning of May.
There is a verse that would have suited him well in this May Day song:
O! Where is St George?
O! Where is he O?
He's out on his long boat
All on the salt sea O.

Ed never stopped surfing, sailing or swimming. He was always out on the water somewhere.

Preheat the oven to 425°F.

Bring 2 quarts water and 1 tablespoon salt to a boil in a large pan. Add the pasta and cook for 9 minutes, or until *al dente*, then drain and leave to cool.

Meanwhile, put the eggplant, onion, red pepper and tomato in a bowl with the garlic, 2 tablespoons of the olive oil and the sea salt and mix together well. Spread out in a small roasting pan and cook in the oven for about 30 minutes, until well colored around the edges. Remove from the oven and leave to cool.

Put the wine or water in a saucepan, add the mussels, then cover and cook over high heat for 3 to 4 minutes, or until they have opened. Discard any that remain closed. Shell the mussels and leave to cool.

Heat 1 tablespoon of the remaining oil in a frying pan. Add the squid and fry over high heat for 2½ minutes, or until lightly browned. Season with salt and pepper and leave to cool.

When the pasta, roasted vegetables, mussels and squid are all cold, put them in a large bowl with the remaining olive oil, shrimp, mussels, sun-dried tomatoes, chili, Parmesan cheese, vinegar, 4 tablespoons of the parsley, 1 teaspoon of salt and 10 turns of the black pepper mill. Toss together lightly, then fold in the arugula. Spoon the salad onto a large serving platter and sprinkle with the remaining chopped parsley.

Seafood Paella

Serves 6

1 cooked lobster, weighing about 1 pound

5 cups *Chicken Stock* (see p. 213)

2 fresh bay leaves

1 large leek, sliced

12 mussels, cleaned (see p. 17)

6 tablespoons extra-virgin olive oil

1 pound monkfish fillet, cut into slices $\frac{1}{2}$ inch thick

$\frac{1}{4}$ pound prepared small squid (see p. 16), sliced

1 medium onion, finely chopped

8 garlic cloves, 4 finely chopped and 4 cut into quarters

1 red bell pepper, seeded and thinly sliced

1 pound ($2\frac{1}{2}$ cups) Arborio or Valencia rice

• Scant $\frac{1}{2}$ teaspoon saffron threads

6 cooked shrimp

I have written this to serve only six people because most recipes for paella feed more people than anybody could possibly have a pan large enough for in their own home. If you are lucky enough to possess an enormous frying pan or, even better, a paellera, *then by all means double up the quantities in this recipe. Paella is one of those dishes that often contain just about everything in the refrigerator. However, what I like about it are the flavors of olive oil, garlic and saffron together with seafood and some good, large-grain rice. Keep it simple, in other words. The best rice to use is Valencia rice but this is still hard to get in most places. I use Italian risotto rice, which I think works nearly as well.*

Pull the claws and legs off the lobster and then detach the head from the tail. Cut the tail into pieces at each section and the claws into 3 and set aside. Put the lobster head and legs into a pan with the stock, bay leaves and the green part of the leek. Bring to a boil, then leave to simmer until reduced to a scant 2 cups. Strain the stock through a sieve into a clean pan and set aside.

Put the mussels into a pan with a splash of the stock. Cover and cook over high heat for 3 to 4 minutes, or until opened. Lift the mussels out of the cooking liquid, discarding any that remain closed, then cover and set aside. Pour all of the liquid back into the stock except the last tablespoonful, which is often gritty.

Heat the oil in a large frying pan or shallow saucepan—you will need one that is about 12 inches across. Add the monkfish and fry for 3 minutes, turning it over after 2 minutes. Remove from the pan and set aside. Add the squid and stir-fry for 2 to 3 minutes, or until lightly browned. Set aside with the monkfish. Add the onion, the chopped and the quartered garlic, the white part of the leek and the red pepper to the pan and fry for 4 to 5 minutes, or until softened and lightly browned. Add the rice and stir until all the grains are well coated with the oil. Add the saffron and stock and bring to a boil. Season with salt and pepper, then lower the heat, cover and simmer gently for 15 minutes.

Uncover the rice and lay the pieces of lobster, monkfish, squid, mussels and shrimp on top. Cover and cook gently for 5 minutes. Remove from the heat and leave for 5 minutes, then uncover and gently fork the seafood and rice together before serving.

Grilled Shark Steaks with Roasted Tomato and Cumin Chutney

Serves 4

- Shark steaks or swordfish steaks, about $1/2$ pound each
- Salt and freshly ground black pepper
- 2 tablespoons olive oil
- Finely grated zest of $1/2$ lime

For the roasted Tomato and Cumin Chutney

- 1 tablespoon black or yellow mustard seeds
- 7 tablespoons malt vinegar
- $2^1/4$ pounds beef tomatoes, peeled
- 6 tablespoons olive oil
- 1 tablespoon cumin seeds
- $1/3$ cup roughly chopped fresh ginger
- 5 garlic cloves, roughly chopped
- 3 red bird's-eye chilies, roughly chopped
- 2 teaspoons sambal oelek or minced red chili
- $1^1/2$ teaspoons ground turmeric
- $1/4$ cup palm sugar or soft light brown sugar
- 2 tablespoons Thai fish sauce (*nam pla*)

The real pleasure of this dish is the accompanying chutney, which comes from one of my favorite cooks, Gay Bilson, who runs the Bennelong Restaurant in Sydney Opera House. If you ever go to Sydney, you've got to have a meal there. I happened to see a jar of it while looking round Leigh Stone Herbert's outside catering kitchen in Sydney. I insisted on taking off the lid of the chutney and trying a spoonful. It was wonderful, and just made to go with a piece of fish. Naturally I have forgotten exactly how Gay makes it. Leigh rattled off the recipe and I only remember the outline— often a good idea since you get the original recipe and a derivative, too. Incidentally, you can equally well use swordfish instead of shark, which you might find easier to obtain, but shark is what we get in Cornwall. Porbeagle or mako shark have the best flavor but, failing that, blue shark is cheaper and easier to come by.

For the chutney, soak the mustard seeds in the vinegar overnight. If you don't have time to do this, you can put them in a small pan and bring to a boil, then take off the heat and leave to soak for 2 hours.

Preheat the oven to 400° F. Place the tomatoes in a small roasting pan, pour over the oil and roast in the oven for $1^1/2$ hours.

Heat a dry, heavy-bottomed frying pan or wok over high heat. Add the cumin seeds and fry for a few seconds until they begin to darken and smell aromatic. Tip into a mortar or spice grinder and grind to a fine powder. Put this powder and the ginger, garlic, chilies, sambal oelek, turmeric, sugar and fish sauce, vinegar and mustard seeds into a blender and blend until smooth. Pour this purée into a pan and simmer very gently for 10 minutes, stirring all the time as it has a tendency to spit quite a lot. Add the roasted tomatoes to the pan and simmer for 10 to 15 minutes, or until the chutney has thickened. Season with salt and pepper.

Season the shark steaks with plenty of salt and pepper. Mix the olive oil with the lime zest and then paint it over both sides of the steaks. Heat a lightly oiled cast-iron ribbed pan, add the steaks and cook for 3 to 4 minutes on each side. Transfer the steaks to 4 warmed plates and serve with the chutney.

Poached Salmon with Mayonnaise, New Potatoes and Cucumber Salad

Serves 4

1   piece salmon, weighing about 3 to 3 1/2 pounds
1 1/2   pounds new potatoes, preferably freshly dug
3   fresh mint sprigs
1   cucumber
1   tablespoon white wine vinegar
1   carrot, thinly sliced
1   onion, thinly sliced
12   black peppercorns
5   tablespoons salt
1   quantity of *Olive Oil Mayonnaise* (see p. 217)

This is the sort of classic dish that is all too often served up at weddings overcooked. In this recipe I've given you precise cooking times and weights, which will always mean that the salmon is slightly pink and moist.

Put the salmon in a fish poacher and pour in enough water to cover. Add the salt, bring to a boil and simmer very gently for 5 minutes. Remove the fish from the heat and set aside to cool for about 20 minutes.

Boil the new potatoes with 1 sprig of mint in salted water until soft. Drain and keep warm.

Peel the cucumber and slice it as thinly as possible, preferably with a mandoline. Chop the leaves of the remaining mint sprigs and mix them together with the sliced cucumber and white wine vinegar. Remove the salmon from the fish poacher and serve with a bowl of new potatoes, the mayonnaise and the cucumber salad.

Fish from Colder Climates

The inspiration for this chapter came from a conversation I had in Sydney in the offices of *Australian Gourmet Traveller,* which is a magazine devoted to the interests of people such as myself, who like to travel around the world and enjoy good food. Why on earth don't we have a similar magazine in this country? I was overwhelmed by the intelligence and enthusiasm of the entire staff and their knowledge of what was going on not only in Australian cooking but everywhere else in the world as well. I had gone to see the editor, Caroline Lockhart, to ask her if she might be interested in visiting the West Country or sending someone over to write about all the good restaurants and hotels we have. When I told her how exciting I found Australian cooking, with its great influences from Thailand, Singapore, Hong Kong, India and the whole of the Pacific, she said, "Yes, but reading your book (*Taste of the Sea*), we don't half hanker sometimes after some good old European butter sauces." So I started thinking and realized that we shouldn't spend all our time fretting about calories and trying to stick to salads and grilled fish. Occasionally we should rejoice in those classic sauces, rich in butter, cream and wine, those hefty fish pies whose delicious, heartwarming fillings are topped with a layer of buttery pastry, or mounds of steaming-hot mashed potatoes enriched with a slick of saffron-scented butter or extra-virgin olive oil. Well, this chapter is where you'll find all these and more. Long may they survive.

Facing page: Baked John Dory with Chili, Cannellini Beans and Thyme (see p. 120).

Turbot Fillet with Montpellier Butter and Creamed Cabbage

Serves 4

4 pieces turbot fillet, weighing about 6 ounces each
• Salt and freshly ground black pepper

For the Montpellier Butter
1 cup spinach leaves
1 cup arugula leaves
3/4 cup chopped mixed fresh parsley, chives, chervil and tarragon
1/4 cup chopped shallot
3 small gherkins, chopped
1 teaspoon capers
2 garlic cloves, chopped
6 anchovy fillets
1 egg yolk
2 hard-boiled egg yolks
1/2 cup butter, softened
1/2 teaspoon salt
6 tablespoons olive oil

For the Creamed Cabbage
1/4 cup butter
1 pound young, tender cabbage, thinly sliced
1/2 pound leeks, thinly sliced
1 tablespoon white wine vinegar
6 tablespoons heavy cream
1/2 cup *Fish Stock* (see p. 212)

I don't know why I've never used creamed cabbage and leeks before with fish because it's very common in France and every time I eat it I vow to include it in a recipe. The idea is that you cook the cabbage very gently with some leeks and butter, then add cream and a little stock to make a sort of vegetable-come-sauce base for the fish—here, fillets of beautifully white turbot topped with slices of green Montpellier butter. You could also use John Dory, brill, sea bass or a thick fillet of cod.

First make the Montpellier butter. Drop the spinach and arugula leaves into a pan of boiling water for 1 minute, then drain and refresh under cold running water. Press out all the excess water and then put the leaves into a food processor with all the remaining ingredients except the oil. Process to a purée, then with the machine still running, pour in the olive oil in a steady stream. Season to taste, then scrape out onto a large sheet of plastic wrap, shape into a roll 1 inch thick and chill until firm.

For the creamed cabbage, melt the butter in a large pan, add the cabbage, leeks and vinegar, then cover and cook over gentle heat for 20 minutes. Add the cream and stock and cook, uncovered, over high heat for about 10 minutes, or until the liquid has reduced but the mixture is still quite creamy.

Meanwhile, preheat the broiler. Season the turbot fillets on both sides with salt and pepper, then put them, skin-side up, on the lightly oiled rack of the broiler pan and cook for 6 minutes. Carefully peel away the skin from the fillets. Remove the Montpellier butter from the refrigerator, cut off 8 thin slices and put 2 slices on each piece of fish.

Put the cabbage mixture on 4 warmed plates. Slide the fish back under the broiler for a few seconds, or until the butter is just beginning to melt. Quickly put the fish on top of the cabbage and serve immediately.

Fillet of Cod with Saffron Mashed Potatoes

Serves 4

4 thick pieces cod fillet, weighing about 6 ounces each, skin on
• Olive oil for brushing
• Coarse sea salt and freshly ground black pepper
2 tomatoes, peeled, seeded and diced
1 tablespoon chopped fresh parsley
• About 8 teaspoons tapenade

For the Sauce
1/3 cup minced carrot
1/3 cup minced onion
1/2 red chili, seeded and minced
• 2-inch piece orange zest
1 tablespoon olive oil
Juice of 1/2 orange
4 tablespoons white wine
1 tomato, chopped
2 1/2 cups *Roasted Fish Stock* or *Fish Stock* (see p. 212)
• Salt and white pepper
4 tablespoons *Olive Oil Mayonnaise* (see p. 217)

For the Potatoes
2 pounds floury potatoes, peeled and cut into chunks
• A good pinch of saffron threads
• Salt
1/2 garlic clove, crushed
1/4 cup olive oil
2 tablespoons heavy cream
• Freshly ground black pepper

This dish is known in our kitchen as cod and saff mash. I got the idea for the potatoes from Simon Hopkinson, the chef and food writer, whose recipes in the Independent are not only a pleasure to read but also usually leave me thinking, blast, I wish I'd come up with that one. Cod with saff mash not only has this delightful purée of potatoes with saffron and olive oil but also a mayonnaise-based sauce flavored with tomato, orange and chili and, on the side, some tapenade, which is a purée of black olives, anchovy and capers. There is a recipe for Tapenade *on p. 218, but you can buy jars of good-quality tapenade in all the major supermarkets these days, so feel free to go and buy your own.*

For the sauce, fry the carrot, onion and chili with the orange zest in the olive oil for 5 minutes. Add the orange juice, white wine, tomato and stock and simmer for 20 minutes. Season with salt and white pepper.

Meanwhile, put the potatoes in a pan and barely cover with cold water. Add the saffron and a pinch of salt, then bring to a boil and cook for 20 minutes or until tender. Drain the cooking liquid off the potatoes into a clean pan and boil rapidly until reduced to 4 to 6 tablespoons. Mash the potatoes until smooth, then beat in the reduced cooking liquid, garlic, olive oil, cream and some salt and pepper to taste. Keep warm.

Strain the sauce into a pitcher. Put the mayonnaise in a small pan and gradually whisk in the sauce. Cook over very gentle heat until it thickens and just coats the back of the spoon. Do not let it boil or it will curdle. Keep warm.

Preheat the broiler. Brush both sides of the cod with olive oil and season with coarse sea salt and pepper. Place on the oiled rack of the broiler pan, skin-side up, and cook for 8 minutes.

To serve, put the saffron mashed potatoes in the center of 4 warmed plates and place the cod on top. Pour the sauce around the edge and sprinkle with the diced tomato and chopped parsley. Put 2 small teaspoons of the tapenade on either side of each plate.

Haddock and Cornish Yarg Pie with a Potato Pastry Crust

Serves 6

2¹⁄₂ cups milk
1¹⁄₄ cups *Fish Stock*
 (see p. 212)
1¹⁄₂ pounds haddock fillet
10 ounces leeks
 5 tablespoons butter
¹⁄₃ cup finely diced carrot
¹⁄₃ cup finely diced celery
¹⁄₃ cup finely chopped
 onion
1¹⁄₂ ounces bacon, thinly
 sliced
¹⁄₃ cup all-purpose flour
¹⁄₄ pound cooked peeled
 shrimp
 1 cup grated Cornish
 Yarg cheese
 • Freshly grated nutmeg
 • Salt and freshly ground
 black pepper

For the Potato Pastry Crust
³⁄₄ pound potatoes, peeled
 and cut into chunks
1³⁄₄ cups self-raising flour
 1 teaspoon salt
15 turns of the black
 pepper mill
³⁄₄ cup butter, cut into
 small pieces
 2 tablespoons cold water
 1 egg, beaten

For the Bouquet Garni
 1 bay leaf
 1 small bunch fresh
 parsley
 • Leaves from the center
 of 1 head of celery
 1 small fresh thyme sprig

Fish pies are always incredibly popular. This one is a result of my continuing attempts to try and produce some genuinely local dishes. Here I've used all local fish and vegetables and that excellent cheese, Cornish Yarg, which is mild and firm and particularly suited to a pie like this. If you can't get Cornish Yarg, use a mild Cheddar.

For the pastry, cook the potatoes in boiling salted water until tender. Drain well and either mash or pass through a potato ricer. Leave to cool.

Meanwhile, put the milk and stock into a large pan and bring to a boil. Add the haddock and simmer for 5 to 7 minutes, or until firm and opaque. Lift the fish out onto a plate and, when cool enough to handle, break the flesh into large flakes, discarding any skin and bones.

Clean the leeks, finely dice 2 ounces of them and set aside. Thinly slice the remainder. Melt 2 tablespoons of the butter in a clean pan, add the sliced leeks and fry gently for 2 to 3 minutes, or until just cooked. Lift out with a slotted spoon and set aside.

Add the diced leek, carrot, celery, onion and bacon to the pan with a little more of the butter if necessary. Fry over gentle heat for 10 minutes without letting them brown. Add the remaining butter to the vegetables, stir in the flour and cook for 1 minute. Remove the pan from the heat and gradually add the cooking liquid from the haddock, stirring all the time to make a smooth sauce. Bring to a boil, stirring. Tie together all the ingredients for the bouquet garni and add to the pan. Simmer gently for 30 minutes, then remove the bouquet garni from the pan and season the sauce with nutmeg, salt and pepper.

Stir the flaked fish, reserved leeks, shrimp and cheese into the sauce, spoon into a deep 7¹⁄₂-cup pie dish and push a pie funnel into the center of the mixture. Set aside to cool.

Meanwhile, for the pastry, sift the flour, salt and pepper into a bowl. Add the butter and rub it in with your fingertips until the mixture looks like fine bread crumbs. Add the cold potato and lightly mix into the flour, then add the water and stir with a round-bladed knife until everything starts to stick together. Form it into a ball, turn out onto a lightly floured work surface and knead briefly until smooth. Chill for 20 to 30 minutes.

Preheat the oven to 400°F.

Roll out the pastry on a floured surface until it is slightly larger than the top of the pie dish. Cut a thin strip off the edge of the pastry, brush with a little water and press it onto the rim of the pie dish. Brush with a little more water. Make a small cut in the center of the remaining pastry and then lay it over the pie so that the pie funnel pokes through the cut. Press it onto the rim of the dish and crimp the edge decoratively with your fingers. Brush the top with beaten egg and decorate with leaves cut from the pastry trimmings, if you wish. Bake in the oven for 35 to 40 minutes, or until the pastry is crisp and golden.

Baked Cod Portuguese

Serves 4

6 tablespoons unsalted butter
2 pounds thick cod fillet, skin on, cut into 4 pieces
1 large onion, cut into quarters and finely sliced
4 plum tomatoes, peeled, seeded and chopped
4 sun-dried tomatoes in oil, drained and finely chopped
1¼ cups *Fish Stock* (see p. 212)
½ cup white wine
2 tablespoons chopped fresh parsley
• Salt and freshly ground black pepper
• Fresh parsley sprigs, to garnish

I have never eaten a cod Portuguese that was anything other than fish in a watery sauce, so I thought it would be fun to take such a standard dish and try and restore it to something like the original. The problem with cooking many Portuguese or Mediterranean dishes in Britain is that they never taste the same using vegetables, particularly tomatoes, that have been grown in northern Europe. You have to zip up these dishes with something to compensate for the lack of sunshine in the vegetables. I have added sun-dried tomatoes to boost the flavor and used fresh plum tomatoes for authenticity. Although the dish is from southern Europe, I don't think of it as particularly summery, so I have included it in this chapter. Call me inconsistent, of course I am!

Melt half the butter in a shallow flameproof baking dish that is big enough to hold all the pieces of cod in a single layer. Fry the cod, skin-side down, for 1 minute, or until crisp and golden. Carefully remove from the dish and set aside.

Add the onion to the dish and fry gently for 5 minutes, or until softened. Add the plum tomatoes, sun-dried tomatoes, stock and white wine. Bring to a boil and simmer for 10 minutes, or until slightly reduced and thickened.

Preheat the oven to 400°F.

Place the cod, skin-side up, on top of the onion and tomato mixture, transfer the dish to the oven and bake for 5 to 6 minutes—less if the pieces of cod are thin. Remove from the oven and lift the cod out onto a warm plate. Return the dish to the stove over high heat, add the remaining butter and reduce by boiling rapidly for about 4 minutes, stirring now and then, to make a really thick sauce. Stir in the parsley, season with salt and pepper and cook for 30 seconds more. Spoon the sauce onto 4 warm plates, put the cod on top and garnish with parsley sprigs. Serve with boiled potatoes and a green salad.

Lobster Pot Pie

Serves 8

1   cooked lobster,
    weighing about $1\frac{1}{2}$
    pounds
$\frac{1}{2}$ pound cod fillet
1   quantity of *Shellfish
    Stock* (see p. 214),
    made with the broken
    lobster shell instead of
    shrimp
$\frac{3}{4}$ pound small waxy
    potatoes, peeled and
    thickly sliced
$\frac{1}{4}$ pound baby carrots
1   cup shelled young peas,
    fresh if possible
$\frac{1}{4}$ cup butter
1   medium onion,
    chopped
$\frac{1}{4}$ cup all-purpose flour
$\frac{2}{3}$ cup heavy cream
•   Salt and freshly ground
    black pepper

For the Pastry
$2\frac{1}{4}$ cups all-purpose flour
$\frac{1}{4}$ teaspoon salt
$\frac{1}{2}$ cup butter, cut into
    small pieces
7   tablespoons lard, cut
    into small pieces
2   tablespoons cold water
1   egg yolk
1   teaspoon milk

This is a fish pie from the other side of the Atlantic, where lobsters are cheap and plentiful. I wouldn't expect you to use one of our British lobsters, they're far too expensive. But you can use cheaper North American lobsters.

Remove the meat from the cooked lobster (see p. 19). Cut the lobster tail meat and the cod into slices $\frac{1}{2}$ inch thick and set aside. Break up the lobster shell into small pieces and use to make the *Shellfish Stock* (see p. 214).

Strain the stock into a clean pan. Add the potatoes and the whole baby carrots and simmer for 5 minutes or until just cooked. Add the peas and simmer for 1 minute. Lift the vegetables out with a slotted spoon and set aside. Add the slices of cod to the pan and simmer for 1 minute, then lift out and set aside. You will need $2\frac{1}{2}$ cups of stock for the sauce. If you have more than this, boil rapidly until reduced to the required amount.

Melt the butter in a pan, add the onion and cook for 5 minutes, or until lightly browned. Stir in the flour and cook for 1 minute. Take the pan off the heat and gradually stir in the stock. Return to the heat and bring to a boil, stirring all the time. Simmer for 5 minutes and then stir in the cream, lobster meat, cod and vegetables. Season with salt and pepper, spoon into a $7\frac{1}{2}$-cup pie dish and push a pie funnel into the center of the mixture. Set aside to cool.

Preheat the oven to 425°F.

For the pastry, sift the flour and salt into a food processor, add the butter and lard and process until the mixture looks like fine bread crumbs. Tip this into a large mixing bowl and stir in the water with a round-bladed knife until everything starts to stick together. Bring together into a ball, turn out onto a lightly floured work surface and knead once or twice until smooth. Roll out the pastry thinly until it is about 1 inch bigger than the top of the pie dish. Cut a thin strip off the edge of the pastry, brush with water and press it onto the rim of the pie dish. Brush the top of the pastry strip with a little more water. Make a small cut in the center of the remaining pastry and then lay it over the pie so that the funnel pokes through the cut. Press it onto the rim of the dish and crimp the edge decoratively with your fingers. Beat the egg yolk with the milk, brush it over the top of the pie and then bake for 35 to 40 minutes, or until the pastry is golden, protecting the edge of the pastry with a strip of foil after 20 minutes, if necessary, to stop it going too brown.

Sautéed Chicken with Mussels, Tarragon and Chardonnay

Serves 4

1 chicken, weighing about 3½ pounds
1 tablespoon olive oil
4 tablespoons butter
2 tablespoons tarragon vinegar or white wine vinegar
1¼ cups *Chicken Stock* (see p. 213)
1¼ cups Chardonnay wine
1 ounce fresh tarragon
4 garlic cloves, peeled
2 pounds mussels, cleaned (see p. 17)
1¼ cups heavy cream
· Juice of ½ lemon
· Salt and freshly ground black pepper

This is just a simple sautéed chicken dish, but live mussels are added right at the end so that there is only time for them just to open in the pan before the dish is served. The cooking liquor from the mussels gives a final salty tang to the tarragon sauce. I took such an aversion to the phrase "surf and turf" when I first heard it in the early eighties that it took me over ten years to accept the fact that a combination of meat and seafood can often be excellent.

Joint the chicken into 8 pieces: to do this, pull one leg away from the body and cut through the skin, down toward where the thighbone joins the main carcass. Twist the leg so that the ball and socket joint is exposed and cut through it to detach the leg. Repeat on the other side. Cut each leg in half through the joint and cut off and discard the feet bones from the end of each drumstick. Now cut through the skin down the center of the breastbone and ease back the breast meat slightly. Cut along either side of the breastbone using kitchen scissors or a sharp knife. Open up the bird and remove the breast and wing joints by cutting horizontally through the rib bones. Cut the breast and wing joint diagonally in half so that each piece has an equal amount of breast meat. Cut off the tips of the wings. The backbone, breastbone, wing tips and feet bones can be discarded or used to make stock (see p. 213).

Season the chicken pieces with a little salt and pepper. Heat the oil and butter in a large, deep frying pan, add the chicken pieces and fry, skin-side down, for 10 minutes or until well browned. Turn over and continue cooking for 5 minutes. Transfer the breast meat portions to a plate and continue to fry the leg and thigh portions for another 5 minutes. This means that all the pieces of chicken will be well browned without the breast meat being overcooked.

Remove the remaining chicken from the pan and pour away the excess fat. Add the vinegar to the pan and boil until it has almost all evaporated. Add the chicken stock and wine and boil until reduced to half its original volume.

Return the chicken to the pan and add half the tarragon with its stems and the whole garlic cloves. Partly cover with a lid and simmer very gently for 30 minutes, or until the chicken is tender and cooked through.

Add the mussels to the chicken in the pan, cover and cook over high heat for about 3 minutes, or until the mussels have opened. Discard any that remain closed. Lift the chicken and mussels out of the pan with a slotted spoon and place in a warmed serving dish; cover and keep warm. Strain the cooking liquid to remove the tarragon and garlic, then return it to the pan and bring back to a boil. Boil until reduced by half, then taste; it should be really well flavored. Chop the remaining tarragon leaves, setting aside a few sprigs for garnish.

Add the cream to the pan and boil for 2 to 3 minutes, or until the sauce thickens slightly. Stir in the lemon juice and chopped tarragon and season with a little salt and pepper if necessary. Simmer for 1 minute to release some of the flavor from the tarragon, then pour the sauce over the chicken and mussels. Serve garnished with the reserved tarragon sprigs and accompanied by a tossed green salad and boiled new potatoes.

Baked John Dory with Chili, Cannellini Beans and Thyme

Serves 6

1 pound (2¼ cups) dried cannellini beans

1 red bell pepper

⅔ cup olive oil, plus extra for brushing

3 garlic cloves, very finely chopped

2 shallots, finely chopped

2 red finger chilies, seeded and finely chopped

2 tablespoons chopped fresh thyme

1 John Dory, weighing about 2½ to 3 pounds, cleaned (see p. 11)

12 black olives, pitted and finely chopped

• Salt and freshly ground black pepper

2 tablespoons white wine vinegar

The cannellini beans are mixed with olive oil, garlic, lots of red chili, roasted red pepper and thyme. Then a whole John Dory is baked on top of them, sprinkled with chopped black olives. Serve with a frisée salad tossed with some Olive Oil Dressing (see p. 216), preferably made with a lemon-flavored olive oil. You can make this dish equally successfully with red snapper, sea bass or tilapia.

Cover the beans with plenty of cold water and leave to soak overnight.

The next day drain the beans, return them to the pan with plenty of fresh water to cover and bring to a boil, skimming off any scum as it rises to the surface. Leave to simmer for 40 minutes, or until tender. Drain the beans, pour the cooking liquid into another pan and bring back to a boil. Boil rapidly until reduced to ⅞ cup.

Meanwhile, preheat the oven to 400°F and preheat the broiler.

Brush the red pepper with a little oil and broil, turning now and then, until the skin is slightly blackened. Leave until cool enough to handle, then peel off the skin, remove the seeds and cut the flesh into fine dice.

Heat the oil in a dutch oven large enough to hold the fish. Add the garlic, shallots, chilies, diced red pepper and thyme and fry gently for 5 minutes. Stir in the beans and reduced cooking liquid and season well with plenty of salt and pepper.

Brush the fish inside and out with olive oil and season well with salt and pepper. Put it on top of the beans and sprinkle with the black olives. Cover and bake for 20 minutes. Then uncover and cook for a further 10 minutes, by which time the fish should be done.

To serve, lift the fish off the beans and remove the flesh from the bones. Put it on 4 warmed plates. Stir the vinegar into the beans and serve them alongside the fish.

Cod with Red Wine Sauce

Serves 4

6 tablespoons unsalted butter

4 pieces cod, cut from a thick fillet, weighing about 6 ounces each

½ cup chopped carrot

½ cup chopped celery

½ cup chopped onion

• A small pinch of ground allspice

• A small pinch of ground cloves

• A small pinch of grated nutmeg

• A large pinch of curry powder

2½ cups red wine

2½ cups Chicken Stock (see p. 213)

• 1 teaspoon sugar

• Coarse sea salt

1 tablespoon all-purpose flour

• Freshly ground black pepper

For the Lentils

¼ cup dried green lentils or Puy lentils

¾ cup Fish Stock (see p. 212)

1 clove

1 fresh or dried bay leaf

2 onion slices

½ teaspoon salt

This dish originated from one of the best restaurants in the world, Giradet at Crissier, near Lausanne in Switzerland. I got the recipe from a book that has given me a great deal of pleasure, Egon Ronay's The Great Dishes In My Life. *Almost better than an autobiography, it's one of those books that everyone who has influenced the way we eat should write. The original recipe calls for a very elaborate fish-scale effect to be made with wafer-thin slices of small potatoes, which are fried and laid on top of the fish. We occasionally do this at the restaurant, but it really is three-star cooking and probably, I think, outside the scope of even an advanced cookery book like this!*

A good accompaniment to the cod would be some zucchini fried very gently in butter with chopped tarragon and chives.

Put all the ingredients for the lentils into a pan and simmer until tender. Drain, remove the clove and bay leaf, then cover and keep warm.

Melt 4 tablespoons of the butter in a medium-sized pan and brush a little over the cod. Set aside, skin-side up, on the greased rack of the broiler pan and sprinkle with sea salt and a little black pepper.

For the sauce, add the carrot, celery, onion and spices to the remaining butter in the pan and fry over high heat for about 10 minutes, or until the vegetables are well browned. Add the red wine, stock, sugar and ¼ teaspoon of salt, bring to a boil and boil until reduced to one-quarter of its original volume. Strain the reduced sauce to remove the vegetables, return to the pan and keep warm.

Preheat the broiler. Broil the cod for 8 minutes, or until the skin is well browned. Meanwhile, mix the remaining butter with the flour to make a smooth paste. Bring the sauce to a boil and then whisk in the paste, a little at a time. Simmer for 2 minutes until the sauce is smooth and thickened. Adjust the seasoning with salt and pepper if necessary.

To serve, put the lentils on 4 warmed plates and place the cod on top, then spoon the sauce around the fish.

Roast Monkfish with Prosciutto and Sauerkraut

Serves 4

2½ cups *Chicken Stock* (see p. 213)

⅔ cup white wine

6 tablespoons heavy cream

4 prepared monkfish fillets (see p. 15), weighing about 6 ounces each

4 thin slices of prosciutto, weighing about ½ ounce each

4 tablespoons unsalted butter

• Salt and freshly ground black pepper

2 teaspoons chopped fresh parsley

For the Sauerkraut

2 tablespoons butter

½ cup very thinly sliced carrot

½ cup thinly sliced celery

½ cup thinly sliced onion

½ pound sauerkraut

This dish works extraordinarily well because the slight blandness of the monkfish contrasts most pleasingly with the acidity of the sauerkraut. Fillets of monkfish are wrapped in thin slices of prosciutto, tied and roasted in the oven. They are then sliced and served on top of some sauerkraut that has been stewed with carrot, celery and onion, accompanied by a sauce made from the roasting juices, a little fish stock and cream, and finished with parsley.

I'm quite happy to use canned sauerkraut for this. To me, sauerkraut is the heart of warm, glowing winter food and I love its slightly smoky, salty flavor. I got the idea for this dish in Obergurgl during one very cold skiing holiday in January. In central Europe sauerkraut was for centuries the only source of vitamin C in the winter months, when no fresh vegetables were available. We don't have to eat it any more but you ought to know that it's very good for you. The lactic acid in foods like sauerkraut is now thought to be part of the secret of longevity in the Balkan diet. So eat more, it's lovely!

Preheat the oven to 400°F.

For the sauerkraut, melt the butter in a pan, add the carrot, celery and onion and cook gently for 5 minutes, or until softened. Add the sauerkraut, cover and cook gently for 20 to 25 minutes.

Put the stock, white wine and cream into a wide-bottomed pan and boil rapidly until reduced to ¾ cup.

Wrap each monkfish fillet in a slice of the prosciutto and tie securely with string in 2 places. Melt 2 tablespoons of the butter in a large, shallow flameproof pan. Add the monkfish, seam-side up, and fry for 1 to 1½ minutes, or until golden brown underneath. Turn over, transfer the pan to the oven and cook for 10 minutes.

Remove the fish from the oven, transfer to a plate and keep warm. Add the reduced stock, wine and cream mixture to the pan and stir to scrape up all the crusty bits from the bottom. Strain into a small pan, bring back to a boil and then whisk in the remaining 2 tablespoons butter. Season with pepper and a little salt if necessary (but remember that the prosciutto is quite salty). To serve, spoon the sauerkraut into the center of 4 warmed plates. Cut each piece of monkfish on the slant into 4 and place on top of the sauerkraut. Pour the sauce around and sprinkle with the chopped parsley.

Grilled Haddock with Potato Gnocchi and Beurre Rouge

Serves 4

4 pieces haddock fillet, weighing about 6 ounces each, skin on
2 tablespoons butter, melted
• Coarse sea salt

For the Gnocchi
1¼ pounds floury potatoes
½ teaspoon salt
2 egg yolks
• Scant ¾ cup all-purpose flour, sifted

For the Beurre Rouge
¼ pound red onions, very finely chopped
⅔ cup red wine
⅔ cup *Fish Stock* (see p. 212)
5 tablespoons red wine vinegar
¼ teaspoon superfine sugar
¾ cup chilled unsalted butter, cut into small pieces
• Salt and freshly ground black pepper

This dish typifies restaurant cooking in that it relies on quite a lot of advance preparation but the actual cooking is very straightforward and easy. The gnocchi can be prepared a long time in advance, as can the base for the beurre rouge. Then, when you are ready to serve, you just poach the gnocchi, whisk the butter into the sauce and broil the fish—none of which takes more than a few minutes. Everything is then assembled on the plate with no last-minute panics. Every dish has to be more or less like this in a busy restaurant kitchen, otherwise we'd all perish from stress!

Preheat the oven to 400°F. Bake the potatoes in their skins for 1 hour, or until soft.

Meanwhile, for the *beurre rouge*, put all the ingredients except the butter into a saucepan with a pinch of salt, bring to a boil and simmer, uncovered, for 15 minutes. Cover and cook gently for another 20 to 25 minutes, or until the onions are very soft.

Remove the potatoes from the oven and, when cool enough to handle, cut in half and scoop out the cooked potato into a bowl. Mash until very smooth, then beat in the salt, egg yolks and flour to make a soft dough. Turn the mixture out onto a very lightly floured surface and knead briefly until smooth. Divide it into 20 pieces and lightly roll each one into a ball. Press a finger into the center of each to form an indentation and then put on a floured baking sheet. You can cover and refrigerate them at this stage, if convenient.

To finish the dish, preheat the broiler. Brush the top of the haddock liberally with the melted butter and season with pepper. Place skin-side up on the rack of the broiler pan and drizzle with more butter, then sprinkle with coarse sea salt. Bring the *beurre rouge* up to a simmer and then whisk in the butter, a few pieces at a time, until thick and creamy. Season and keep warm.

Broil the haddock for 3 to 6 minutes, depending on the thickness of the fillet. Meanwhile, drop the gnocchi in batches into a pan of simmering water and cook for 2 minutes, or until they float to the surface. Lift out with a slotted spoon and put them in a lightly buttered dish as soon as they are cooked.

To serve, put the haddock on 4 warmed plates and pile the gnocchi alongside. Spoon the *beurre rouge* over and around the haddock.

Skate au Poivre with Béarnaise Sauce

Serves 4

2 tablespoons black peppercorns

4 pieces skate, weighing about 7 ounces each, peeled

4 tablespoons olive oil

1 teaspoon salt

For the Béarnaise Sauce

1 tablespoon chopped fresh tarragon

2 shallots, very finely chopped

20 turns of the black pepper mill

4 tablespoons white wine vinegar

½ cup unsalted butter

2 egg yolks

2 tablespoons water

½ teaspoon salt

The skate is strewn with coarsely crushed peppercorns, seasoned and then fried in olive oil and served with a classic butter sauce. Do be careful when buying skate that it doesn't smell at all of ammonia. I don't care what other books say; if you can smell it, don't buy it.

If the béarnaise sauce strikes fear into your heart, use the Quick Hollandaise Sauce *on p. 215 and simply add the tarragon, shallot, pepper and vinegar reduction to it.*

Coarsely crush the black peppercorns in a mortar or simply in a bowl with the end of a rolling pin. Trim about 1 inch from the edge of the skate, otherwise it will break off during cooking and look unattractive.

For the béarnaise sauce, put the tarragon, shallots, pepper and vinegar in a small pan, bring to a boil and boil until reduced to 1 tablespoon, then set aside. Clarify the butter by melting it in a pan over low heat, then pouring off the clear butter, leaving the white solids behind. Put the egg yolks and water in a bowl set over a pan of simmering water, making sure the bowl is not touching the water. Whisk until the mixture is voluminous and creamy. Remove the bowl from the heat and whisk in the clarified butter a little at a time. Rest the bowl in a bowl of warm water to keep it warm. Stir the tarragon and shallot reduction into the sauce.

To cook the skate, heat the olive oil in a large frying pan. Brush the peppercorns on both sides of each piece of skate with a pastry brush, then sprinkle with the salt. Fry 2 pieces at a time for about 4 to 5 minutes on each side, depending on their thickness. Transfer to a warm plate and keep hot while you cook the rest. To serve, put the skate on 4 warmed plates and spoon the béarnaise sauce to one side.

Tourte of Scallops, Crab and Mussels

Serves 6

20 mussels, cleaned
(see p. 17)

3 to 4 tablespoons dry
white wine or water

1 pound puff pastry,
either homemade or
the best-quality bought
puff pastry

6 prepared scallops
(see p. 18)

¼ pound crabmeat

1 egg, beaten

• Salt and freshly ground
black pepper

For the Mousseline

6 ounces whiting or
pollack fillets, peeled

3 tablespoons *Shellfish
Reduction* (see p. 214)

1 egg

1 small shallot, finely
chopped

¾ teaspoon salt

½ cup heavy cream

For the Sauce

5 tablespoons *Shellfish
Reduction* (see p. 214)

⅔ cup heavy cream

6 tablespoons chilled
unsalted butter, cut into
small pieces

2 teaspoons lemon juice

I suppose if any dish typified a slight return in British cooking to more substantial, warming—dare I say, comforting—food, this would be it. We used to sell individual tourtes made with crawfish in the restaurant about ten years ago, but then gave up when the wave of Mediterranean food began to sweep over northern Europe. However, we've slipped the dish back onto the menu recently and it has gone down very well indeed. A tourte is a round, savory, covered tart from France, made with the very best puff pastry, which is glazed with egg to give it a beautiful brown finish and cut in radiating curves like a Pithiviers gâteau. This one is filled with seafood, then a rich shellfish sauce is poured into the tart and served with it. Tourtes are very old in origin. The founder of classic French cookery, Antoine Carême, noted with sadness in the early 1800s that the tourte served by "our great cooks in the old days at the table of princes" was by then thought to be too common for sophisticated gastronomes because it was round.

Make the *Shellfish Reduction* if you have not already done so (see p. 214). Leave to cool.

For the mousseline, cut the fish fillets into small pieces and put them in a food processor with the shellfish reduction, egg, shallot and salt. Process until smooth, then, with the motor still running, add the cream in a steady stream, taking care not to process for more than 10 seconds or the mixture may curdle. Scrape into a bowl, cover and chill for 1 hour.

Put the mussels and white wine or water in a large pan over fairly high heat, cover and cook for 3 to 4 minutes, or until the mussels have opened. Discard any that remain closed. Shell the mussels and leave to cool.

Preheat the oven to 425°F.

Cut the pastry in half and roll out one piece into a 10-inch round. Roll out the second piece into an 11-inch round. Put the smaller piece of pastry on a lightly greased baking sheet and spread half the mousseline over it to within 1½ inches of the edge. Cut each scallop in half horizontally and arrange over the mousseline with the crab and the cooked mussels. Season with salt and pepper and then carefully spread the remaining mousseline over the top.

Brush the edge of the pastry with a little water, cover with the larger round of pastry and press the edges together to seal. Crimp the edges decoratively, then brush the top with the beaten egg. Using the tip of a small, sharp knife, either score crisscross lines on top or mark radiating curves from the center. Make a hole in the center and bake for 25 minutes.

Shortly before the tourte is ready, make the sauce. Put the shellfish reduction and cream into a pan, bring to a boil and simmer for 5 minutes. Whisk in the butter a piece at a time, followed by the lemon juice.

Take the tourte out of the oven, pour about 2 tablespoons of the sauce into it through the hole in the top, then return it to the oven for 5 minutes. Slide the pie onto a warm serving plate and serve the rest of the sauce separately.

Classic Hake in Parsley Sauce

Serves 4

2½ quarts water
1 lemon slice
1 tablespoon salt
1½ to 2 pounds hake fillet, skin on
6 tablespoons unsalted butter
1½ tablespoons flour
2½ cups milk
1 fresh parsley, stems removed and chopped

This is the joke dish that people always use as an example of boring British cooking but in fact, if you use perfectly fresh hake, haddock or cod and make this simple white sauce properly (i.e., not out of a mix) and use freshly chopped parsley, the joke is on everyone else as it is very good.

Put the water, lemon and salt in a large pan. Bring to a boil, then simmer for 5 minutes. Add the hake and simmer for 2 minutes. Remove the pan from the heat and leave to finish cooking gently in the cooking liquid.

Melt 2 tablespoons butter in a heavy-bottomed pan and sprinkle over the flour. Stir continuously with a wooden spoon to mix, then cook until the mixture smells nutty. Gradually pour in the milk, stirring all the time, to make a smooth sauce. Add 1¼ cups of the fish cooking liquid and leave to simmer for 12 minutes.

Drain the hake and cut into 4 portions. Place on 4 warmed plates. Stir the chopped parsley and the rest of the butter into the sauce. Pour the sauce over half the fish. I think dishes like this look more attractive if the fish is only partly covered. Serve with some potatoes boiled in salted water and a sprig of mint.

Herrings in Oatmeal with Bacon

Serves 4

4 herrings, weighing about ½ pound each
1⅓ cups rolled oats
2 tablespoons vegetable oil
4 slices bacon, cut into thin strips
• Salt and freshly ground black pepper
1 lemon, cut into wedges

We filmed this dish and five or six other dishes on the theme of simplicity in the series and in the end, nothing seems to bring out the creamy, nutty flavor of fresh herrings better than this straightforward British dish.

Fillet the herrings (see p. 13). Season and press with oatmeal until they are well covered. Heat the oil in a frying pan and fry the bacon until crisp. Remove from the pan and keep warm. Fry the herrings in the same oil, flesh side first, until golden brown. Sprinkle the fillets with the bacon. Serve with lemon wedges and some boiled potatoes with chopped parsley.

Fillets of Brill with a Ginger and Monbazillac Sauce and Pappardelle Pasta

Serves 4

2½ cups *Fish Stock* (see p. 212)

6 tablespoons Monbazillac (or another sweet wine such as Sauternes or Muscat Beaumes de Venise)

6 tablespoons unsalted butter

1 shallot, very finely chopped

4 brill fillets, 6 ounces each, skinned

• Salt and freshly ground black pepper

1½ tablespoons very finely chopped fresh ginger

For the pasta

2 tablespoons extra-virgin olive oil

2 tomatoes, peeled, seeded and diced

6 fresh basil leaves, very finely shredded

• Juice of ¼ lemon

¼ pound pappardelle pasta

You can use John Dory or turbot equally successfully in this dish. Like many of my recipes, I look to build up complexity of flavors by combining two or more different, but complementary, tastes on the plate. Here I have combined a butter and ginger sauce with a tomato and olive dressing for the pasta. The trick is to aim to be complex but not over complicated.

Put the stock and wine into a pan (the larger the better because it will reduce more quickly) and boil rapidly until reduced to one quarter of its original volume (about ¾ cup).

Preheat the oven to 400°F. Meanwhile, lightly grease a shallow baking dish with some of the butter and then sprinkle the base with the chopped shallots. Bring 2 quarts water and 1 tablespoon of salt to a boil in a large pan.

Season the brill fillets on both sides with salt and pepper and lay on top of the shallots. As soon as the stock is ready, cool slightly and then pour over the fish and cover with a piece buttered parchment paper. Bake for 8 minutes.

Put the olive oil, diced tomatoes, basil and lemon juice for the pasta into a small pan and leave over very low heat to warm through. Drop the pappardelle pasta into a boiling water and cook for 3 to 4 minutes (or according to the manufacturer's instructions).

Drain the pasta well, return to the pan with the olive oil and tomato mixture and a little salt and toss together gently. Keep warm.

Remove the fish from the oven and lift the fillets out of the sauce onto a plate. Cover and keep warm. Strain the sauce into a small pan and add the chopped ginger. Bring to a boil and then whisk in the remaining butter a small piece at a time. Season with a little salt and pepper. Keep warm.

To serve, put the brill onto 4 warmed plates and spoon the ginger butter sauce over and around the fish. Place four little piles of pasta to the side and serve with a slightly off-dry white wine.

Elegant Fish Dishes

The dishes in this chapter are not necessarily ones that require hours of commitment in the kitchen, though some of them do. They are more a collection of recipes that you might even feel embarrassed to serve at anything but a formal occasion. You would feel a bit self-conscious about bringing out a plateful of *Braised Fillet of Turbot with Slivers of Potato, Mushrooms and Truffle Oil* for the children.

"What's for supper?"

"Braised Fillet of Turbot with Slivers of Potato, Mushrooms and Truffle Oil."

To which, with children there is only one answer: "But I wanted fish sticks."

I have a bit of a theory about dinner parties, a theory born of having held very few, since I spend most of my evenings cooking in the restaurant. Lack of knowledge is rarely a hindrance when it comes to pronouncing on anything! A dinner party should contain only one elaborate and stylish dish. The rest of the meal should be simple and composed of things with which your guests feel familiar. I almost feel that it is bad manners to impose too much cooking on your friends. This idea also underpins the menu at the restaurant: keep it simple and don't show off too much, because what counts is people's relaxed enjoyment. The food should almost be forgotten, just coming along effortlessly and reinforcing everyone's sense of well being, except for that one dish that everyone will remember so well.

Hopefully this is a chapter of memorable dishes. Certainly the *Spiny Lobster with Vanilla Sauce* (see p. 140) would be, or the *Fillet of Bass on a Crisp Risotto Cake with Saffron Sauce* (see p. 134). These are time-consuming to prepare but terribly worthwhile. Others are equally elevated but really quite easy to make, such as *Fillets of Bass with Vanilla Butter Vinaigrette* (see p. 137) and *Escalopes of Salmon with Champagne and Chive Sauce* (see p. 150). This, then, is the chapter for really flying.

Facing page: Poached Lobster with Butter and Basil (see p. 132).

Poached Lobster with Butter and Basil

Serves 4 as a first course

1 quantity of *Shellfish Nage* (see p. 214), made using 2$\frac{1}{2}$ quarts water and 1$\frac{1}{4}$ cups wine

1 live lobster, weighing about 1$\frac{1}{2}$ pounds, or 2 small lobsters, weighing about 1 pound each

1 carrot, sliced

1 baby turnip, sliced in half

2 celery stalks, sliced

1 small onion, sliced

4 oz haricots verts, halved

$\frac{1}{2}$ cup chilled unsalted butter, cut into small pieces

6 fresh basil leaves, very finely shredded, plus basil sprigs, to garnish

• Salt

The lobster is poached in a delicate shellfish nage, then some root vegetables are added. The poaching liquor is reduced right down and whisked with a little butter and a chiffonade of basil (very finely shredded basil). The reduction of the nage takes a long time, as you have to boil about 2$\frac{1}{2}$ quarts of liquid down to a mere cupful, but the fruits of your labor will be so very worthwhile that you will be amazed how much flavor there is in the shell of a smallish lobster. The finished sauce is truly wonderful. Do try it. I add some baby turnips to the bouillon for cooking this lobster. I love the taste of young turnips, so sweet and yet slightly bitter, and this flavor comes through in the final sauce as a subtle hint.

Put the nage into a pan just large enough to accommodate the lobster. Bring to a rapid boil, then add the lobster. Bring back to a boil and simmer for 12 minutes. Remove the lobster and set aside until cool enough to handle. Remove the meat from the lobster (see p. 19), reserving the shell.

Add the carrot, turnip, celery, onion and the reserved lobster shells to the nage and boil rapidly until the liquid has reduced to about $\frac{2}{3}$ cup, but remove the 2 pieces of turnip after 10 minutes, otherwise the flavor will overpower the final sauce.

Bring a small pan of salted water to a boil. Add the haricots verts and cook for about 3 minutes, or until just tender. Drain and keep warm.

Strain the reduced stock into a small pan. Bring back to a boil and gradually whisk in the butter, a few pieces at a time. Check the seasoning, adding salt if necessary. Stir in the basil and leave over very low heat for about 5 minutes, to allow the flavor to infuse the sauce. Strain the sauce into a clean pan to remove the basil if you wish.

To serve, slice the lobster meat, reheat gently and arrange it on 4 warmed plates. Pour the sauce around, then pile the haricots verts alongside the lobster and garnish with basil sprigs.

Broiled Fillets of Dover Sole with Sautéed Potatoes, Caramelized Apples and Cider Sauce

Serves 4

2 pounds potatoes
2 tablespoons olive oil
6 tablespoons unsalted butter
$\frac{2}{3}$ cup dry cider
$\frac{2}{3}$ cup *Fish Stock* (see p. 212)
8 Dover sole fillets, weighing about 3 to 4 ounces each, skinned
• Salt and freshly ground black pepper
3 pippin apples
$\frac{1}{4}$ teaspoon superfine sugar
1 tablespoon finely chopped fresh parsley

A simple dish inspired by one I ate in Brittany, where apples, cider and Dover sole are as plentiful as they are here in the West Country. You can use plenty of other types of fish for this, such as lemon sole, flounder, sand dab, or even small cod (codling), hake or whiting.

Peel the potatoes, cut them in half lengthwise and then cut each half into slices $\frac{1}{4}$ inch thick. Cook in boiling salted water for about 8 minutes, or until just tender, then drain and pat dry. Heat the olive oil and 2 tablespoons of the butter in a large frying pan. Add the potato slices, season well with salt and pepper and fry for about 7 to 8 minutes on each side, or until they are pleasantly brown and sandy. Transfer to a baking sheet and keep warm in a low oven.

Put the cider, stock and another 2 tablespoons of the butter in the frying pan, bring to a boil and boil for a few minutes, until reduced to a thick, well-flavored sauce. Season with salt and pepper, pour into a small pan and keep warm.

Preheat the broiler. Melt the remaining butter in the cleaned frying pan. Brush the sole fillets with a little of the butter and lay them on the rack of the broiler pan. Season with salt and pepper. Peel and core the apples, then cut each one into 8 wedges.

Broil the fish fillets for 3 minutes on one side only. Meanwhile, put the apple slices in the frying pan, sprinkle over the sugar and fry for about 1 minute on each side, or until golden. Stir into the sautéed potatoes.

To serve, arrange the sole fillets down the center of a warmed oval serving dish and put the apples and potatoes around the edge. Bring the sauce back to a boil, stir in the parsley and pour it over the fish. Serve immediately.

Fillet of Bass on a Crisp Risotto Cake with Saffron Sauce

Serves 6

1 quantity of *Shellfish Stock* (see p. 214)

$\frac{1}{2}$ teaspoon saffron threads

3 tablespoons *Olive Oil Mayonnaise* (see p. 217)

6 sea bass fillets, weighing about $\frac{1}{4}$ pound each, skin on

1 tablespoon unsalted butter, melted

1 tablespoon olive oil

• Salt and freshly ground black pepper

• Chopped fresh parsley, to garnish

For the Risotto

2 tablespoons olive oil

1 small onion, finely chopped

1 garlic clove, very finely chopped

$1\frac{1}{8}$ cups risotto rice such as Arborio

6 tablespoons dry white wine

• Salt and freshly ground black pepper

All the flavors in this dish—the bass, the shellfish-flavored risotto cake under it and the warm, mayonnaise-based saffron sauce—complement one another in a beguiling way. At the time of writing, this recipe has not had its premiere at the restaurant but I have a feeling it will go down rather well.

Make the stock (see p. 214) if you haven't already done so, adding most of the saffron with the rest of the ingredients just before simmering. You should end up with about $4\frac{1}{2}$ cups—if you have any less, make it up with a little more fish stock.

For the risotto, heat the olive oil in a heavy-bottomed pan. Add the onion and garlic and cook over medium heat until soft and lightly browned. Add the rice and stir around for a couple of minutes, or until well coated with the oil. Pour in the wine, bring to a boil and stir until the rice has absorbed all the liquid. Now add 4 cups of the warm shellfish stock in 3 batches, stirring well until all the stock has been absorbed before adding the next amount. Season with salt and pepper. The risotto will take about 20 minutes to cook, by which time the rice should be tender and will have absorbed all the liquid. Since the risotto is to be molded into cakes it should be allowed to become really quite thick.

Put six $3\frac{1}{2}$-inch pastry cutters or egg poaching rings on a baking sheet and line each one with a small sheet of plastic wrap, leaving the edges overhanging. Divide the risotto among them, level the surface and cover with the overhanging plastic wrap. Chill for at least 3 hours.

Preheat the broiler. For the sauce, bring the last $\frac{1}{2}$ to $\frac{2}{3}$ cup of stock to a boil and add the remaining saffron threads. Gradually whisk it into the mayonnaise, then pour it back into the pan and cook over a gentle heat for a couple of minutes, stirring constantly, until the sauce is thick enough to coat the back of a spoon. Do not let it get too hot or it will curdle. Keep warm while you finish the dish.

Cut each fillet of fish in half, brush both sides with a little of the melted butter and season with a little salt and pepper. Place skin-side up on the rack of the broiler pan.

Heat the remaining melted butter and the oil in a large frying pan until quite hot. Unwrap the risotto cakes, put them in the pan and fry for $1\frac{1}{2}$ to 2 minutes, or until richly golden. Carefully turn them over, lower the heat to medium-high and fry for another 3 to 4 minutes, or until they have heated right through. Meanwhile broil the fish for 2 minutes, skin-side up only.

To serve, put the risotto cakes on 6 warmed plates. Put 2 pieces of sea bass on top of each one, pour the sauce around and sprinkle lightly with chopped parsley.

Braised Fillet of Turbot with Slivers of Potato, Mushrooms and Truffle Oil

Serves 4

6 ounces waxy potatoes,
$\frac{1}{2}$ cup unsalted butter
1 thin slice cooked ham, weighing about 1 ounce, cut into very fine cubes
3 tablespoons finely chopped shallots
6 tablespoons dry vermouth, such as Noilly Prat or Martini
$1\frac{1}{4}$ cups *Concentrated Chicken Stock* (see p. 213)
$\frac{1}{4}$ pound button mushrooms, thinly sliced
2 teaspoons lemon juice
1 tablespoon truffle oil
• Salt and freshly ground black pepper
$1\frac{1}{2}$ pounds turbot fillet, skin on, cut into 8 pieces
1 tablespoon chopped fresh parsley

I originally devised this recipe using fresh black truffles, but these are pretty impossible (and pretty expensive) to get, especially outside the restaurant business. However, the flavor of truffles is so good that it seemed a shame not to try and incorporate them somewhere. Then I found an Italian olive oil flavored with white truffles. It is fantastic and quite easy to get in any good delicatessen. A little bottle is also fiendishly expensive, but it goes a long way.

Peel and slice the potatoes as thinly as you can and then cut them across into thin matchsticks. Melt half the butter in a frying pan that is large enough to hold all the pieces of fish in one layer. Add the potatoes, ham and shallots and cook gently for 4 to 5 minutes. Add the vermouth and chicken stock and simmer for about 8 minutes, or until the potatoes are almost, but not quite, cooked. You can prepare the dish to this stage some time in advance, if you wish.

Stir the mushrooms, lemon juice, truffle oil and some salt and pepper into the pan and then rest the pieces of turbot on top, skin-side up. Cover and simmer for about 6 minutes or until the fish is cooked through. Lift the fish onto a plate and keep hot. Add the remaining butter to the pan and boil rapidly for 10 minutes, or until the sauce has thickened and the potatoes are just beginning to break up.

To serve, peel the skin off the turbot and place the fish on 4 warmed plates. Stir the parsley into the sauce and spoon it on top of the fish.

Fillets of Bass with Vanilla Butter Vinaigrette

Serves 4

$^1/_2$	cup unsalted butter
4	sea bass fillets, weighing about $^1/_4$ pound each, skinned
•	Salt and freshly ground black pepper
$^1/_2$	vanilla bean
4	tablespoons Noilly Prat
2	teaspoons white wine vinegar
1	shallot, halved
$^2/_3$	cup *Fish Stock* (see p. 212)
3	tablespoons peeled, seeded and diced tomato
1	tablespoon coarsely chopped fresh chervil

I cooked this dish for a friend of mine, Henry Gilbey, who is the most enthusiastic fisherman I have ever met. His whole life is geared toward fishing and yet he doesn't like fish. This is the dish I chose for him because it works so well together and all the flavors are pretty irresistible. A simple fillet of bass is cooked on a cast-iron ribbed pan to give that flavor, then served with a warm vinaigrette made with a good fish stock reduction, dry vermouth and vanilla. Maybe Henry was just being polite but he did say it was very good.

Clarify the butter by melting it gently in a small pan, then skimming off any froth and pouring off the clear liquid into another pan, leaving behind the butter solids that will have collected at the bottom.

Brush both sides of the sea bass fillets with a little of the clarified butter and season with salt and pepper.

For the vinaigrette, split the vanilla bean open lengthwise, scrape out the seeds with a small teaspoon and then chop the bean halves very finely. Put the seeds and beans into a small pan with the Noilly Prat, vinegar and shallot, bring to a boil and boil for a few minutes until reduced to about 1 tablespoon. Add the stock and boil once more until reduced to about 3 tablespoons. Remove the shallot halves, then add the remaining clarified butter, plus the tomato, chervil, $^1/_4$ teaspoon of salt and 6 turns of the black pepper mill. Keep just warm over very low heat.

Heat a lightly oiled cast-iron ribbed pan until very hot. Cook the fish fillets, skin-side down, for 1 minute, pressing down on top of each fillet in turn with a spatula to help mark them with the lines from the griddle. Turn over and cook for 30 seconds on the other side.

To serve, put the fish fillets on 4 warmed plates and spoon the vinaigrette to the side.

Mille Feuille of Sashimi with Wasabi Mayonnaise and Ginger Dressing

Serves 4 as a first course

$^1/_4$ pound small lemon sole or flounder fillets, skinned

6 prepared scallops (see p. 18)

4 sheets filo pastry, about 12 by 16 inches

2 tablespoons butter, melted

2 green onions

2 tablespoons Japanese soy sauce

• $^1/_2$-inch piece fresh ginger, peeled and very finely chopped

1 tablespoon cold-pressed sesame oil

4 teaspoons *Mustard Mayonnaise* (see p. 216)

1 teaspoon wasabi paste

I had this dish in an excellent restaurant in Sydney called The Pier, which is in Rose Bay on the eastern side of the harbor. The chef there, Greg Doyle, is one of those exceptionally imaginative cooks who can just think up a new dish for virtually every service of lunch or dinner. I don't know whether this one ever appeared on the menu again there but it certainly should. It is such a sensible way of serving up the delicious raw fish flavors of sashimi in an elegant style. As with all my recipes calling for raw fish, it is essential that the fish is extremely fresh, otherwise there is no point in doing this dish at all.

Cut the fish fillets into small, thin slices by cutting at a slight angle across the top of each fillet as if you were slicing smoked salmon. Detach the coral from each scallop and, if large, cut in half lengthwise. Cut each scallop horizontally into 4 thin slices. Cover the fish and set aside in the refrigerator.

Preheat the oven to 400°F.

Lay 2 sheets of filo pastry on a work surface and brush with melted butter. Cover each one with a second sheet and brush with more butter. Now cut out twelve $3^1/_2$-inch circles. Place on a lightly greased baking sheet and bake for about 5 minutes, or until crisp and golden. Remove and leave to cool.

Cut the green onions into 2-inch lengths and then cut lengthwise into very fine shreds.

To serve, place 4 filo pastry circles on 4 large plates. Cover each one with about 4 pieces of fish fillet and 3 pieces of scallop. Drizzle each layer of fish with very small amount of the soy sauce and then sprinkle with a few of the green onions. Place another pastry circle on top of each one, repeat the filling once more, then cover with the remaining pieces of pastry.

Mix the remaining soy sauce with the chopped ginger and sesame oil to make a dressing. Mix the mayonnaise with the wasabi paste. Using a teaspoon, spoon little drops of the dressing around each mille feuille and spoon some of the wasabi mayonnaise to one side. Serve immediately, otherwise the filo pastry will go soft.

Spiny Lobster with Vanilla Sauce

Serves 4

1 live spiny lobster, weighing about 3 to 4 pounds, or 2 live lobsters, weighing about 1$\frac{1}{2}$ to 2$\frac{1}{4}$ pounds each

$\frac{1}{2}$ vanilla bean

1$\frac{1}{4}$ cups *Fish Stock* (see p. 212)

2 tablespoons Noilly Prat

1 quantity of *Quick Hollandaise Sauce* (see p. 215)

• Salt and freshly ground black pepper

I make no apologies for using vanilla in two of my dishes, this and the sea bass recipe on p. 137. The sauces are completely different but the flavor of vanilla is so good with seafood. The other great plus of using vanilla in a savory sauce like this is that it has a particular affinity with Chardonnay or, more particularly, oaked Chardonnay. Wine writers often describe a good Chardonnay as having vanillary overtones. This comes from the flavor of the oak, and a dish like this, spiny lobster (often called crawfish or cray-fish in Cornwall) with a sweet and aromatic sauce, cries out for a really good oaked Chardonnay.

For the sauce, split the vanilla bean open lengthwise and scrape out the seeds. Put the fish stock, vanilla bean and seeds and the Noilly Prat into a pan and boil rapidly until reduced to about 1$\frac{1}{2}$ to 2 tablespoons. Set aside.

Remove the meat from the lobster (see p. 19). Lift out the tail meat in one piece and slice on a slant into $\frac{1}{2}$-inch pieces (see p. 19).

Meanwhile make the hollandaise (see p. 215), adding the reduced hot fish stock with the melted butter. Season with salt and pepper.

To serve, heat the lobster gently and arrange the slices of tail meat on 4 warmed plates. Put a little pile of the warmed head meat to one side and a spoonful of the vanilla sauce to the other.

The Finest Seafood in a Small Ragout with a Deep Red Wine Sauce

Serves 4 as a first course

1   cooked lobster, weighing about 1 pound
1   Dover sole, weighing about ³/₄ pound, filleted and skinned (see pp. 14–15)
4   prepared scallops (see p. 18)
•   A pinch of paprika
•   Salt and freshly ground black pepper

For the Croutons
2   medium-thick slices white bread
2   tablespoons sunflower oil
•   A small knob of unsalted butter

For the Red Wine Sauce
2¹/₂   cups *Fish Stock* (see p. 212)
2¹/₂   cups red wine
¹/₂   cup port
6   tablespoons chilled unsalted butter, cut into small pieces

This is unashamedly a real show-off dish. The quantities are small but the seafood is the best and the sauce contains an expensive amount of red wine, reduced by boiling to give the richest, deepest flavor imaginable. Some people are put off by the idea of fish in a red wine sauce, but when wine and fish are joined as the dish is served and the red wine has been reduced down and sweetened with port, then finished with butter, the combination is irresistible.

Remove the meat from the lobster (see p. 19), trying to remove the claw meat in as large pieces as possible. Slice the tail meat across into pieces ¹/₂ inch thick. Lay the fish fillets and the scallops on the lightly greased rack of the broiler pan and season with a little salt and pepper and the paprika. This will give them a pleasing color.

For the croutons, cut four 2-inch rounds from the bread. Heat the oil and butter in a frying pan and fry the croutons for 1 to 2 minutes on each side, until golden. Drain on paper towels and keep warm.

For the sauce, put the stock, wine and port into a pan, bring to a boil and boil rapidly until reduced to about ¹/₂ cup. Whisk in the butter a little at a time and keep warm over low heat.

Preheat the broiler. Broil the fish fillets and scallops for 2 minutes. Add the pieces of lobster meat to the rack and broil for a further minute.

To serve, pile up the seafood in the center of 4 warmed plates, drizzle some of the sauce over the top and pour more around the edges. Lay a crouton on top of each pile.

Ravioli of Creamed Cod with Arugula Pesto

Serves 4 as a first course

1   quantity of *Egg Pasta Dough* (see p. 218)

•   Freshly shaved Parmesan cheese, to serve

For the Creamed Cod Filling

3   ounces cod fillet

•   Salt

2   tablespoons extra-virgin olive oil, preferably lemon-flavored

4   tablespoons heavy cream

4   garlic cloves, sliced

For the Arugula Pesto

6   tablespoons olive oil

1   cup arugula leaves, tough stems removed

1   garlic clove, roughly chopped

$\frac{1}{4}$ cup grated Parmesan cheese

2   tablespoons pine nuts

•   Salt and freshly ground black pepper

Commercial salted and dried cod needs long soaking and has a distinctive flavor that is addictive once you are used to it. You can make your own salt cod for this, which is easy to make and less assertively flavored. Arugula is available everywhere now, but for this dish to succeed it really needs to be a good, strong-leaved, peppery arugula, not the rather wishy-washy, limp stuff that is probably grown in hothouses out of season.

To make your own salt cod, put the cod in a plastic container and completely cover with a thick layer of salt. Refrigerate for 24 hours—the salt will turn to brine overnight.

The next day, remove the cod from the brine and soak it in cold water for 2 hours. If using commercial salt cod, soak in plenty of cold water for 12 hours. Make the pasta (see p. 218), leaving it to rest while you make the creamed cod filling.

Drain the salt cod, put it in a pan and cover with fresh water. Bring to a boil and simmer for 5 minutes. Lift out and, when cool enough to handle, flake the flesh, discarding the skin and bones.

Put the oil and cream into a small pan and bring to a boil. Put the flaked cod into a food processor with the garlic and the hot cream mixture and blend until smooth. Leave to cool.

For the arugula pesto, put all the ingredients into a food processor and blend until smooth. Scrape into a bowl and set aside.

Make the ravioli (see opposite). If you are not going to eat them immediately, drop them into a pan of boiling water and cook for just 1 minute. Drop into a bowl of cold water, then lift out and drain. Store in the refrigerator on oiled trays covered with plastic wrap.

Otherwise, bring 2 quarts of water to a boil with 1 tablespoon of salt. Add the ravioli and cook for 4 minutes (3 minutes if they have already been blanched). Drain well, then return the ravioli to the pan with the arugula pesto and toss together well. Spoon the ravioli into 4 large warmed pasta plates and serve sprinkled with a few shavings of fresh Parmesan.

Making Ravioli

1. Roll out the pasta dough on a lightly floured work surface into a 15- inch square. Then with your fingertip, make small marks at 3 cm 11/2-inch intervals in even rows over one half of the square.

2. Place a teaspoon of the creamed cod filling on each mark.

3. Brush lines of water between the piles of mixture and then fold over the other half of the square so that the edges meet.

4. Working from the center of the folded side, outward and downward, press firmly around each pile of mixture with your fingers to push out any trapped air and seal in the filling.

5. Trim off the edges of the dough and cut between the rows with a sharp knife or a fluted pasta wheel.

Open Ravioli of Lobster with Tomato and Basil Sauce

Serves 4 as a first course

½ quantity of *Egg Pasta Dough* (see p. 218)

6 ounces cooked lobster tail, thinly sliced (see p. 19)

• Fresh basil sprigs, to garnish

For the Tomato and Basil Sauce

2 tomatoes, peeled, seeded and diced

6 fresh basil leaves, finely sliced

4 tablespoons extra-virgin olive oil

• Salt and freshly ground black pepper

For the Cream Sauce

⅔ cup *Fish Stock* (see p. 212)

2 tablespoons heavy cream

2 tablespoons white wine

4 tablespoons *Olive Oil Mayonnaise* (see p. 217)

Here, cooked lobster is combined with some fresh basil, uncooked tomato and virgin olive oil, then loosely sandwiched between al dente pasta squares to form an "open ravioli." The accompanying sauce is simply some mayonnaise whisked with a white wine and fish stock reduction. I must admit that this is one of those restaurant dishes designed to make a small amount of lobster go a long way, but why not? The finished dish looks very professional and actually part of the art of a good cook is to present a small amount of expensive protein in an appetizing and imaginative way. You need to do plenty of advance preparation because the final assembly is a bit fiddly.

Bring a large pan of salted water to a boil. Roll out the pasta dough on a lightly floured surface into a 6-by-12-inch rectangle. Cut into eight 3-inch squares.

For the tomato and basil sauce, put all the ingredients into a small pan and set aside.

Reheat the slices of lobster meat. Meanwhile, drop the pasta squares into a boiling water and cook for 3 to 4 minutes, or until *al dente*, then drain and lay out on a sheet of plastic wrap. Put the tomato and basil sauce over very low heat and leave just to warm through.

For the cream sauce, bring the stock, heavy cream and white wine to a boil and boil until reduced in volume by half. Put the mayonnaise into a bowl and gradually whisk the hot stock reduction into it. Season to taste with salt.

To serve, put a square of pasta in the center of each of 4 warmed plates. Spoon a little of the cream sauce onto each one, divide the lobster meat among them and then spoon over half the tomato and basil sauce. Now cover with the remaining pasta squares and pour the remaining cream sauce over and around each ravioli. Finally spoon on the rest of the tomato and basil sauce. Serve immediately, garnished with basil sprigs.

Pavé of Salmon with Easter Fennel and New Potatoes

Serves 4

4 thick pieces salmon fillet, weighing about 6 ounces each, skin on (they should measure about 4 inches square)
· Salt and freshly ground black pepper
6 tablespoons unsalted butter

For the Potatoes
1 pound new potatoes
3 tablespoons extra-virgin olive oil
1 shallot, very finely chopped
2 large plum tomatoes, peeled, seeded and chopped
1 tablespoon red wine vinegar
3 tablespoons chopped fresh fennel tops
1/2 teaspoon salt
· Freshly ground black pepper

Why Easter fennel, you may ask. There is a dead time between the depth of winter and the real arrival of spring. On the coast in February and March we get disconcertingly sharp easterly winds and the country seems covered in a layer of salt, with a gray bleakness about it and a smell of cold seas. Then you notice one or two bright green shoots of fennel with a sudden clean scent of aniseed, bringing a returning memory of summer and light, far more acute than some basil from the supermarket. I thought I'd celebrate that return of life in spring with a dish that uses fennel and new potatoes. The potatoes will have been grown under plastic and, though not of great flavor, are fresh tasting and confirmation of the skill of a local market gardener. They go well with local salmon, which reappears in the kitchen in March. Pavé is French for paving stone or slab, which perfectly suggests the shape of a thick fillet of salmon cut from the loin.

Season the salmon on both sides with salt and pepper. Clarify the butter by melting it over low heat and then pouring off the liquid into a frying pan, leaving behind the milky solids that will have collected at the bottom.

Peel the potatoes, cut them into slices $^1/_4$ inch thick and then cut the slices lengthwise into matchsticks. Drop them into a pan of well-salted boiling water and simmer for 3 to 4 minutes, or until just tender. Drain and keep warm.

Meanwhile, heat the clarified butter in the frying pan, add the salmon, skin-side down, and cook for 3 to 4 minutes, pressing down on the fish with the back of a spatula to make sure that the skin browns evenly. Turn over and cook for another 1 to $1^1/_2$ minutes.

Stir the olive oil, shallot, tomatoes, red wine vinegar, chopped fennel tops, salt and some pepper into the potatoes. Put the salmon skin-side up on 4 warmed plates and spoon the warm potatoes alongside.

Grilled Goatfish with Spiced Fish Sausage and Tomato and Basil Dressing

Serves 4

4 goatfish or bream, weighing about ¹/₂ pound each, filleted
• Extra-virgin olive oil for brushing
• Salt and freshly ground black pepper

For the Tomato and Basil Dressing
6 tablespoons extra-virgin olive oil
• Finely grated zest and juice of ¹/₄ lemon
¹/₂ red finger chili, seeded and very finely chopped
1 tomato, peeled, seeded and diced
12 fresh basil leaves, finely shredded
¹/₂ teaspoon salt

For the Spiced Fish Sausage
¹/₂ pound conger eel or shark fillet
3 tablespoons olive oil
1 tablespoon beaten egg
1 anchovy fillet
¹/₄ teaspoon salt
7 turns of the black pepper mill
1 small garlic clove, chopped
1 teaspoon harissa paste
¹/₂ teaspoon lemon juice
¹/₄ cup finely chopped canned pimiento or roasted red pepper

I cook a lot of fish fillets on a cast-iron ribbed pan to give that attractive branded look. Here, broiled red mullet is served with a simple tomato and basil dressing and, more unusually, some sliced fish sausage made of conger eel and flavored with harissa. You should be able to buy this fiery North African chili paste in small cans from good delicatessens and some large supermarkets.

For the spiced fish sausage, put everything except the pimiento or red pepper in a food processor and blend until smooth. Stir in the pimiento or red pepper, then spoon the mixture in a thick line onto a large sheet of plastic wrap. Fold over the edge of the plastic wrap nearest to you, roll the mixture over once or twice until well encased in the plastic wrap and then use your hands to shape it into a sausage 2 inches thick. Firmly twist the ends of the plastic wrap to make a watertight package. Bring some water to a boil in a large, deep frying pan, reduce to a simmer and add the fish sausage. Poach for 10 minutes, then transfer to a bowl of cold water and leave to cool for 2 minutes. You can make this some time before the final cooking. Keep it wrapped in the refrigerator. Remove the plastic wrap and cut on the diagonal into 12 slices ¹/₄ inch thick.

Place a cast-iron ribbed pan over high heat. Brush the slices of fish sausage with a little oil, season with salt and pepper and broil for 1 minute on just one side. Set aside on a plate and keep warm.

Reheat the pan until very hot. Brush the fish fillets with oil, season and broil for 1 minute on each side.

To make the dressing, whisk the oil with the lemon zest and juice, then stir in the chili, tomato, shredded basil and salt. Warm through over low heat.

To serve, put the fish fillets on 4 warmed plates and arrange the fish sausage to one side. Spoon a little of the dressing around the edge of the plate.

Ragout of Turbot and Scallops with Vouvray, Butter and Basil

Serves 4

2½ cups *Fish Stock*
     (see p. 212), made from
     the turbot bones
1   piece turbot, 2 pounds,
     filleted and skinned
     (see pp. 14 to 15)
2   ounces carrot
2   ounces celeriac
2   ounces white of leek
6   tablespoons butter
4   tablespoons Vouvray or
     other medium-dry
     white wine
2   ounces button
     mushrooms, thinly
     sliced
•   Salt and freshly ground
     white pepper
8   large scallops,
     prepared (see p. 18)
10   fresh basil leaves, finely
     shredded
¾   cup heavy cream
•   Lemon juice
•   Fresh basil sprigs, to
     garnish

The essential point of this dish is not to exceed the cooking times by a second so that the seafood is beautifully succulent. Don't feel you have to buy Vouvray for this dish—any medium-dry white wine will suffice, but Vouvray is the best.

Pour the stock into a pan and boil rapidly until reduced to ⅔ cup.

Cut the turbot fillet across into slices ¾ inch thick. Cut the carrot, celeriac and leek into 1-inch pieces and then cut each piece into thin slices. Heat the butter and half the Vouvray in a wide, heavy-bottomed pan large enough to hold the slices of turbot in one layer. Add the carrot, celeriac and leek strips, cover and cook gently for 5 minutes, or until just tender. Stir in the mushrooms and a little seasoning.

Lay the slices of turbot on top of the vegetables, spoon over the rest of the Vouvray and the reduced fish stock and season lightly. Cover and cook over a gentle heat for 3 minutes. Add the scallops to the pan, cover and cook for a further 1 to 2 minutes, or until both the turbot and scallops are just cooked.

Carefully lift the turbot and scallops out of the pan onto a warmed plate and keep warm. Add the basil to the vegetables in the pan with the cream. Bring to a boil and cook for 1 to 2 minutes, or until the sauce has thickened slightly. Season with salt and pepper and add a little freshly squeezed lemon juice to taste.

Spoon the vegetables onto 4 warmed plates. Arrange the turbot and scallops on top and serve garnished with sprigs of fresh basil.

Lobster à L'Américaine

Serves 4

2	live lobsters, each weighing about 1½ to 2 pounds
6	tablespoons olive oil
⅓	cup finely chopped onion
1	tablespoon cognac
2	garlic cloves, finely chopped
1½	pounds tomatoes, peeled, seeded and chopped
1	tablespoon roughly chopped tarragon
6	tablespoons dry white wine
1	teaspoon sugar
2½	cups *Fish Stock* (see p. 212)

I like to keep good things simple and the best way, to me, of eating lobster is to serve it simply boiled and split in half with new potatoes and some melted butter. However, there are one or two more complicated lobster dishes that I do approve of and this is one of them. Many people add cream in the recipe for Lobster à l'Américaine, but to me it's gilding the lily. The advantage with this recipe, rather than a more simple approach, is that you use all the intense flavor in the shell to make the tomato, white wine and tarragon sauce.

Cut the live lobsters in half lengthwise. Pull each tail section away from the head section and cut each section of tail into 4 or 5 pieces. Break the claw sections apart and crack each section so that the meat can be extracted easily later (see p. 19). The easiest way to do this is with the thickest part of a large knife.

Put the olive oil into a heavy-bottomed pan, big enough to hold all the pieces of lobster. Cook the onion and garlic in the olive oil until they are beginning to soften, then add all the pieces of lobster. Turn up the heat a little and turn the lobster pieces over until they are beginning to color red. Add the cognac and let the alcohol boil off. Add the tomatoes, chopped tarragon, white wine, sugar and stock. Cover. Leave the lobsters to cook through for about 8 minutes.

Remove the lobster pieces and keep warm. Return the pan to the heat and reduce the sauce by half.

When the sauce has reduced, return the lobster pieces to the sauce, heat through, and transfer to an attractive serving dish.

Escalopes of Salmon with Champagne and Chive Sauce

Serves 4

1 salmon fillet,
1$\frac{1}{2}$ pounds, taken from
a good-sized salmon
2 tablespoons sunflower
oil
• Salt

*For the Champagne and
Chive Sauce*
2 tablespoons unsalted
butter
1 small shallot, finely
chopped
$\frac{1}{2}$ cup champagne plus
1 tablespoon
2$\frac{1}{2}$ cups *Fish Stock*
(see p. 212)
$\frac{1}{2}$ teaspoon superfine
sugar
$\frac{1}{2}$ cup heavy cream
1 tablespoon chopped
fresh chives

What a shame. You're going to have to open a whole bottle of champagne to make this dish. Now what are you going to do with the rest of the champagne!

For the sauce, melt 1$\frac{1}{4}$ teaspoons of the butter in a saucepan, add the shallot and cook, without coloring, until softened. Add the $\frac{1}{2}$ cup of champagne and boil for 2 minutes, then add the stock and sugar. Boil rapidly until reduced by three-quarters. Add half the cream, bring to a boil and reduce until the sauce is thick enough to coat the back of a spoon.

Meanwhile, prepare the salmon escalopes. Remove any bones from the fillet with tweezers or by trapping them between the point of a small, sharp knife and your thumb. Then, with a large filleting knife or a carving knife, cut the salmon into 12 slices about $\frac{1}{4}$ inch thick, holding the knife at a 45-degree angle to the fillet and cutting at a slant down toward the skin. This will give you wider slices. Brush each escalope with a little of the oil, season lightly with salt and then put them on a lightly oiled baking sheet.

Preheat the broiler. For the sauce, whisk the remaining cream with the tablespoon of champagne and 2 teaspoons of the chopped chives until it forms soft peaks. Set aside.

To finish the dish, broil the salmon escalopes for about 1 minute, then put them on 4 warmed plates. Bring the reduced sauce back to a boil, whisk in the remaining butter, then the whipped cream mixture and pour around the salmon. Sprinkle with the remaining chives and serve immediately, while the sauce is still foaming.

Fillet of Turbot with Clams, Cockles and Chardonnay

Serves 4

16	small clams, such as cherrystone clams
20	cockles
4	pieces turbot fillet, weighing about 6 ounces each, skin on
2	shallots, finely chopped
6	tablespoons Chardonnay wine
1¼	cups *Fish Stock* (see p. 212)
¾	cup chilled unsalted butter, cut into small pieces
2	tablespoons chopped fresh flat-leaf parsley
•	Salt

The clams and cockles are steamed open in a rich Chardonnay, then a butter sauce is made with the cooking liquor and plenty of flat-leaf parsley. I thought up this dish as an attractive way of using the small clams called butterfish, which live at one end of the estuary, and the small cockles that live at the other, combining them in a main course with that magnificent fish, the turbot. The steamed turbot fillets are served covered in the parsley and butter sauce with cockles and clams both in and out of the shell, the idea being to use some of the shells as a garnish. If you can't get small live clams and cockles, however, use small mussels instead. We quite often do the dish with mussels in the restaurant.

Scrub the clams and cockles with a stiff brush to remove any sand or dirt, then wash in plenty of cold water and set aside.

If you don't have a steamer big enough for cooking the turbot, take very large saucepan into which a dinner plate will fit and put some sort of trivet in the bottom, such as a small upturned bowl. Add about 2 inches of water and bring to a boil. Season the turbot fillets lightly with salt, then put them on the plate, rest it on the trivet, cover and steam for about 10 minutes.

Meanwhile, put the shallots, Chardonnay, clams and cockles into a pan, cover and cook over high heat, shaking the pan every now and then, for 2 to 3 minutes, or until the clams have opened. Discard any that remain closed. Pour the shellfish through a colander set over a shallow pan, keeping back the last tablespoon of so of liquid, as this will contain some grit. Shell half the clams and cockles. Add the stock to the cooking liquor in the pan and boil rapidly until reduced to about 6 tablespoons. Whisk in the butter, a piece at the time. Return all the shellfish to the sauce with the parsley.

To serve, put the turbot fillets onto 4 warmed plates and pour the sauce right over them. Rearrange the shells so that they look attractive and then serve with, naturally, a bottle of good Chardonnay.

Sea Bass Baked in a Salt Crust with a Lemon Sauce and Potato, Tomato and Basil Confit

This method of baking in a salt crust ensures perfectly cooked, moist fish. It is served with a simple mayonnaise flavored with lemon, white wine and fennel seeds and also a great potato dish that I got from the south of France. You can cook any of the bream family, goatfish, John Dory and even searobin in the same way.

Serves 4

4	pounds table salt or coarse sea salt
2	egg whites
1	sea bass, weighing about 3 pounds, gutted but not scaled (see p. 11)

For the Lemon Sauce

$2^1/_2$	cups *Fish Stock* (see p. 212)
1	tablespoon fennel seeds
1	small lemon, sliced
$^1/_2$	cup white wine
1	egg
1	egg yolk
$1^1/_4$	cups olive oil
•	Salt and freshly ground black pepper

For the Potato, Tomato and Basil Confit

4	tablespoons olive oil
1	small onion, finely chopped
1	garlic clove, finely chopped
1	pound waxy new potatoes, peeled and cut into quarters
1	beefsteak tomato or 2 large plum tomatoes, peeled and chopped
2	tablespoons finely shredded fresh basil

Preheat the oven to 400°F.

For the sauce, put the stock, fennel seeds, sliced lemon and white wine into a pan and boil rapidly until the liquid has reduced to about 4 tablespoons. Strain into a small bowl and leave to cool. Put the whole egg, egg yolk, reduced stock mixture and some salt and pepper in a blender. With the motor running, gradually pour in the oil until you have a thick mayonnaise. Transfer to a bowl and season to taste.

For the potato confit, heat the olive oil in a pan, add the onion and garlic and cook for 5 minutes, or until softened and lightly browned. Add the potatoes, tomato and basil and cook gently for 25 minutes, or until the potatoes are tender. Season with salt and pepper and keep warm.

For the fish, mix the salt with the egg whites and spread a layer of this mixture in a roasting pan. Put the sea bass on top and then completely cover with the remaining salt mixture, making sure that there are no gaps (but don't worry if the tail is still exposed). Bake in the oven for 30 minutes.

To serve, crack the salt crust by giving it a sharp tap with the back of a knife, lift it away from the top of the fish and then carefully transfer the whole fish to a serving plate, leaving behind the rest of the salt crust. Pull away the skin from the top of the fish and gently lift the flesh away from the bones. Lift the bones off the remaining fish and discard, then remove the remaining fillets. Put the fish on 4 warmed plates, spoon a little of the sauce to the side and serve with the potato, tomato and basil confit.

Quick and Simple Fish

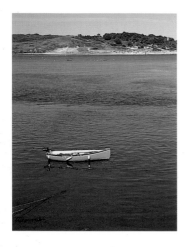

Most people don't have time to cook elaborate dishes these days, so fish, as it does not need lengthy cooking, is ideal.Often it tastes all the better for simple treatment, and lends itself well to quick cooking methods such as stir-frying and broiling, which appear many times in this chapter.

Funnily enough, in my first book I said people ought to spend a bit more time cooking and, although I have conceded to the pressure of modern life in this chapter, I still feel the same way. Cooking is therapeutic. It calms you down and puts you back in touch with the things that really matter.

I thought it might be apt to quote part of a poem that I read recently called "Ratatouille," on the subject of the need for people to get back into the kitchen.

See p. 98 for a good recipe using ratatouille.

Men who forget
Lovingly chopped-up cloves of *ail,* who scorn
The job of slicing two good peppers thinly,
Then two large onions and six aubergines—
Those long, impassioned and imperial purples—
Which, with six courgettes, you sift with salt
And cover with a plate for one round hour;
Or men who do not care to know about
The eight ripe *pommes d'amour* their wives have need of,
Preparing ratatouille, who give no thought to
The cup of olive oil that's heated in

Their heaviest pan, or onions, fried with garlic
For five observant minutes, before they add
Aubergines, courgettes, peppers, tomatoes;
Or men who give no thought to what their wives
Are thinking as they stand beside their stoves
When seasoning is sprinkled on, before
A bouquet garni is dropped in—these men
Invade Afghanistan, boycott the Games
Call off their fixtures and prepare for war.

Douglas Dunn (Saint Kilda's Parliament, 1981)

Facing page: Basque-Style Stuffed Crab (Shangurro) (see p. 170).

Grilled Hake Steaks with Champ and Black Bean Butter

Serves 4

4 hake steaks, weighing about 6 ounces each
2 tablespoons butter, melted
• Salt and freshly ground black pepper

For the Champ
2 pounds floury potatoes, peeled and cut into chunks
4 tablespoons butter
1¼ cups milk
6 green onions, thinly sliced

For the Black Bean Butter
1¼ cups *Fish Stock* (see p. 212)
1½ tablespoons black bean sauce
½ tablespoon lemon juice
4 tablespoons unsalted butter
1 tomato, peeled, seeded and diced
1 tablespoon chopped fresh leaf celery or celery leaves from head celery
• Salt

This is a very popular dish at our bistro. If you can't get the celery herb specified in the recipe, use the leaves from a head of celery instead. I grow a lot of leaf celery in my herb garden, which is very closely related to ordinary celery but with a much stronger flavor. This dish is a bit of an eclectic mix of East—the black bean sauce—and West—the champ, an Irish recipe for mashed potato with plenty of green onions. There is butter in the sauce as well, and tomato, and it's very easy to make. Really, the most time-consuming part of the whole recipe is the mashed potato.

For the champ, cook the potatoes in boiling salted water until tender, then drain. Return to the pan and mash until smooth. Beat in the butter, milk, green onions and salt and pepper to taste. Keep hot.

Meanwhile, for the sauce, put the stock, black bean sauce, lemon juice and butter into a wide pan and boil over high heat for about 12 minutes, or until reduced and thickened to the consistency of light cream. Set aside and keep warm.

Preheat the broiler. Brush both sides of the fish steaks with the melted butter and season well with salt and pepper. Place on the oiled rack of the broiler pan and broil for 3 minutes on each side. Bring the sauce back to a boil, take off the heat and stir in the diced tomato, juices from the broiler pan and celery herb. Season to taste with a little salt if necessary.

To serve, put the hake steaks on 4 warmed plates with the champ, then spoon the sauce around the fish.

Carpetshell Clams with Aïoli

Serves 4

¹⁄₂ quantity of *Olive Oil Mayonnaise* (see p. 217)

5 garlic cloves, very finely chopped

2 pounds carpetshell clams or other clams

4 tablespoons dry white wine

1 tablespoon finely chopped fresh parsley

I came across this dish in the Camargue region of the south of France, where it is made with tiny clams called tellines. *These are virtually impossible to find in Britain, but* palourdes, *or carpetshells as they are known here, are getting easier and easier to obtain. However, if you can't get any live clams for this dish, do try it with small mussels instead. You simply steam open the shellfish with a little white wine, then stir in some aïoli, a garlic mayonnaise. And that's it. Plenty of French bread. Pure delight.*

To make the aïoli, mix the mayonnaise with the garlic and set aside.

Scrub the clams with a stiff brush to remove any sand or dirt, then wash in plenty of cold water. Put the clams in a large pan with the white wine, then cover and cook over high heat, shaking the pan occasionally, for 2 to 3 minutes, or until they have opened. Discard any clams that remain closed. Take the pan off the heat and stir in the garlic mayonnaise and the parsley. Serve hot or cold, with lots of crusty French bread.

A Hash of Fresh Salmon with Parsley and Chives

Serves 4

2 pounds floury potatoes, peeled and cut into 1-inch chunks

· Salt and freshly ground black pepper

1 pound salmon fillet, cooked

4 tablespoons butter

1 large onion, chopped

· A pinch of cayenne pepper

2 tablespoons chopped fresh parsley

1 tablespoon chopped fresh chives or green onion tops

This dish is just fried potatoes, onion and salmon—an ideal way of using up leftover salmon or, indeed, any other leftover fish. It is based on corned beef hash and just as good, in my view. Put in plenty of parsley to lift the color.

Cook the potatoes in boiling salted water for 6 minutes or until tender, then drain well. Break the salmon into pieces roughly the same size as the potatoes and season well with salt and pepper. Melt 3 tablespoons of the butter in a frying pan large enough to take the salmon and potatoes in one layer. Add the onion and fry gently for 2 to 3 minutes, or until softened but not browned. Add the potatoes and fry for 7 to 10 minutes, turning now and then, until lightly browned. Now add the salmon and the rest of the butter and fry for 1 to 2 minutes, or until the salmon has heated through, turning the mixture over gently so as not to break up the salmon too much. Season with salt and cayenne pepper and serve sprinkled with the parsley and chives or green onion tops.

Sautéed Squid with Garlic, Parsley, Tomato and Zucchini

Serves 4

3 zucchini
4 tablespoons olive oil
1½ pounds prepared squid (see p. 16), cut into narrow rings
2 garlic cloves, finely chopped
1 red chili, seeded and finely chopped
3 plum tomatoes, peeled, seeded and chopped
2 tablespoons chopped fresh parsley
• Salt and freshly ground black pepper

Another dish from the south of France, which I ate in a restaurant in Marseilles called Le Lunch. A great name, I thought, and it harks back to the 1920s when the British first started going to the Mediterranean. This is a very simple dish. The squid is fried with garlic, parsley, chili, tomatoes and some small pieces of zucchini, which add a crisp textural note. When I had it in France, it was made with cuttlefish that tastes almost nicer than squid, but it is a little hard to get hold of here.

Cut the zucchini lengthwise into quarters and then across into slices ½ inch thick. Heat the olive oil in a large frying pan, add the squid and fry over high heat, stirring, for 2 minutes, or until lightly browned. Lower the heat, add the garlic, chili and zucchini and cook gently for 2 minutes. Add the tomatoes, parsley and seasoning, toss together and serve with crusty bread.

Chinese Conchs with Bean Sprouts and Button Mushrooms

Serves 4

½ pound shelled conchs
3 tablespoons sunflower oil
3 garlic cloves, very finely chopped
• 2-inch piece fresh ginger, peeled and very finely chopped
1 large red finger chili, seeded and sliced
¼ pound button mushrooms, thinly sliced
2 ounces mustard greens or bok choy, coarsely shredded
2 ounces bean sprouts
2 tablespoons oyster sauce
½ tablespoon soy sauce
2 tablespoons dry sherry

Traditionally, conchs are served with malt vinegar, freshly ground white pepper and lots of fresh brown bread and butter. But actually, they're incredibly good thinly sliced and stirred into a Chinese stir-fry.

Thinly slice the conch and set aside.

Heat the oil in a wok or large deep frying pan. Add the garlic, ginger and chili and stir-fry over high heat for 30 seconds. Add the sliced conch and stir-fry for 1 minute. Add the mushrooms and stir-fry for 30 seconds, then add the greens and the bean sprouts and stir-fry for another 30 seconds, or until the leaves have just wilted into the bottom of the pan. Add the oyster sauce, soy sauce and sherry and cook for another 1 minute. Serve immediately with some steamed rice or noodles.

Facing page: Sautéed Squid with Garlic, Parsley, Tomato and Zucchini.

Poached Ling Served with Sauce Messine

Serves 4

1 piece ling, 2¼ pounds,
 cut from just behind the
 cavity

For the Court Bouillon
2 quarts water
3 tablespoons salt
6 tablespoons cider
 vinegar
1 teaspoon superfine
 sugar
10 black peppercorns,
 lightly crushed
3 fresh bay leaves, finely
 shredded
1 onion, sliced
¼ teaspoon red pepper
 flakes

For the Sauce Messine
1 quantity of *Hollandaise
 Sauce* (see p. 215)
1 teaspoon French
 mustard
2 shallots, very finely
 chopped
4 tablespoons heavy
 cream
1 teaspoon finely
 chopped fresh tarragon
1 teaspoon finely
 chopped fresh chervil
1 teaspoon finely
 chopped fresh chives

I think that ling is a much underrated fish. It is always dismissed into the same sort of category as pollack, but I think it has a good flavor and, more importantly, an excellent firm texture, particularly the smaller fish. Nevertheless, being one of the cod family it is a bit bland, so I have used a well-flavored court bouillon to cook it in here and accompanied it with a butter sauce with lots of herbs and a little finely chopped shallot, which I think you will find partners the fish extremely well. If you wish to use a more upmarket fish, salmon would be a very good choice.

Put all the ingredients for the court bouillon in a large saucepan, bring to a boil and simmer for 10 minutes. Add the piece of ling, cover and simmer very gently for 10 minutes. Don't worry if it seems a little undercooked at this stage; it will be fine. Set aside for 5 minutes in the court bouillon.

Meanwhile, make the hollandaise. Put the mustard, shallots and cream in a small pan and bring to a boil. Stir into the hollandaise sauce with the chopped herbs, then set aside in a bowl of warm water.

Lift the ling out of the courtbouillon and leave to cool slightly. Then cut through the skin along both edges of the joint and carefully peel it off. You will now see a natural break in the flesh, about halfway down. Divide the fish into 2 fillets by cutting down along this line, then turn the knife and ease one fillet off, keeping the knife close to the bones. Remove the other fillet in the same way. Turn the ling over and repeat on the other side.

Serve the ling with the sauce, accompanied by boiled waxy potatoes.

Mussels with a Cream and White Wine Sabayon

Serves 4

¼   onion, sliced
1   small bay leaf
⅔   cup dry white wine
4   pounds mussels, cleaned (see p. 17)
3   medium egg yolks
⅔   cup heavy cream
½   cup unsalted butter
•   Fresh lemon juice
•   Salt and freshly ground black pepper
2   tablespoons chopped fresh parsley

In the days before cheap flights I used to drive everywhere on the continent with a group of friends in a series of ancient VW vans. Every time the ferry docked at Calais, we went to the nearby town of Gravelines and ordered immense bowls of this superb mussel dish. This first taste of France would always fill us with excited anticipation, because in those days you couldn't possibly imagine eating a dish like this on the other side of the Channel.

Put the onion, bay leaf and wine into a large saucepan. Bring to a boil and leave to simmer for 5 minutes. Add the mussels to the pan, cover and cook over high heat for 3 to 4 minutes, or until the mussels have opened. Discard any that remain closed. Lift the mussels into a large serving dish with a slotted spoon, cover and keep hot.

Whisk the egg yolks and cream together in a large bowl. Strain the mussel cooking liquor into the bowl, rest it over a pan of just simmering water and continue to whisk briskly until the mixture is light and frothy. Make sure not to let the sauce get too hot or the eggs will curdle. Whisk in the butter, a small piece at a time. Remove the bowl from the heat and season to taste with the lemon juice, salt and pepper. Pour the sauce over the mussels, sprinkle with the chopped parsley and serve.

Sautéed Goatfish with Parsley, Garlic and Spaghettini

Serves 4

4   small goatfish, weighing about 5 ounces each, filleted (see p. 13), skin on

•   Freshly ground black pepper

1   pound spaghettini

4   tablespoons olive oil

•   Salt

2   garlic cloves, finely chopped

1   red finger chili, seeded and finely chopped

4   plum tomatoes, peeled, seeded and chopped

3/4   cup fresh flat-leaf parsley, finely chopped

•   Extra-virgin olive oil, to serve

The quantities in this recipe make four hearty servings, but I always think that a good pile of pasta is what everybody really likes. I've never seen a recipe for this dish anywhere in Britain, but my good friend and the director of my television series, David Pritchard, rang me up from Italy, where he was filming with the mushroom expert Antonio Carluccio, to say how excited he was to have just eaten this fantastic fish pasta. As he explained, the great thing about it is that the well-flavored skin of the fish goes slightly grainy when it is fried and seems to coat the spaghettini with the sweet taste of seafood.

Cut the fish fillets across into strips 3/4 inch wide. Bring 3½ quarts of water to a boil in a large pan with 2 tablespoons of salt. Add the pasta, bring back to a boil and cook for 5 minutes, or until *al dente*.

Meanwhile, heat the olive oil in a large frying pan. Fry the strips of fish fillets, skin-side down, for 3 minutes. Turn them over, fry for 1 minute and then season with salt and pepper.

Drain the pasta well and tip it into a large, warmed serving bowl. Add the garlic and red chili to the frying pan with the fish and fry for 30 seconds. Add the tomatoes and fry for a further 30 seconds. Tip everything into the bowl with the pasta, scraping up all the little bits that may have stuck to the bottom of the pan, then add 3 tablespoons of the parsley and gently toss everything together so that the fish just begins to break up. Serve immediately, drizzled with extra-virgin olive oil and sprinkled with the remaining parsley.

Mussels with Black Beans, Garlic and Ginger

Serves 4

1 teaspoon salted black beans
1/4 teaspoon sugar
3 green onions
2 tablespoons peanut oil
4 garlic cloves, finely chopped
2 tablespoons finely chopped fresh ginger
3 pounds mussels, cleaned (see p. 17)
1 tablespoon dark soy sauce
2 tablespoons Chinese rice wine or dry sherry
3 tablespoons *Chicken Stock* (see p. 213)
1 tablespoon chopped fresh cilantro

In her excellent Classic Chinese Cookbook, *Yan-Kit So comments that black beans and clams go together for the Chinese as horseradish and roast beef do for us. This dish is based on her recipe for clams in black bean sauce.*

Rinse the black beans and mash them with the sugar. Thinly slice the green onions, keeping the white part separate from the green.

Heat the peanut oil in a wok or a large, deep frying pan until smoking hot. Add the garlic, ginger and black beans and stir-fry until the smell of hot ginger and garlic rises. Stir in the white of the green onions and stir-fry for a few seconds. Add the mussels, soy sauce, rice wine or sherry and stock. Cover and cook for about 3 minutes, or until the mussels open. Discard any that remain closed. Add the cilantro and green part of the green onions, toss together and serve.

Conch Fritters

Serves 4

8 to 10 cooked conchs
2 medium eggs, separated
2 plum tomatoes, peeled seeded and chopped
1/3 cup very finely chopped onion
2 cloves garlic, very finely chopped
2 tablespoons chopped fresh parsley
3/4 cup matzo meal or fresh bread crumbs
• Salt and freshly ground black pepper
• Sunflower oil for frying

I've got a lot of time for conchs. This recipe is adapted from one using giant clams, and you can in fact use large clams in place of conchs.

Remove the cooked conchs from their shells (you will need about 2 ounces) and roughly chop. Put the egg yolks into a bowl and lightly break up with a fork. Stir in the chopped conchs, tomatoes, onion, garlic, parsley, matzo meal or bread crumbs and some salt and pepper to taste.

In another bowl, whisk the egg whites into soft peaks and then gently fold them into the main fritter mixture.

Pour a good layer of sunflower oil into a large heavy-bottomed frying pan and leave over high heat until very hot. Lower the temperature a little, then drop 4 large spoonfuls of the batter into the pan and fry for about 1 1/2 minutes on each side, or until golden brown. Lift out onto paper towels and keep hot while you cook the rest. You should end up with about 12 fritters. Serve immediately.

Stir-fried Chicken and Monkfish with Shrimp, Cucumber and Water Chestnuts

Serves 4

¹⁄₂ cucumber

1 can (7 ounces) water chestnuts, drained

1 bunch of green onions

2 tablespoons sunflower oil

1 teaspoon Asian sesame oil

3 garlic cloves, very finely chopped

· 1-inch piece fresh ginger, peeled and very finely chopped

6 ounces boneless, skinless chicken thighs or breasts, cut into short, chunky strips

6 ounces monkfish fillet, cut into short, chunky strips

¹⁄₂ pound headless, shrimp, peeled and deveined (see p. 18)

1 lemon zest strip, very finely shredded

2 tablespoons dark soy sauce

1 tablespoon dry sherry

· Salt and freshly ground black pepper (or Sichuan pepper, if possible)

I have purposely kept the soy sauce and other Asian flavorings quite muted in this dish. Sometimes I think these stir-fries are too salty and spicy and you miss the taste of the fish, meat and vegetables. So this one is light and full of fresh flavors.

Cut the cucumber into 2-inch lengths, cut these into slices ¹⁄₂ inch thick and then cut into matchsticks. Cut each water chestnut into 3. Cut the green onions into 2-inch lengths and then lengthwise into fine shreds.

Put a wok or a large, deep frying pan over high heat and, when hot, add the sunflower and sesame oils. Add the garlic and ginger and stir-fry for 30 seconds. Add the chicken and stir-fry for 3 minutes. Add the monkfish and stir-fry for about 1 minute, or until just firm. Add the shrimp and lemon zest and stir-fry for another minute. Add the soy sauce and dry sherry and stir-fry for 1 minute, or until the liquid is slightly reduced. Add the cucumber and water chestnuts and toss for 30 seconds. Add the green onions, season with salt and pepper and toss together quickly. Serve straight away.

Fillets of Flounder with Pancetta and Beurre Noisette

Serves 4

16   small, very thin slices pancetta or 8 thin slices bacon, halved

2   tablespoons sunflower oil

3   tablespoons unsalted butter

3   tablespoons all-purpose flour

1/2   teaspoon salt

10   turns of the white pepper mill

8   flounder fillets, weighing about 3 to 4 ounces each, skinned

•   Juice of 1/4 lemon

2   teaspoons chopped fresh *fines herbes* (parsley, chervil, chives and tarragon)

This incredibly simple dish relies on presentation for its effect. The fillets of fish are arranged down the center of a nice oval serving dish, interleaved with thin slices of fried pancetta or, if you can't get it, extremely thinly sliced bacon. It looks wonderful when surrounded with beurre noisette, *which is simply butter heated until brown and nutty smelling, then sharpened with lemon juice. Next time you're in France and wandering through a market, do make sure you buy one of those long, narrow, elegant, white oval fish dishes for presenting food like this. Owing to the demise of silver service in restaurants, it is all too rare to see dishes served up in a formal manner from the kitchen, but if it's done well it is extremely effective. I suspect that, as everything in restaurant cooking appears to be of a cyclical nature, the era of presenting beautiful large platters of food at the table will return.*

Preheat the broiler. Broil the slices of pancetta or bacon for 1 to 1 1/2 minutes on each side, or until crisp. Set aside and keep warm.

Heat the oil and 1 tablespoon of the butter in a large frying pan. Season the flour with the salt and white pepper and spread it over a large plate. Cut each fish fillet across in half and then dip the pieces in the seasoned flour. Fry for 2 minutes on each side, or until lightly golden, then arrange them down the center of a warmed oval serving platter, interleaving them with the slices of grilled pancetta or bacon.

Discard the frying oil, add the remaining butter and allow it to melt over medium heat. When the butter starts to smell nutty and turn light brown, quickly add the lemon juice and herbs and then pour it right over the fish and bacon. Serve straight away.

English Sole and Porcini with Tagliatelle in a Cream Sauce

Serves 4

½ ounce dried porcini
3 cups water
2 English soles, weighing about 14 ounces each, filleted and skinned (see pp. 14–15)
6 tablespoons dry white wine
1 medium onion, sliced
⅔ cup heavy cream
2 tablespoons butter, cut into pieces
¾ pound egg tagliatelle
• Salt and freshly ground black pepper

You can use any pasta for this, but thin, flat ribbons such as tagliatelle seem to go particularly well. The dish is made with dried porcini; if you can get fresh, of course, that's even better. All you need to do is make a quick stock with the fish trimmings, boil the pasta, then make a simple cream sauce with the stock, porcini soaking liquid and some pieces of Dover sole.

Soak the dried porcini in ½ cup of the water for 10 minutes. Cut the fish fillets diagonally into strips 1 inch wide and set aside. Put the fish bones into a pan with the wine, onion and the remaining water, bring to a boil and simmer for 15 minutes. Strain this stock into a clean pan, bring to a boil and add the cream, butter pieces and the porcini with their soaking liquid. Boil rapidly until reduced by about three-quarters to a sauce that is thick enough to coat the back of a spoon (about the consistency of light cream).

Cook the tagliatelle in a large pan of boiling salted water for about 4 minutes, or until *al dente*, then drain.

Put the pieces of sole in the sauce and poach gently for about 2 minutes, then season with salt and pepper. Tip the pasta into a large warmed serving bowl. Add the sauce, toss together lightly and serve immediately.

Sautéed Scallops with Caramelized Endive

Serves 4

10 good-sized scallops
6 small Belgian endive
½ cup unsalted butter
½ cup *Fish Stock* (see p. 212) or *Chicken Stock* (see p. 213)
• Juice of ½ lemon
1 teaspoon chopped fresh parsley
• Salt and freshly ground white pepper

The sweetness of scallops goes well with the slight bitterness of endive, particularly when the endive is lightly browned and slightly crisp around the edges.

Detach the corals from the scallops, remove the white ligament from the side of each scallop meat and then slice the meat horizontally in half.

Remove the outer leaves of the chicory if they are damaged. Trim the base if it is brown but don't cut off too much or the leaves will detach themselves from the base. Cut them lengthwise through the base into 3 thin slices.

Melt 2 tablespoons of the butter in a large frying pan. As soon as it starts to turn brown and smell slightly nutty, add the scallop slices and corals and cook briefly for about 30 seconds on each side. Remove from the pan and keep warm. Add a little more butter to the pan if necessary and fry the endive slices in batches for about 1 minute on each side, or until lightly browned. Transfer to another plate and keep warm while you cook the rest.

Add the stock and remaining butter to the pan, bring to a boil and boil until the sauce is thick enough to coat the back of a spoon. Add the lemon juice, season with a little salt and pepper and stir in the chopped parsley.

To serve, put the endive on 4 warmed plates, top with the scallops and then spoon over the sauce.

Grilled Whole English Sole with Sea Salt and Lime

Serves 4

4   English soles, each weighing about 14 to 16 ounces, skin on
·   Vegetable oil, for brushing
·   Sea salt

For the Sauce
1¼ cups *Fish Stock* (see p. 212)
1½ teaspoons Thai fish sauce (*nam pla*)
3   limes
1   tablespoon unsalted butter
1¼ small red onion, finely diced
1   bunch fresh flat-leaf parsley, roughly chopped, a few sprigs reserved for a garnish

The sauce with this sole goes very well with all fresh fish. Its pure simplicity makes it a winner at my restaurant.

Scale the soles and cut off the fins. Dry the fish with paper towels.

To make the sauce put the stock and fish sauce in a small pan. Grate the zest of 1 lime and add to the pan with its juice.

Preheat the broiler until it's very hot. Then brush the fish with vegetable oil and sprinkle the dark side with sea salt. Place on the oiled rack of the broiler pan and cook for about 10 minutes. Remove the fish from the broiler and sprinkle with more sea salt.

Place each fish on a warmed plate, then finish the sauce. Bring the ingredients in the pan to a boil and add the butter. Whisk until it has all melted, then add the chopped red onion and the chopped parsley. Simmer for 30 seconds, then pour the sauce around the fish and garnish with the remaining limes, cut into wedges, and sprigs of parsley.

Basque-style Stuffed Crab (Shangurro)

Serves 4

2 large cooked Dungeness crabs, or approximately 1¼ pounds crabmeat

3 tablespoons olive oil

2 onions, finely chopped

8 small garlic cloves, finely chopped

½ pound plum tomatoes, peeled, seeded and chopped

4 tablespoons dry white wine

1 teaspoon superfine sugar

¼ teaspoon red pepper flakes

• Salt and freshly ground black pepper

3 tablespoons chopped fresh parsley

1 cup fresh white bread crumbs

1 tablespoon butter, melted

1 garlic clove, very finely chopped

I like using shells as natural containers for seafood. Mussels, scallops, clams and crabs all look much more appetizing to me presented in this way. The great charm of shangurro, *which comes from the Basque coast of northern Spain, is that in San Sebastian, Santander and Bilbao it is normally served using the back shell of a snow crab as a gratin dish for the combination of crabmeat, tomato, garlic, chili, olive oil, parsley and bread crumbs. I must admit, however, that if you have time to pick out four snow crabs, you would hardly call this a quick and simple dish. It is so good, however, it is worth using Dungeness crabmeat and gratin dishes rather than shells.*

Preheat the oven to 400°F.

If using cooked crabs, remove the meat from the shell (see pp. 20–21). Wash out the back shells and then break away the edge along the visible natural line to give a flat open shell. Set aside.

Heat the oil in a heavy-bottomed frying pan, then add the onions and all except 1 chopped garlic clove. Fry over a gentle heat for 2 minutes, or until softened. Increase the heat, add the tomatoes, wine, sugar, red pepper flakes and some salt and pepper and simmer for about 4 minutes, or until the mixture has reduced to a thick sauce. Stir in 2 tablespoons of the parsley and the flaked crabmeat and spoon the mixture into the crab shells, if using, or individual gratin dishes. If using crab shells, rest them in a shallow ovenproof dish. Mix the bread crumbs with the melted butter and the rest of the parsley and garlic, sprinkle this mixture over the crab and bake in the oven for 10 minutes, or until the topping is crisp and golden.

Panfried Whiting with Lime Butter and Salsify

Serves 4

4 whiting or pin hake, weighing 1 pound each

2 tablespoons unsalted butter

3 tablespoons all-purpose flour seasoned with salt and freshly ground black pepper

1 tablespoon sunflower oil

For the Lime Butter

4 tablespoons unsalted butter, softened

• Finely grated zest of 1 lime

2 teaspoons chopped fresh thyme

½ teaspoon finely grated fresh ginger

• Salt and freshly ground white pepper

For the Salsify

1 pound salsify, peeled and cut in half, then cut in half lengthwise

2 tablespoons unsalted butter

• Salt and freshly ground black pepper

2 teaspoons fresh lime juice

1 tablespoon chopped fresh parsley

I wrote this recipe in Australia using their version of whiting called sand whiting, which is actually rather better tasting than ours. But small, perfectly fresh whiting are well worth eating. However, if you should ever get the chance to buy some small hake instead, called pin hake, then you're in for a treat. You can get hold of the vegetable salsify (oyster plant) from all good greengrocers. I hope you like the lime butter.

For the lime butter, beat all the ingredients together, spoon onto a large sheet of plastic wrap and shape into a roll 1 inch wide. Chill in the freezer or refrigerator until firm. For the salad dressing, mix the olive oil and lime juice with some salt and pepper and set to one side.

Scale and trim the fish (see p. 11). Melt the butter in a small pan, spoon off the scum from the surface and then pour the clarified butter into a large, heavy-bottomed frying pan, leaving behind the milky-white liquid.

Coat the fish in the seasoned flour. Add the oil to the butter in the frying pan and, when hot, add two of the fish and fry for 4 to 5 minutes on each side, or until crisp and golden. Remove and keep warm while you cook the other two fish.

Cut the lime butter into 12 thin slices. Lift the fish onto 4 warmed plates and place 3 slices of butter down the center of each fish while you cook the other two fish. Meanwhile, fry the salsify gently in the butter until soft, then turn up the heat to brown a little, season with salt and pepper, add the lime juice and parsley and keep warm. Serve the salsify beside the fish.

Seared Bay Scallops with Garlic, Ginger and Greens

Serves 4

6 green onions

· Salt

2 ounces watercress or arugula, larger stems removed

2 tablespoons sunflower oil

16 prepared scallops or 24 bay scallops (see p. 18)

2 garlic cloves, very finely chopped

· 1-inch piece fresh ginger, peeled and very finely chopped

2 tablespoons Thai fish sauce (*nam pla*)

2 tablespoons oyster sauce

½ cup water

I cooked this dish of bay scallops for the Padstow Carnival Queen last year. The "Queen" turned out to be George Masters, who doesn't exactly fit the bill for a carnival queen, as he usually works behind the bar in the London Inn, but there you go, that's Padstow. George was highly delighted with my spicy dish—to which I added some mustard greens and cress from my garden, which is what you get if you allow those little flats of salad cress to grow on. We sat on the roof of the restaurant drinking champagne, eating the scallops with George dressed up in his taffeta finery, including a bouffant wig and high-heeled shoes. The whole thing seemed a bit like something out of a Fellini film.

Cut the green onions in half and then cut each half lengthwise into very fine shreds. Set aside.

Bring a large pan of salted water to a boil. Add the watercress or arugula and cook for just 2 minutes. Drain, divide equally among 16 cleaned scallop shells or 4 soup plates and keep hot.

Heat a large, heavy-bottomed frying pan until very hot. Add 1 tablespoon of the oil and the scallops in a single layer and fry over high heat for about 2 minutes, turning once, or until they are richly caramelized on both sides but only just cooked in the center. This is very important to the flavor and appearance of the finished dish.

Lift out the scallops and divide equally among the scallop shells or bowls. Add the garlic, ginger and the remaining oil to the pan and stir-fry for about 30 seconds. Add the Thai fish sauce, oyster sauce and water, bring to a boil and then quickly spoon this sauce over the scallops. Sprinkle with the shredded green onions and serve immediately.

Warm Crab Pancakes with Lemongrass and Cilantro

Serves 4

For the Pancakes
1/3 cup all-purpose flour
1/4 teaspoon salt
1/2 beaten egg
2/3 cup milk
1 1/2 teaspoons unsalted butter, melted, plus extra for frying

For the Filling
• 2-inch piece lemongrass, finely chopped
1/4 pound crabmeat
1/2 green chili, seeded and very finely chopped
• Finely grated zest of 1/2 lime
1 teaspoon fresh lime juice
1 teaspoon Thai fish sauce (*nam pla*)
2 teaspoons chopped fresh cilantro, plus a few sprigs to garnish
1/3 cup very finely shredded iceberg lettuce

For the Sauce
2/3 cup water
1 tablespoon Asian sesame oil
1 teaspoon Thai fish sauce (*nam pla*)
• Juice of 1/2 lime
1 tablespoon unsalted butter
• A pinch of salt
1 teaspoon chopped fresh cilantro

You will need a 4-inch frying pan for these delicate little pancakes, which are filled with crabmeat and lots of Thai flavorings, all kept very mild. They are warmed through in the oven and served with a light sauce of sesame oil, Thai fish sauce, lime juice and cilantro. Serve, I would suggest, with an ice-cold bottle of Alsace Pinot Blanc or similar wine.

For the pancakes, sift the flour and salt into a bowl, make a slight dip in the center and add the egg. Gradually whisk in the milk and then the melted butter to make a smooth batter.

Preheat the oven to 400°F.

Heat a 4-inch frying pan. Brush with a little melted butter, pour in a little of the batter and swirl it around so that it coats the base of the pan. Cook for about 1 minute, flipping the pancake over as soon as it has browned underneath. Repeat this process to make 8 pancakes.

Mix together all the ingredients for the filling and divide among the pancakes. Roll them up and lay side by side, seam-side down, in a lightly buttered oven-proof dish. Cover loosely with foil and warm through in the oven for 8 to 10 minutes.

Just before the pancakes are ready, put all the ingredients for the sauce into a small pan and whisk over high heat until it comes to a boil. To serve, put the pancakes on 4 plates and spoon a little of the sauce over and around them. Garnish with sprigs of cilantro.

Handheld and Party Food

This chapter contains the sort of dishes you can eat in your hand and also the little items you might pick up and nibble at a cocktail party. Several of the recipes were inspired by the type of food that is sold by street vendors. I have a great affection for street food. After all, what is a Cornish pasty if not that sort of cheap, convenient and nourishing hand-held food? There is a recipe for *Crab Pasties with Leek and Saffron* here (see p. 177), which perhaps takes handheld food into the realms of *haute cuisine*, but I still think it should be eaten in the hand. I think there's something a bit second rate about eating a pasty with a knife and fork.

My other source of inspiration was bars. The fishermen of Spain are not particularly well liked in Cornwall because there is a theory that they are taking all our fish, particularly undersized ones, and should never have been allowed to fish the rich waters between Cornwall and Ireland, known as the Irish Box. I've always had a slight ambivalence about this because, while I support our local fishermen, I have a sneaking regard for the way the Spanish cook fish and their immense enthusiasm for it. So I went on a long weekend break to Madrid, partly because I wanted to see the Goya paintings but also to check out Spanish seafood. I've long been told that if you want to eat the best seafood in Spain you should go not to the coast, where it is normally very good, but to Madrid where it is excellent. So for about five days and nights we visited lots of restaurants and did the rounds of the tapas bars. It was an exhilarating experience and the fish cookery was just as I would have expected: simple, relying on the freshest ingredients, and showing a deep respect for the raw materials—a respect that I sometimes think we lack in this country. In one restaurant the couple at the next table ordered a snow crab and that's what they got: just one large snow crab between two. I remarked to my wife, Jill, that I wouldn't be surprised if it had come from Cornwall. Wouldn't it be nice if you could sell something like that in Britain—just plain, freshly boiled crab, and have people eating it with such enthusiasm and leaving absolutely nothing afterward.

All the tapas in this chapter—the *empanadas* and the two mussel dishes—were the result of that trip to Madrid.

Empanadas with Conger Eel, Sun-dried Tomato and Chorizo Sausage

Makes 20 slices

½ pound new potatoes, sliced

4 tablespoons olive oil

1 leek, thinly sliced

2 garlic cloves, finely chopped

2 ounces *chorizo* sausage, finely chopped

1 ounce sun-dried tomatoes in oil, drained and thinly sliced (about 2 tablespoons)

1 tablespoon white wine

• Leaves from 2 fresh thyme sprigs

• A small pinch of saffron threads

• A pinch of cayenne pepper

• Salt and freshly ground black pepper

1 pound conger eel fillet, skinned
Beaten egg, to glaze

For the Olive Oil Pastry

1²⁄₃ cups all-purpose flour

1 teaspoon salt

1 egg, beaten

7 tablespoons olive oil

3 to 4 tablespoons tepid water

These large, oblong pies made with olive oil pastry are sliced and served as tapas in Spain. They make ideal drinks party food. Serve with glasses of ice-cold beer or with manzanilla sherry. In tapas bars beer is served in small glasses so that you've drunk it before it has a chance to get at all warm. They do the same in Queensland, too.

I have suggested conger eel for the filling but you can use any thick fillets of white fish such as cod, pollack or ling.

For the pastry, sift the flour and salt into a bowl. Make a well in the center and add the egg, olive oil and 3 tablespoons of warm water. Gradually work the flour into the liquid ingredients, adding more water if necessary. Gather the dough into a ball, turn out onto a lightly floured surface and knead briefly until smooth. Wrap in plastic wrap and leave to rest at room temperature for 1 hour.

Meanwhile, cook the potato slices in boiling salted water for about 4 to 5 minutes, or until only just tender. Heat the olive oil in a pan, add the leek and garlic and fry for 2 minutes, or until softened. Add the chorizo sausage and fry for 2 minutes, then stir in the cooked potatoes, sun-dried tomatoes, white wine, thyme, saffron, cayenne and a little salt and pepper. Set aside to cool.

Preheat the oven to 400°F.

Cut the pastry in half and roll out each piece into a 12-by-9-inch rectangle. Place each one on a lightly oiled baking sheet and spoon the filling lengthwise along one-half of each piece of pastry. Cut the piece of conger eel lengthwise into 2 thick strips. Slice each one across thinly and put on top of the filling, overlapping the slices slightly. Season with salt and black pepper.

Brush the edges of the pastry with a little water. Fold the pastry over the filling so that the edges meet, then pinch and twist over the edge to make a good seal. Brush with beaten egg and bake in the oven for 20 to 25 minutes, or until golden. Remove from the oven and set aside to cool slightly. Then cut across on the diagonal into slices 1 inch thick and serve.

Crab Pasties with Leek and Saffron

Makes 6

2 pounds chilled puff pastry

$\frac{1}{4}$ teaspoon saffron strands

2 teaspoons hot water

• Scant 1 pound crabmeat

$\frac{1}{2}$ pound leeks, thinly sliced

1 cup fresh white bread crumbs

1 teaspoon salt

10 turns of the white pepper mill

2 tablespoons butter, melted

We make these pasties at our bakery and they are enormously popular. I wrote the recipe with, essentially, a Cornish theme in mind: local vegetables, local crabs and saffron, which has long been connected with the county in the form of saffron cake. At one time saffron was grown in Cornwall just as in Essex.

Preheat the oven to 400°F.

Divide the pastry into 6 pieces. Roll out each piece on a lightly floured surface and cut into a $7\frac{1}{2}$-inch round.

For the filling, soak the saffron in the hot water for 5 minutes. Put the crabmeat, leeks, bread crumbs, salt and pepper into a bowl and stir together until well mixed. Crush the saffron a little into the water to release the color and flavor, then stir it into the melted butter. Now stir this into the rest of the filling ingredients.

Divide the filling mixture among the pastry rounds. Brush the edge of one-half with a little water, bring both sides together over the top of the filling and pinch together well to seal. Crimp the edge of each pasty decoratively between your fingers, transfer to a lightly oiled baking sheet and bake for 35 minutes, or until golden brown. Serve hot or cold.

Fish Tacos from Baja California

Serves 4

2   sea bream or sea bass,
    weighing about
    2³/₄ pounds each,
    filleted (see p. 13)
·   Salt and freshly ground
    black pepper
8   flour tortillas
¹/₂ pound iceberg lettuce,
    finely shredded
1¹/₄ cups sour cream
·   Sunflower oil for
    deep-frying

For the Batter
1²/₃ cups all-purpose flour
2   eggs
⁷/₈ cups water

For the Salsa
1   medium red onion,
    finely chopped
5   tomatoes, peeled,
    seeded and finely
    chopped
3   or 4 red chilies, seeded
    and finely chopped
1   teaspoon sugar
·   Juice of 1 lime
4   tablespoons chopped
    fresh cilantro
·   Salt

Perhaps the most thoroughly irresistible dish in this chapter. I've never been to Baja California in Mexico, but I got the idea for this recipe from the television presenter and food journalist, Hugh Fearnley-Whittingstall, who lent me a book on Baja because I'm very keen on surfing and the waves there are fantastic. He told me about this great dish consisting of a tortilla filled with deep-fried fish, cilantro, chili, tomato, a little sour cream and some salad. I knocked it all up according to how it sounded to me and it's brilliant. One day I'll make the trip to Ensenada with my big old Malibu and ride the odd small wave that may just happen down there.

First make the salsa by mixing together all the ingredients with a pinch of salt. Set aside.

Cut the fish fillets across into strips ¹/₂ inch wide and season with plenty of salt and pepper. For the batter, put the flour, eggs, water and a pinch of salt into a blender and blend until smooth.

Pour the sunflower oil into a pan until it is about one-third full and heat to 375°F, or until a small piece of white bread dropped into the oil browns and rises to the surface in 1 minute. Warm the tortillas in a low oven or a microwave.

Dip the strips of fish into the batter and then drop them into the hot oil and fry for 4 minutes, or until crisp and golden. Lift out with a slotted spoon and drain briefly on paper towels.

To serve, put some lettuce down the center of each tortilla, top with the fried fish, then spoon over some salsa and sour cream. Fold in the sides, roll up as tightly as you can and serve straight away, with some cold Mexican beer.

Mussels with Tomato and Serrano Ham

Serves 4 to 6

2 pounds mussels, cleaned (see p. 17)

4 tablespoons dry white wine

4 tablespoons extra-virgin olive oil

²⁄₃ cup very finely chopped onions

2 garlic cloves, very finely chopped

1 red finger chili, seeded and very finely chopped

1 cup sieved canned chopped tomatoes

12 sun-dried tomatoes in oil, drained and very finely chopped

• Leaves from 4 fresh thyme sprigs, finely chopped, plus a few whole leaves to garnish

4 thin slices Serrano ham

The mussels are steamed open with a little white wine and lots of fresh chili, then served on the half shell with a rich tomato sauce and thin strips of Serrano ham. If you can't get Serrano ham, just use prosciutto instead. Serve with a glass of chilled manzanilla or fino sherry.

Put the mussels into a large pan with the wine. Cover and cook over high heat for about 3 to 4 minutes, shaking the pan every now and then, until the mussels have opened. Discard any that remain closed. Remove the top half of each shell, leaving the mussel in the other half. Reserve the cooking liquor.

Heat the olive oil in a small pan. Add the onion and garlic and fry for a few minutes, or until softened but not browned. Add the chilies, canned tomatoes, sun-dried tomatoes, thyme and the mussel cooking liquor. Bring to a boil and simmer for 7 to 10 minutes, or until reduced to a thick sauce.

Cut the Serrano ham into very small, fine strips and stir into the sauce. Spoon about 1 teaspoon of the sauce over each mussel, sprinkle with a few thyme leaves and serve.

Monkfish Satays with a Spicy Peanut Sauce

Serves 4

1 pound prepared monk-fish fillet (see p. 15), cut into $^3/_4$-inch pieces

16 bamboo skewers, each 6 inches long

For the Marinade

3 large garlic cloves, very finely chopped

• 1-inch piece fresh ginger, peeled and finely chopped

$^1/_2$ teaspoon ground turmeric

3 tablespoons Thai fish sauce (*nam pla*)

1 tablespoon fresh lime juice

1 teaspoon palm sugar or soft dark brown sugar

$^1/_2$ teaspoon cayenne pepper

2 tablespoons vegetable oil

For the Spicy Peanut Sauce

2 tablespoons sunflower oil

2 shallots, finely chopped

2 garlic cloves, chopped

1 red finger chili, seeded and chopped

$^1/_2$ teaspoon cayenne pepper

3 tablespoons roasted peanuts

2 tablespoons crunchy peanut butter

4 teaspoons fresh lime juice

1 tablespoon palm sugar or soft dark brown sugar

$^1/_2$ teaspoon salt

$^3/_4$ cup coconut milk

If you travel to Singapore you must go to the park in Orchard Road, where you can eat Chinese, Indian, Indonesian or Malay food from stalls all in the same place and all really cheap. It's a bit like an Asian food fair and almost worth a trip to Singapore just to visit it. All the food is very good but the barbecued satays are exceptional. The operators crouch next to their charcoal barbecues, endlessly fanning the flames and producing a tireless succession of chicken or fish satays with the hot but sweet peanut sauce that I know will never taste quite so good anywhere else. This recipe is based on my memory of those uniquely satisfying satays.

Put the monkfish in a bowl with all the marinade ingredients and mix together well. Set aside for 20 minutes. Cover the bamboo skewers with cold water and leave to soak. This stops them burning under the broiler.

For the spicy peanut sauce, heat the oil in a pan, add the shallots or onion, garlic, chili and cayenne pepper and fry for 7 minutes, or until soft and lightly golden. Coarsely grind the roasted peanuts in a spice grinder, then stir them into the fried onion mixture with all the remaining sauce ingredients. Simmer gently for 4 to 5 minutes, or until thickened. Keep warm while you cook the fish.

Preheat the broiler.

Thread the fish onto the bamboo skewers and put them on the lightly oiled rack of the broiler pan. Cook for about 8 minutes, turning them over halfway through. Serve with the spicy peanut sauce.

Mussels with Tomato, Celery and Saffron Butter

Serves 4 to 6

2 pounds mussels, cleaned (see p. 17)

4 tablespoons dry white wine

2½ cups *Fish Stock* (see p. 212)

¼ teaspoon saffron threads

3 ounces inner stalks of celery, finely diced (about ⅔ cup)

3 tomatoes, peeled, seeded and finely diced

¾ cup chilled unsalted butter, cut into small pieces

• Juice of ¼ lemon

• Salt and freshly ground black pepper

Like the recipe on p. 180, this uses mussel shells as a natural container for serving at a drinks party, without need of knives, forks or plates. The mussels are served on the half shell with a rich saffron butter sauce, some finely chopped celery that has been lightly cooked so it is still a little crunchy, and some finely diced good, sweet tomatoes.

Put the mussels into a large pan with 1 tablespoon of the wine. Cover and cook over high heat for about 3 to 4 minutes, shaking the pan every now and then, until the mussels have opened. Discard any that remain closed. Remove from the heat, strain off the juice and stir 2 tablespoons of it into the stock. Discard the remainder.

Bring the stock, the remaining wine and the saffron to a boil and boil rapidly until reduced to about 4 tablespoons.

Meanwhile, bring a small pan of salted water to a boil, add the celery and cook for 1 minute. Drain and refresh under cold running water, then set aside.

Preheat the oven to 275°F.

Remove the top half of each mussel shell, leaving the mussel in the other half. Lay them side by side in a shallow ovenproof serving dish. Put the diced celery and tomato on top of the mussels and season with a little salt and black pepper. You can do this up to an hour beforehand if you wish, but don't refrigerate the cooked mussels as they never taste the same again. Cover with plastic wrap, however, to stop them drying out.

When you are ready to serve, remove the plastic wrap and cover the mussels with aluminum foil. Warm through in the oven for just a few minutes. Meanwhile, bring the reduced stock back to a boil and then whisk in the butter a few pieces at a time, adding more as the butter amalgamates. I prefer to make these mounted butter sauces over a brisk heat, adding the butter and whisking all the time. The action of boiling stock with the butter causes a natural liaison. If the sauce separates, simply add a little more water, bring it back to a boil and it will cohere again. Stir in the lemon juice and season with salt and pepper to taste. Remove the mussels from the oven, uncover, and spoon a little of the sauce over each one. Serve immediately.

Bruschetta of Anchovies with Tomato and Red Onions

Serves 4

1 ciabatta loaf

3 garlic cloves, peeled

6 tablespoons olive oil

2 ounces anchovy fillet or salt sardines fillets, very finely chopped

²/₃ cup finely chopped red onion

6 plum tomatoes, peeled, seeded and finely chopped

3 tablespoons coarsely chopped fresh flat-leaf parsley

20 turns of the black pepper mill

• Fresh flat-leaf parsley sprigs, to garnish (optional)

I got this recipe from a friend of mine in Newlyn, Nick Howell, who runs the only sardine salting and pressing sheds left in Cornwall. If it weren't for the enthusiasm of the Italians for this old method of preserving the most famous of Cornish fish, there would be none left, but they still import them from Cornwall. Nick Howell is trying to reintroduce chilled salt sardine fillet in Britain, and if he succeeds maybe you will be able to prepare this piquant and savory bruschetta with sardine, as he does, rather than anchovy. It's not everyone's cup of tea, being raw, earthy and salty, but I love it, particularly when made with sardines.

Preheat the broiler. Slice the ciabatta in half horizontally and toast the cut side only for about 2 minutes, or until lightly golden. Rub with one of the peeled cloves of garlic. Drizzle each half with 1 tablespoon of the olive oil and slice diagonally into quarters.

Finely chop the remaining garlic. Gently mix with the anchovies or sardines, red onion, tomatoes, parsley, remaining oil, and black pepper. Spoon a little of the mixture onto each piece of bread, garnish with sprigs of parsley, if liked, and serve straight away, before the bread becomes soft again.

Deep-fried Shredded Fish Wrapped in Lettuce with Chili, Shrimp and Cilantro

Serves 4

2   sea bream, red snapper, searobin, mullet or mackerel, weighing about $^3/_4$ pound each, filleted (see p. 13)

6   cooked large shrimp, thinly sliced

2   red finger chilies, seeded and very finely chopped

3   tablespoons chopped fresh cilantro
    Juice of 2 limes

3   tablespoons Thai fish sauce (*nam pla*)

16   to 20 medium-sized romaine lettuce leaves, stems trimmed off
    Sunflower oil for deep-frying

A great combination of textures and flavors, this works marginally better with oily fish, which has a more pronounced flavor, but it is also a good way of using cold leftover fish and slightly less than perfectly fresh fish. For cocktail pieces, simply make them all up at once, tie in place with long chives and serve immediately before the lettuce leaves go too limp.

Bring $2^1/_2$ cups water and 1 tablespoon of salt to a boil in a frying pan. Reduce to a simmer, add the fish fillets and poach for 3 minutes, turning them over halfway through. Lift out with a slotted spoon onto plenty of paper towels and leave to go cold. Remove any skin and bones and finely shred the flesh using 2 forks. Blot the excess moisture from the fish with more paper towels—this is important because if it is too wet it will cause the oil to foam up and possibly overflow.

Put the sliced shrimp, red chilies, chopped cilantro, lime juice, fish sauce and lettuce leaves into separate bowls and place in the center of the table.

Pour the oil into a large pan so that it is about one-third full and heat to 375°F, or until a small cube of white bread dropped into the oil browns and rises to the surface in 1 minute. Place the flaked fish in the hot oil and deep-fry for 2 minutes. Lift out with a slotted spoon and drain briefly on paper towels, then transfer to a bowl and take to the table. Instruct your guests to take a lettuce leaf and place a small amount of fish, shrimp, chili and cilantro toward the fatter end. Sprinkle with a little lime juice and fish sauce, roll up and eat straight away.

Warm Oysters with Black Beans, Ginger and Cilantro

Serves 4

20   Pacific oysters

·   1-inch piece fresh ginger, peeled and very finely chopped

·   3-inch piece cucumber

1   tablespoon chopped fresh cilantro

1   teaspoon chopped fresh chives

1   tablespoon salted black beans or black bean sauce

1   garlic clove, very finely chopped

1   tablespoon dark soy sauce

2   tablespoons dry sherry

4   tablespoons cold-pressed sesame oil

The oysters are opened, leaving about half the liquor that surrounds the oyster meats in the shell, and then grilled until just set. The liquor gives a delightful salty tang to the sauce, but do discard half of it otherwise the sauce will be too salty. If you can get the fermented and salted black beans available in Chinese food shops you will be glad I suggested trying, because they keep for ages and are a great addition to so many stir-fry dishes. However, these oysters are also very well worth preparing with black bean sauce; try and get the type with whole black beans in it rather than the smooth one.

Preheat the broiler. Open the oysters (see p. 17), pour away half the liquor surrounding the meats and nestle the oysters in the broiler pan so that they can't roll over during cooking. Sprinkle each one with the chopped ginger and set aside.

Cut the cucumber into 1-inch pieces, then thinly slice each piece and cut lengthwise into matchstick-width shreds. Mix with the cilantro and chives and set aside.

If using salted black beans, rinse them and then chop them up a little. Put the salted black beans or black bean sauce in a small pan with the garlic, soy sauce, sherry and sesame oil. Leave over very low heat to warm through.

Broil the oysters for 3 minutes. Arrange on 4 warmed plates and sprinkle a little of the cucumber mixture over each one. Spoon over a little of the sauce and serve immediately.

Spring Rolls with Squid, Crab, Bean Sprouts and Shiitake Mushrooms

Makes 12

¼ pound prepared squid (see p. 16)

6 ounces boneless pork loin

6 green onions

2 tablespoons Asian sesame oil

2 garlic cloves, finely chopped

• ½-inch piece fresh ginger, peeled and finely chopped

¼ pound bean sprouts

2 ounces shiitake mushrooms, thinly sliced

6 ounces crabmeat

1 tablespoon dark soy sauce

• A pinch of superfine sugar

1 teaspoon salt
Freshly ground Sichuan pepper

2 tablespoons all-purpose flour

12 large spring roll wrappers

• Sunflower oil for deep-frying

The filling for these spring rolls is stir-fried briefly, then rolled up in spring roll wrappers and deep-fried. The wrappers are easy to get hold of in Asian food shops, but you can use filo pastry instead. This is not an authentic recipe, but spring rolls are such a good idea and generally I find the fillings a bit dull—often little more than cabbage, bean sprouts and soy sauce. I think seafood and Asian mushrooms work rather well, but you could also try shredded green cabbage, pork, shredded cooked skate with soy sauce, a pinch or two of star anise and a little finely diced red chili. Alternatively use the crab, leek and saffron filling for the pasties on p. 177.

Slit the squid pouch open along one side and cut it into thin strips about 4 inches long. Cut the pork into similar-sized pieces. Cut the spring onions into 3-inch lengths and then cut lengthwise into fine shreds.

Heat the sesame oil in a wok or a large deep frying pan. Add the garlic and ginger and stir-fry for a few seconds. Add the squid and pork and stir-fry over high heat for 3 minutes. Add the bean sprouts and mushrooms and stir-fry for 30 seconds only. Tip into a bowl and gently stir in the green onions, crabmeat, soy sauce, sugar, salt and Sichuan pepper.

Mix the flour with 2 tablespoons of cold water to make a paste. Fill the spring roll wrappers (see opposite).

Pour the oil into a large pan so that it is about one-third full and heat to 375°F, or until a small piece of white bread dropped into the oil browns and rises to the surface in 1 minute. Deep-fry the spring rolls, 4 at a time, for 5 to 6 minutes, or until crisp and golden. They tend to float in the oil, so a good trick is to rest a frying basket or sieve on top of them to keep them submerged during cooking.

Mix together all the ingredients for the dipping sauce and pour into small saucers or bowls. Serve with the hot spring rolls.

Making Spring Rolls

For the Dipping Sauce

2 tablespoons dark soy sauce
1 tablespoon sweet chili sauce
1 tablespoon cold water
• 1-inch piece fresh ginger, peeled and finely grated
1 garlic clove, very finely chopped
1 small red finger chili, seeded and very finely chopped
1 tablespoon chopped fresh cilantro

1. Put a spring roll wrapper on a work surface with one corner facing you. (Keep the other wrappers covered with a slightly damp cloth to prevent them drying out.) Put 3 heaped teaspoons of the filling in a line about 2 inches in from the corner.

2. Fold the corner of the spring roll wrapper over the line of filling and give it a little roll, making sure that the filling stays in place.

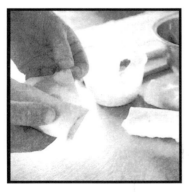

3. Fold in first one side of the wrapper and then the other, so that they overlap in the center and the filling is completely enclosed.

4. Roll up the spring roll tightly, holding in the sides as you do so. Seal the end with a little of the flour-and-water paste.

Make the remaining spring rolls in the same way, keeping them covered with a damp cloth.

Food to Finish With

At long last I've been able to include pudding recipes in one of my books. Although I write about fish, when you think about it I've got recipes for first courses and main courses, so why not some puddings, too? All the recipes in this chapter come from the restaurant and have been particularly successful. We've always tried to keep our puddings simple, like everything else. So, not for us those rather elaborate and extravagant concoctions you get in starred restaurants in Britain and France, with about seven different little piles of this and that all artfully arranged on one plate. I prefer simple tarts, classic English puddings, and fruit-and-cream combinations. I suppose the most original dish in this chapter is the *Crème Brûlée Ice Cream,* which I can honestly say was my invention, albeit one that arose from a mistake (see p. 196 for the full story). Extraordinarily enough, two or three years after the pudding first appeared on the menu, with an explanation of how it came about, somebody from Canada came to the restaurant and said they had seen exactly the same remarks about the very same pudding on a menu in a restaurant in Canada. Whether somebody had copied us, or whether the *doppelgänger* theory really does apply and there are exact replicas—my restaurant on the other side of the world—I don't know.

The trick with creating a good pudding menu is to balance wholesome and substantial puddings and tarts with light fruit, cream and ice confections. Throw in the obligatory and ever-popular chocolate dessert and maybe some cheese-and-fruit combinations and you're there. I hope you like them.

Facing page: Pine Nut and Ricotta Tart (see p. 201).

Prune Tart with Armagnac

Serves 6

1 quantity of *Basic Sweet Pastry* (see p. 220)

6 ounces Agen prunes or other good-quality moist pitted prunes

2 eggs

5 tablespoons heavy cream

4 tablespoons vanilla sugar (see Note below), or use superfine sugar and a few drops of vanilla extract

3 tablespoons ground almonds

2 tablespoons Armagnac or cognac

2 tablespoons cold water

2 tablespoons butter, melted

• Confectioners' sugar, for dusting

I just don't remember where this recipe came from, but it was designed to use those fantastic prunes from Agen, in the southwest of France, which are so moist and heavy. It really does depend on having a good juicy prune, and if you can't get any Agen ones, the Californians are now producing something pretty similar. Prunes are the sort of thing that when I was a boy you had with rice pudding at school and nobody thought much of. But how wrong we were.

Roll out the pastry thinly on a lightly floured surface and use to line a lightly greased 8½-inch tart pan 1 inch deep and with a removable bottom. Prick the base with a fork and chill for 20 minutes.

Preheat the oven to 400°F.

Line the pastry shell with a sheet of parchment paper, then cover the base with a generous layer of pie weights. Bake blind for 15 minutes. Remove the weights and paper and return the pastry to the oven for a further 3 to 4 minutes. Set aside while you make the filling.

Arrange the prunes in a single layer over the base of the pastry shell. Put the eggs, cream, sugar, almonds, Armagnac or cognac and water into a bowl and whisk together until smooth. Stir in the melted butter. Pour the batter over the prunes and bake in the oven for 25 to 30 minutes, or until set and lightly golden. Remove from the oven and leave to cool slightly, then dust with confectioners' sugar. Serve with a little unwhipped heavy cream.

Note: To make vanilla sugar, slit a vanilla bean open and put it in a jar of superfine sugar. Leave for 1 week before use.

Poached Peaches with Fresh Fruit and Basil Ice Cream

Serves 8

1   quantity of *Stock Syrup*
    (see p. 220)

(see p. 220)

8   firm, ripe peaches

1/4   pound mixed fresh
    summer berries,
    such as raspberries,
    strawberries and
    blueberries (about
    1 cup)

For the Basil Ice Cream

1¼   cups milk

1¼   cups heavy cream

½   vanilla bean

½   cup fresh basil leaves

5   egg yolks

¾   cup superfine sugar

•   Fresh basil sprigs,
    to decorate

The idea for this came from Michel Guérard's restaurant at Eugénie-les-Bains in France. He serves an identical dish but with an ice cream made from verbena, a lemon-scented leaf rather like lemon balm. I haven't been able to get hold of verbena and neither have I been able to grow it very successfully. Then I went to Franco Taruschio's restaurant, The Walnut Tree Inn at Abergavenny in Wales—a place of such joy, good humor and great food. I had basil ice cream there and thought, that's the one for this dish. I've since found that Joyce Molyneux of The Carved Angel in Dartmouth also has a recipe for it, and I think that Franco may have got it from her. So you see how we all share recipes and borrow and nip and tuck!

First make the ice cream. Put the milk, cream, vanilla bean and half the basil leaves into a pan and bring slowly to a boil over gentle heat. Set aside for 5 minutes to allow the flavor of the basil to infuse the milk.

Meanwhile, beat the egg yolks and sugar together until pale and creamy. Strain the hot milk mixture onto the egg yolks and mix together well. Return to the pan and cook over gentle heat, stirring all the time, until the mixture is thick enough to coat the back of the spoon. Do not let the custard boil or it will curdle. Remove from the heat and leave to cool.

Freeze the ice cream in an ice cream maker if you have one. If not, strain the mixture into a plastic container and freeze for 2 hours or until almost set, then scrape it into a food processor and blend until smooth. Finely shred the remaining basil and stir it into the ice cream. Return it to the freezer and leave for 3 hours or until firm.

Meanwhile, bring the syrup to a boil. Make a small, shallow cross in the top of each peach, lower them into the hot syrup and simmer for 3 to 4 minutes, or until just tender. Lift the peaches out of the syrup and peel off the skin. When the syrup has cooled, return the peaches to it, cover and chill until needed.

To serve, put the peaches in 8 chilled dessert bowls, add one or two scoops of ice cream to one side of each peach and a few summer berries to the other. Decorate with sprigs of fresh basil and serve immediately.

Pear Bavarois with a Fresh Passion Fruit Coulis

Serves 8

1 quantity of *Stock Syrup* (see p. 220)

3 firm, ripe dessert pears, peeled, quartered and cored

1¼ cups milk

3 eggs, separated

⅓ cup superfine sugar

1 tablespoon unflavored gelatin

2½ tablespoons Poire William, kirsch or brandy

1¼ cups heavy cream

• Fresh mint sprigs, to decorate (optional)

For the Passion Fruit Coulis

⅔ cup fresh orange juice

• Juice of 1 small lemon

4 ripe passion fruits

1 teaspoon arrowroot or cornstarch

I got this recipe from a restaurant quite near Rheims in France. It is one of those places where you don't really expect to get much of interest in your 95-franc meal but that's the great thing about eating out in France: you often come across just one dish that is really worth having. I'm always looking for puddings out of the summer season that don't rely on rather tasteless imported soft fruit from warmer countries, and this fits the bill exactly. At the restaurant we turn the bavarois out of its mold, dust it thickly with confectioners' sugar and caramelize it with a blowtorch, which gives the whole thing a new dimension of texture and visual appeal. As a matter of fact, no kitchen should be without a blowtorch. Surely you've got one lurking around in the tool shed somewhere! It's ideal for making quick tops for crème brûlées or even for glazing a fruit tart that has been dusted with confectioners' sugar. However, if you don't have one, don't worry; just cover the bavarois with the passion fruit sauce. I always leave the seeds in passion fruit sauces like this because I love their crunchy texture and acidic taste.

Bring the syrup to a boil, add the quartered pears and simmer until just tender. Lift the pears out with a slotted spoon and leave to cool, then chop them into small pieces. Reserve the syrup for the coulis (and for later use—it will keep in the refrigerator).

Put the milk in a pan and bring just to a boil. Put the egg yolks into a bowl with the superfine sugar and beat together until pale and creamy. Gradually beat in the hot milk, then return the mixture to the pan and cook over low heat, stirring all the time, or until it is thick enough to coat the back of the spoon. Do not let the custard boil or it will curdle. Pour into a bowl, press a sheet of plastic wrap on the surface and leave to cool. Meanwhile, line the base of eight scant-1-cup ramekins or similar-sized molds with parchment paper.

Put 3 tablespoons of cold water in a small pan and sprinkle the gelatin over it. Set aside for 5 minutes, then heat gently until clear. Stir into the cooled custard with the chopped pears and the Poire William, kirsch or brandy.

Lightly whip the cream until it forms soft peaks. Now rest the bowl of custard in a larger bowl filled with ice water and stir gently until the mixture begins to show signs of thickening and setting. Remove from the cold water and fold in the whipped cream. Whisk the egg whites into soft peaks and gently fold them in. Spoon the mixture into the prepared molds, cover loosely with plastic wrap and chill for 3 hours, or until set.

For the passion fruit coulis, strain the orange and lemon juice into a small pan. Add $1\frac{1}{4}$ cups of the reserved syrup, bring to a boil and boil rapidly until reduced to $\frac{3}{4}$ cup. Halve the passion fruit and scoop the pulp out into the pan. Mix the arrowroot or cornstarch with 1 teaspoon cold water to form a binder. Bring the coulis back to a boil, then stir in the binder and simmer for 1 minute. Pour into a bowl, leave to cool and then chill.

To serve, unmold the bavarois onto 8 plates and spoon the passion fruit coulis over and around them. Decorate with sprigs of mint, if liked.

Crème Brûlée Ice Cream

Serves 8

$7/8$ cup milk

$1^2/3$ cups heavy cream

1 teaspoon vanilla extract

5 egg yolks

• Scant $2/3$ cup superfine sugar

This ice cream was invented quite by accident when Christine Hope, who is now our head baker, curdled a rich custard intended for a crème brûlée and asked me whether she should throw it away and start again. "No," I said, "it would be a waste. Sprinkle it with sugar, burn the top as you would normally under a broiler and then bung it in the ice cream machine and we'll see what happens." And what happened was that it turned into the most superbly flavored and textured ice cream because the caramel broke up into exquisite little crunchy pieces. We normally serve it with pears poached in port and cinnamon, or just a pile of fresh berries and maybe a little fruit coulis and a sprig of mint.

Put the milk, cream and vanilla extract into a pan and bring slowly to a boil. Meanwhile, beat the egg yolks with $1/4$ cup of the superfine sugar until pale and creamy. Gradually beat in the hot milk and cream, then return the mixture to the pan and cook over gentle heat until it is thick enough to coat the back of the spoon. Do not let it boil or it will curdle.

Pour the custard into a shallow flameproof dish—it should be about 1 inch deep and come near the top of the dish. Leave to cool, then cover and chill for 6 hours or until set.

Preheat the broiler. Remove the custard from the refrigerator and sprinkle with the remaining superfine sugar. Put it under the broiler for about 5 minutes, or until the sugar has caramelized. Alternatively, if you have a blowtorch you can achieve the same results by playing the flame across the top of the sugar. Remove and leave to cool, then break up the caramel topping here and there with the handle of a kitchen knife and stir the pieces into the creamy mixture below. Transfer to an ice cream maker or a plastic container and freeze for 3 hours, or until firm.

Hot Bread Pudding with Armagnac Sauce

Serves 8

5 ounces day-old white bread

7 ounces day-old *Walnut Bread* (see p. 219)

7 ounces day-old whole-grain bread

$^1/_2$ cup golden raisins

$^1/_2$ cup dried currants

$^1/_2$ teaspoon freshly grated nutmeg

$^3/_4$ teaspoon ground cinnamon

• Finely grated zest of $^1/_2$ orange

• Finely grated zest of $^1/_2$ lemon

2 small eggs, beaten

7 tablespoons unsalted butter, softened

$^3/_4$ cup raw sugar

For the Armagnac Sauce

$^3/_4$ cup milk

$^3/_4$ cup heavy cream

2 large egg yolks

3 tablespoons superfine sugar

2 tablespoons Armagnac or cognac

Like so many apparently mundane nursery puddings, this is really good when made with the best ingredients. I've specified three different types of bread only to give the idea that a mixture should be used. Bread pudding is a great way of using up stale bread. Although originally it was the most economical of northern puddings and also eaten as a cake, it's recently been elevated to restaurant status, particularly when served with a rich Armagnac custard like this.

Cut the bread into 1-inch cubes, put them into a large bowl and cover with cold water. Leave to soak for 15 minutes.

Preheat the oven to 325°F.

Tip the soaked bread into a colander. Take a handful at a time and squeeze out all the excess water. Put the bread back into the bowl and add the dried fruits, spices, orange and lemon zest, eggs, butter and two-thirds of the sugar. Mix together well and then put the mixture into a greased and lined 8-by-10-inch cake pan, 1$^1/_2$ inches deep. Sprinkle with the remaining sugar and bake for 1 hour.

Meanwhile, for the sauce, bring the milk and cream just to a boil in a small pan. Whisk the egg yolks and sugar together in a small bowl until pale and creamy. Gradually beat in the hot milk, then return the mixture to the pan and cook over gentle heat, stirring all the time, or until it is thick enough to coat the back of the spoon. Do not let it boil or it will curdle. Stir the Armagnac into the sauce.

Cut the bread pudding into squares and serve with the Armagnac sauce.

Pain Perdu with Cinnamon Sugar and Caramel Apples

Serves 8

²/₃ cup unsalted butter
• Scant 4 cups milk
• Scant ¹/₂ cup superfine sugar
1 vanilla bean
4 large eggs, beaten
¹/₂ teaspoon ground cinnamon

For the Brioche
1 tablespoon active dry yeast
3 tablespoons warm water
4 tablespoons superfine sugar
3 tablespoons tepid milk
3 cups bread flour
1 teaspoon salt
4 eggs
¹/₂ cup unsalted butter, melted and cooled
• Beaten egg, to glaze

For the Caramel Apples
¹/₂ cup unsalted butter
8 dessert apples, such as pippins, peeled, cored and thickly sliced
²/₃ cup sugar
²/₃ cup heavy cream
2 tablespoons Calvados

I suppose you could call pain perdu France's answer to bread and butter pudding. You dip some slices of bread in sweet milk and beaten egg and fry them in butter to give a set, slightly crispy outside and a soft center. If you then sprinkle the pain perdu *with a little sugar spiced with cinnamon and serve it with some caramelized apple slices and caramel sauce, you're in heaven. This recipe is a luxurious version made with homemade brioche but you could use a good-quality bought brioche or any good white bread.*

For the brioche, put the yeast, water, 2 tablespoons of the sugar, the milk and 1 tablespoon of the flour in a bowl and whisk together until smooth. Cover with a damp tea towel and leave in a warm place for about 1 hour, or until the mixture has become frothy. Sift the rest of the flour and sugar and the salt into a large mixing bowl, make a well in the center and add the yeast mixture, eggs and melted butter. Gradually mix the flour into the wet ingredients to make a sticky dough. Beat it with your hand for 2 to 3 minutes, then cover with a damp tea towel and leave in a warm place for 1 to 2 hours, or until doubled in size.

Preheat the oven to 400°F.

Punch down the dough, turn it out onto a floured surface and knead for a couple of minutes until smooth. Put it in a buttered 9-by-5-inch loaf pan, cover and leave in a warm place until the mixture has risen to the top of the pan. Glaze the top with beaten egg and bake for 30 to 35 minutes, or until the loaf is golden brown on top and sounds hollow when tapped on the base. Remove from the pan and leave to cool on a wire rack.

For the caramel apples, clarify the butter by melting it over low heat, then pouring off the clear butter into a bowl, leaving behind the milky solids that will have collected at the bottom. Pour a little of the clarified butter into a large frying pan, add a layer of apple slices and fry for about 3 minutes, turning them over halfway through, or until they are just soft. Lift out with a slotted spoon and cook the remaining apples in the same way.

Add the rest of the clarified butter to the pan with the sugar and leave over very low heat, stirring occasionally. It will look very dry and grainy to start with but eventually the sugar will melt and turn into a toffee-colored mixture. Take the pan off the heat and add the cream and Calvados. Return the pan to low heat and cook, stirring, or until all the pieces of hardened toffee have melted. Return the apples to the pan and keep warm.

For the *pain perdu*, clarify the butter as for the apples and set aside. Put the milk, two-thirds of the sugar and the vanilla bean into a pan and leave over gentle heat until almost boiling. Take off the heat and leave to cool. Remove the vanilla bean and pour the milk into a wide, shallow dish. Pour the beaten eggs into another shallow dish. Cut the brioche into slices $\frac{1}{2}$ inch thick (you will need 8 slices) and then cut each slice in half diagonally. Mix the rest of the sugar with the cinnamon and set aside.

Heat a little of the clarified butter in a large nonstick frying pan. Put a couple of slices of brioche in the milk, leave for 30 seconds, then turn them over and leave for another 30 seconds—the bread should have absorbed the milk but not gone soggy. Now dip the soaked brioche into the beaten egg, put in the frying pan and fry over medium heat for 1 minute on each side, or until golden. Lift out onto a serving plate and keep warm in a low oven while you cook the rest.

Sprinkle the *pain perdu* lightly with the cinnamon sugar and serve immediately with the caramel apples.

Baked Chocolate Mousse with Cornish Clotted Cream

Serves 6 to 8

5   ounces good-quality bittersweet chocolate

$\frac{2}{3}$ cup softened unsalted butter, plus extra for greasing

$\frac{2}{3}$ cup superfine sugar

3   eggs, separated

•   Confectioners' sugar, for dusting

•   Clotted cream, preferably Cornish, to serve

It's funny how often people describe extremely dark, rich chocolate cakes as wicked or sinful. Yet there is something indefinably seductive about really good chocolate desserts, and this one must top the bill for the most sensual chocolate gâteau in the world. Most so-called chocolate gâteaux leave me cold, and they should more appropriately be described as chocolate cakes to serve for afternoon tea. But this one is so dark and moist and delicate.

Preheat the oven to 325°F. Grease an 8-inch springform pan with a little butter and then line the base with parchment paper.

Melt the chocolate in a bowl set over a pan of barely simmering water, making sure the bowl isn't touching the water. Leave to cool.

Beat the butter and sugar together until pale and fluffy. Beat in the egg yolks, one at a time, then fold in the melted chocolate.

In another bowl whisk the egg whites until they stand in soft peaks. Stir 2 large spoonfuls into the chocolate mixture to loosen it slightly and then gently fold in the remainder. Put the mixture into the pan and bake for 1 hour, or until a crust has formed on top and there is no movement if you shake the pan gently. The cake will rise up dramatically during cooking but will sink once you take it out of the oven. Leave to cool on a wire rack, then remove it from the pan.

Serve the cake dusted lightly with confectioners' sugar and accompanied by scoops of clotted cream.

Lemon Meringue Tart

Serves 6

1   quantity of *Basic Sweet Pastry* (see p. 220)

3   eggs

$1\frac{1}{4}$ cups superfine sugar

$\frac{2}{3}$ cup heavy cream

4   tablespoons lemon juice

Much as I've always liked lemon meringue pie, I find that most recipes call for a rather bland cornstarch mixture to make the lemon filling. If you use a proper lemon tart filling in a deep pastry shell the result is so much better.

Roll out the pastry on a lightly floured surface and use to line a lightly greased 8-inch tart pan $1\frac{1}{2}$ inches deep and with a removable bottom. Prick the base with a fork and chill for 20 minutes. Preheat the oven to 400°F.

Line the pastry shell with a sheet of parchment paper, cover the base with pie weights and bake for 15 minutes. Remove the weights and paper and return

- Finely grated zest of
  1 large lemon
2 egg whites

the pastry shell to the oven for 3 to 4 minutes. Remove from the oven and set aside. Reduce the oven temperature to 300°F.

For the filling, lightly stir together the eggs, $^2/_3$ cup of the sugar and the cream. Gradually stir in the lemon juice, then strain into a pitcher and stir in the zest. Pour the mixture into the pastry shell and bake for 50 minutes, or until set. Remove from the oven and leave to cool. Raise the oven temperature to 350°F.

Whisk the egg whites into stiff peaks. Very gradually beat in the remaining sugar to produce a stiff, glossy meringue. Spread it over the cooled tart, making sure it makes a good seal with the pastry edge. Swirl the top with the tip of a knife and bake for 15 minutes, or until lightly browned. Serve the tart warm or cold.

Pine Nut and Ricotta Tart

The filling of this delicious tart is considerably enhanced by the inclusion of a little lemon zest. It's an Italian recipe, a sort of light baked cheesecake.

Serves 6

2 quantities of *Basic Sweet Pastry* (see p. 220), each made with grated zest of $^1/_2$ lemon
$^1/_3$ cup pine nuts
$1^1/_2$ cups ($^3/_4$ pound) ricotta cheese
3 egg yolks
· Finely grated zest of 1 small lemon
$^2/_3$ cup superfine sugar
4 tablespoons heavy cream
· Confectioners' sugar, for dusting

Roll out half the pastry thinly on a lightly floured surface and use to line a lightly greased $8^1/_2$-inch tart pan 1 inch deep and with a removable bottom. Prick the base with a fork and chill for 20 minutes.

Preheat the oven to 400°F.

Line the pastry shell with a sheet of parchment paper, cover the base with pie weights and bake blind for 15 minutes. Remove the weights and paper and bake for a further 3 to 4 minutes. Remove from the oven and set aside.

For the filling, toast the pine nuts in the oven for about 6 minutes, or until golden, then leave to cool. Lower the oven temperature to 325°F.

Beat together the ricotta, egg yolks, lemon zest and sugar until smooth. Stir in the cream and pine nuts. Pour the filling into the pastry shell. Roll out the remaining pastry and cut it into strips $^1/_4$ inch wide. Lay some of them over the tart about 1 inch apart, then lay the remaining strips crosswise on top to make a lattice. Seal the ends with a little water and then bake the tart for 1 hour, or until set and lightly golden. Dust with confectioners' sugar and serve with unwhipped heavy cream. It can be eaten hot, but is exceptionally good cold, too.

Panna Cotta with Stewed Rhubarb

Serves 6

1 vanilla bean
1¼ cups heavy cream
1¼ cups milk
6 tablespoons superfine sugar
2 teaspoons unflavored gelatin

For the Stewed Rhubarb
¾ pound young rhubarb
1 cup granulated sugar
1 cup water
1 orange
1 lemon
1¼ cups red wine
4 tablespoons port
1 tablespoon soft dark brown sugar
• 3-inch piece cinnamon stick
1 clove

This Italian light set cream can be served with rhubarb in winter and, in summer, with whatever fresh berries you like, but I always favor raspberries—particularly puréed and very lightly sweetened to make a coulis. A great thing about panna cotta *is that it is set with only a tiny amount of gelatin, and in this particular recipe the cream only just holds its shape. For the television series accompanying this book, we filmed the making of this dish during a splendid day where I instructed a dozen or so chefs on a four-course menu I had written for a special dinner for 100 guests at Blenheim Palace that evening. I demonstrated the dishes and then we all prepared them together. However, disaster loomed when it looked extremely doubtful whether the tiny amount of gelatin I had allowed for the 100 portions of* panna cotta *would, in fact, set the cream. In the end I reluctantly decided that we would have to tip the mixture out into a big bowl and add more gelatin, which would firm it up more than I wanted. Just as we were about to do that, Paul Ripley, our head chef, came in bearing a plate of* panna cotta *that had just set in the softest, most melting way. At some stage in any "away match," as I like to call it, things start to go wrong and you think it is all going to collapse. It just takes a little moment like that to make you think, "Oh yes, it's going to be all right after all." And it was. The star turn, in spite of all the brilliant fish, was the* panna cotta, *which everybody said tasted so fresh.*

For the *panna cotta*, split open the vanilla bean and scrape out the seeds. Put both the pod and seeds into a small pan with the cream, milk and sugar and simmer gently for 5 minutes, then remove from the heat. Meanwhile, put 2 tablespoons of cold water in a small pan and sprinkle the gelatin over it. Set aside for 5 minutes, then heat gently until clear.

Remove the vanilla bean from the cream and stir in the dissolved gelatin. Pour into 6 dariole molds or 2½-inch ramekins, cover and chill for 3 hours, or until set.

Peel the rhubarb if it is woody, but if it is very young this shouldn't be necessary. Cut it into 1-inch lengths. Put the sugar and water into a pan and leave over low heat until the sugar has completely dissolved. Bring to a boil and boil for 2 minutes. Pour half this syrup into another pan and stir in half the prepared rhubarb. Simmer it for 1 to 2 minutes, or until only just tender—it should still be slightly firm. Cover and leave to cool.

Pare the zest off a quarter of the orange and a quarter of the lemon, being careful not to remove any of the bitter white pith underneath. Squeeze out the juice of both the orange and the lemon and add to the remaining syrup with the pared zests, red wine, port, dark brown sugar, cinnamon and clove. Bring to a boil and boil until the liquid has reduced to $^2/_3$ cup. Strain into another pan, stir in the remaining rhubarb and simmer gently for 2 to 3 minutes, or until just tender. It should be a little more cooked through than the first batch but not falling apart. Transfer to a bowl and leave to cool. (Remember the rhubarb will continue to cook in the syrup after it has been removed from the heat.)

To serve, unmold the *panna cotta* onto 6 serving plates and arrange a pile of each type of rhubarb to the side, along with a little of the syrup.

Light Fig Tarts with Yogurt Sour Cream

Serves 8

2 pounds chilled puff
   pastry
12 fresh figs
4 teaspoons granulated
   sugar
3 tablespoons red
   currant jelly
2 teaspoons water

*For the Yogurt Sour
Cream*
1¼ cups heavy cream
5 tablespoons plain
   natural yogurt

These are simply some sliced fresh figs baked on puff pastry rounds, then glazed and served with what I call yogurt sour cream. I developed this type of sour cream in the days before we could buy crème fraîche in Britain but actually I almost prefer it. You just mix some yogurt and heavy cream together, leave it in a warm place overnight, then put it in cheesecloth and let it drain. The result is a superb, slightly acidic cream that makes the perfect accompaniment to the fig tarts. You need to start making the cream a good 24 hours before you wish to serve it.

For the yogurt sour cream, bring the cream to a boil in a small pan and then set aside to cool. Stir in the yogurt, cover the pan with a cloth and leave in a warm place (about 70°F) overnight.

The next morning, spoon the cream into a cheesecloth-lined sieve and rest it over a bowl. Cover and leave in the refrigerator for 12 hours to drain.

Preheat the oven to 425°F.

Divide the pastry into 8, roll out each piece thinly on a lightly floured surface and cut into a 6-inch oval. Put them spaced well apart on 2 lightly greased baking sheets.

Cut each fig across into 4 or 5 slices and arrange them slightly overlapping on the pastry ovals, leaving a ½-inch border. Sprinkle each tart with ½ teaspoon granulated sugar and bake for about 12 minutes, or until the pastry is puffed up and golden and the sugar has lightly caramelized.

Meanwhile, put the red currant jelly into a pan with the water and leave over gentle heat until melted. Set aside to cool slightly but do not let it set.

Remove the tarts from the oven and brush the fruit with the red currant glaze. Slide each tart onto a warmed plate and serve with the yogurt sour cream.

Saffron Ice Cream with Brandy Snaps

Serves 8

$^1/_2$ teaspoon saffron threads

$1^1/_4$ cups milk

$1^1/_4$ cups heavy cream

4 egg yolks

• Scant $^2/_3$ cup superfine sugar

For the Brandy Snaps

$4^1/_2$ tablespoons unsalted butter

4 tablespoons all-purpose flour

$^1/_2$ teaspoon ground ginger

• Scant $^2/_3$ cup superfine sugar

3 tablespoons golden syrup

The recipe is for quite a lot of ice cream. I thought of cutting it down and, of course, you can halve everything if you feel so inclined but we find, with a family of children, that the ice cream has a habit of disappearing from the freezer in the most mysterious circumstances.

For the ice cream, grind the saffron to a powder in a mortar or with the end of a rolling pin in a small bowl. Put the milk, cream and ground saffron into a pan and bring slowly to a boil over gentle heat. Meanwhile, beat the egg yolks and superfine sugar together until pale and creamy. Pour on the hot milk, mix well and return to the pan. Cook over gentle heat, stirring all the time, until the mixture is thick enough to coat the back of the spoon. Do not let it boil or it will curdle. Strain the mixture, then leave to cool. Freeze in an ice cream maker, if you have one. Alternatively, pour it into a plastic container and freeze for 2 to 3 hours, or until almost set, then scrape it into a food processor and process until smooth. Pour back into the container and freeze for another 3 hours or until firm.

Preheat the oven to 350°F.

For the brandy snaps, melt the butter in a pan, add all the remaining ingredients and beat until smooth. Drop 4 teaspoons of the mixture about 6 inches apart on a nonstick baking sheet and bake for 11 to 12 minutes, or until richly golden. Leave to cool and set a little—about 1 minute—then use a flexible metal icing knife to lift them off the sheet and drape them over a rolling pin for an open shape (or wrap them round a wooden spoon or sharpening steel for a cigar shape). Press down lightly to curve them and leave until cold. Repeat with the remaining mixture; you should have about 16 brandy snaps in total.

To serve, scoop the ice cream into chilled dessert glasses and push 2 brandy snaps into the top of each one. Serve immediately.

Hot Chocolate Tarts with a Compote of Dried Fruits

Serves 8

2 quantities of *Basic Sweet Pastry* (see p. 220)

4 ounces good-quality bittersweet chocolate

2 eggs

$1\frac{1}{2}$ tablespoons superfine sugar

$\frac{2}{3}$ cup heavy cream

For the Compote of Dried Fruits

6 ounces mixed dried fruits, such as apples, pears, peaches, prunes, apricots and figs

5 tablespoons white wine

$\frac{1}{2}$ cup granulated sugar

5 cloves

• 2-inch piece cinnamon stick

1 orange zest strip

1 lemon zest strip

• Juice of $\frac{1}{2}$ lemon

These little individual chocolate tarts puff up into a wonderful light extravagance when baked. They are served with dried fruits that have been poached in a syrup spiced with cloves, cinnamon and orange and lemon zests. This is the sort of winter pudding that makes you feel the colder months, when soft, ripe summer fruits are not available, have some tremendous compensations after all. Remember you need to soak the dried fruits the night before.

First make the dried fruit compote. Cover the dried fruits with plenty of cold water and leave to soak overnight. The next day, drain the fruit, reserving the soaking liquid. Cut any large pieces of fruit in half. Put $1\frac{1}{4}$ cups of the soaking liquid into a pan with the rest of the compote ingredients (except the fruits). Bring to a boil and simmer for 10 minutes. Add the fruits and simmer for 15 minutes. Leave to cool and then chill until needed.

Preheat the oven to 400°F.

Cut the pastry into 8 and roll out each piece thinly on a lightly floured surface. Use to line eight 4-inch tartlet tins with removable bottoms and chill for 20 minutes.

Line the pastry shells with sheets of parchment paper, cover the bases with a generous layer of pie weights and bake blind for 15 minutes. Remove the weights and paper and return the pastry shells to the oven for 2 to 3 minutes. Remove from the oven and set aside. Lower the oven temperature to 375°F.

Melt the chocolate in a bowl set over a pan of barely simmering water, making sure the bowl doesn't touch the water. Leave the chocolate to cool.

Lightly whisk the eggs and sugar together, then stir in the melted chocolate and the cream. Pour the mixture into the tartlet shells and bake for about 15 minutes, or until set. Serve the warm chocolate tarts with the chilled fruit compote.

Sticky Toffee Pudding

Serves 8

1¼ cups water
6 dates, pitted and
 coarsely chopped
1 teaspoon baking soda
1 teaspoon vanilla
 extract
4 tablespoons butter
¾ cup superfine sugar
2 eggs
1⅔ cups all-purpose flour
1 teaspoon baking
 powder
⅔ cup clotted cream or
 whipped heavy cream,
 to serve

For the Sauce
1¼ cups heavy cream
1 cup soft dark brown
 sugar
½ cup butter

This is the famous and original sticky pudding from Sharrow Bay, that delightful hotel in Ullswater in the Lake District. Francis Coulson and Brian Sack are two of the country's best exponents of British food. Whenever I go there I am filled with a real enthusiasm for the food of this country and the whole experience of staying there fills me with optimism, as all good hotels and restaurants should. Francis Coulson invented this sweet, perhaps the most well loved of all our puddings.

Preheat the oven to 350°F.

Put the water, dates, baking soda and vanilla extract into a pan and bring to a boil. Meanwhile, cream the butter and sugar together until pale and fluffy. Beat in the eggs one at a time, adding a tablespoon of the flour with the second egg if the mixture looks as if it is about to curdle. Sift the remaining flour with the baking powder and gently fold in.

Bring the date mixture back to a boil. Slowly beat the liquid into the creamed mixture to make a smooth batter, then stir in the dates. Pour into a greased and lined 8-by-10-inch cake pan 1½ inches deep, and bake for 30 minutes, or until a skewer inserted in the center of the pudding comes away clean.

For the sauce, put the cream, sugar and butter into a pan and leave over low heat until the sugar has melted.

To serve, cut the pudding into 8 pieces and put them on warmed serving plates. Bring the sauce to a boil, pour it over the pudding and serve with clotted cream or whipped heavy cream.

Crémets de Saumur with Fresh Raspberries

Serves 4

1½   cups heavy cream
1   teaspoon superfine sugar, plus extra to serve
2   egg whites
½   to ¾ cup fresh raspberries

This recipe comes from Elizabeth David's French Provincial Cooking *and differs from the more familiar* coeurs à la crème *in that no cream cheese is used. We serve these crémets sprinkled with lemon sugar (made by drying pared lemon zest and then powdering it with superfine sugar in a blender) and fresh berries and accompanied by a simple coulis. You can buy molds for draining cream quite easily. Alternatively you can just drain the cream mixture in a cheesecloth bag and serve it from a bowl.*

Line 4 *coeur à la crème* molds with cheesecloth, leaving some overlapping the sides. Whip 1¼ cups of the cream with the sugar into soft peaks. Whisk the egg whites into soft peaks and then gently fold them into the cream. Spoon the mixture into the lined molds and lightly level the tops. Cover with the overhanging pieces of cheesecloth and place in the refrigerator with a plate underneath to catch the liquid. Leave for about 12 hours or overnight.

Unmold the creams onto plates and pour the remaining cream around them. Add some raspberries to each plate and sprinkle with a little sugar.

Fruit and Cheese Combinations

I often find in restaurants that, after a fairly filling meal, all I want is something light and not necessarily too sweet. It is rare to find something that fits the bill. In Italy, menus often give you the option of fresh fruit served with cheese—say, Parmesan or pecorino. I like to order a glass of Vin Santo, that sweet, slightly earthy dessert wine, to go with this. The perfect finish to a meal.

So how about some fresh peaches, preferably those white ones with an ephemeral fragrance, served with slivers of Parmesan? Or maybe some slices of the large pears that you get in the autumn in Italy, beautifully tender and moist, with some dolcelatte just spooned out onto the plate. Or perhaps a little pile of mascarpone cheese and some fresh, sweet figs to eat with it. Some nutty farmhouse Cheddar would go well with a good pippin apple. Or you could try that excellent Scottish cheese, Lanark Blue, with a pile of tayberries. Not a recipe but just a few suggestions.

Basics

I used to play rugby in the front row of the scrum and though one naturally assumes that wherever you play in a team sport is the most important position, I do think that games of rugby are won or lost in the front two rows of the scrum. This is a perfect analogy with cooking. Many dishes are won or lost through good or bad basics, particularly stock. And to make a good stock, to prepare bones and vegetables and simmer everything gently to produce a clear and well-flavored liquid, that's real cooking. I mean by real cooking, the care and attention to the background details in a dish. Many recipes today involve the last-minute cooking of good ingredients and don't involve long slow cooking or elaborate sauces and long labored garnishes. Most of the dishes in this book are like that because those are the sort of dishes we all like to eat now, but when a dish calls for a stock or one of the other basic recipes in this chapter it needs to be made properly. I suppose my style of cooking would be described as simple, straightforward, those sort of words, but it's not quite as simple as that! "In my salad days when I was green in judgment" I used to think that the only way to succeed as a restaurant chef was to pile ingredients on ingredients. I once had a dish on the menu that had three fish cooked in three different ways with three different sauces. Now I like a minimum of ingredients but everything has to be just right.

It's really well worth taking care with these basics, what after all is better in this world than a freshly boiled crab with a fluffy mayonnaise or a slab of turbot with a rich, lemony hollandaise. The curry pastes too will be better than anything you can buy in a bottle. Again, a lot of work will go into assembling the ingredients, but it will be well worth it.

Fish Stock

Makes about 5 cups

2¼ pounds fish bones, such as lemon sole, brill and flounder
2½ quarts water
¼ pound onions, chopped
¼ pound celery stalks, chopped
¼ pound carrots, chopped
⅓ cup sliced button mushrooms
1 teaspoon chopped fresh thyme

Unlike meat stocks, fish stock should only be simmered for 20 minutes to extract all the flavor from the bones. A longer simmering time will make it taste bitter and a bit gluey. You can use any fish for stock except oily ones such as herring and mackerel, although in an emergency I have used these without the heads, which is where all the oil is.

Put the fish bones and water in a pan, bring just to a boil and simmer very gently for 20 minutes. Strain through a sieve lined with cheesecloth into a clean pan, add the vegetables and thyme and bring back to a boil. Simmer for 35 minutes, or until reduced to about 5 cups. Strain once more. The stock is now ready to use or store.

Roasted Fish Stock

Makes about 5 cups

2 tablespoons butter
2¼ pounds fish bones, such as lemon sole, brill and flounder
¼ pound onions, chopped
¼ pound celery stalks, chopped
¼ pound carrots, chopped
1 teaspoon chopped fresh thyme
2½ quarts water

This robust stock has a slightly caramelized flavor from the roasted vegetables. It can be used in any dish in which a strong flavor is required.

Preheat the oven to 400°F.

Melt the butter in a large roasting pan. Add the fish bones, vegetables and thyme and turn them over a few times until they are well coated in the butter. Roast in the oven for 30 minutes, then transfer the mixture to a saucepan, add the water and bring just to a boil. Simmer for 20 minutes and then strain through a sieve lined with cheesecloth into a clean pan. Bring back to a boil and boil until reduced to about 5 cups. The stock is now ready to use or store.

Chicken Stock

This light, clear chicken stock crops up quite frequently in my recipes where the particular flavor of a fish-based stock is not important but the clean and fragrant body of a good, clean chicken stock will count for a great deal. A good stock is often what makes a dish like a paella or risotto memorable. I have enjoyed those dishes with very little else in them other than rice and a good stock. I use chicken stock in fish dishes when I want plenty of savory body for a well-flavored sauce, such as the robust red wine sauce with cod and lentils on p. 121.

This chicken stock should be made with fresh carcasses or drumettes. Much as I like stocks made from the leftovers of a roast chicken for vegetable soups and to enrich gravy, the dishes in this book need something a bit more refined.

Put all the ingredients into a large pan and bring just to a boil, skimming any scum from the surface as it appears. Leave to simmer very gently for 2 hours—it is important not to let it boil as this will force the fat from even the leanest chicken and make the stock cloudy. Regularly skim off any fat that does collect on top of the stock.

Strain through a sieve lined with cheesecloth and leave to cool, then chill. Remove the film of fat from the surface. The stock is now ready to use or store.

Concentrated Chicken Stock For a really good concentrated chicken stock, simmer the strained stock until reduced in volume by half.

Light Asian Chicken Stock

Use this for any dish with Asian flavors.

Put the chicken carcasses into a large pan and cover with cold water. Slowly bring to a boil, skimming any scum from the surface. Trim the green tops off the green onions and split the onions in half lengthwise. Lightly crush the garlic, leaving the skin on. Add the green onions, garlic, ginger and star anise, if using, to the pan and simmer very gently for 1½ hours, skimming off any fat as it collects on the surface. Strain and leave to cool. The stock is now ready to use or store.

Shellfish Nage

Makes about 7 cups

1	leek, thinly sliced
2	celery stalks, sliced
1	onion, thinly sliced
1	fennel bulb, thinly sliced
•	Zest and flesh of $^1/_2$ lemon
•	Zest and flesh of $^1/_2$ orange
2	fresh bay leaves
15	black peppercorns, cracked
7	cups water
$^2/_3$	cup dry white wine

A nage is a well-flavored court bouillon used for poaching shellfish. The court bouillon can then be reduced and butter whisked in to make a simple, fresh sauce, as in the recipe for Poached Lobster with Butter and Basil *(see p. 132)*

Put all the ingredients except the white wine into a large pan, bring to a boil and simmer for 25 minutes. Add the white wine and simmer for a further 5 minutes, then strain. The nage is now ready to use.

Shellfish Stock and Shellfish Reduction

Makes about 4 cups stock or $^2/_3$ cup reduction

$^1/_2$	cup chopped carrot
$^1/_2$	cup chopped onion
$^1/_2$	cup chopped celery
1	tablespoon unsalted butter
$^3/_4$	pound shrimp in their shells or small crabs
1	tablespoon cognac
2	tablespoons white wine
1	teaspoon chopped fresh tarragon
$^1/_2$	cup roughly chopped tomato
5	cups *Fish Stock* (see p. 212)
•	A pinch of cayenne pepper

To make the shellfish stock, fry the carrot, onion and celery in the butter for 2 to 3 minutes. Add the shrimp or crabs and the cognac and fry for 2 minutes. Add the remaining ingredients and simmer for 40 minutes, then strain through a sieve lined with cheesecloth. The stock is now ready to use or store.

To make the shellfish reduction, process the stock in a blender before straining. Pass it through a regular sieve and then through a very fine-mesh or cheesecloth-lined sieve, squeezing out as much of the liquid as possible. Return the strained liquid to a clean pan, bring to a boil and boil until reduced to about $^2/_3$ cup. It is now ready to use or store.

Hollandaise Sauce

Serves 4

1 cup unsalted butter
2 tablespoons water
2 egg yolks
• Juice of 1 lemon
• A good pinch of
 cayenne pepper
1/2 teaspoon salt

I like my hollandaise sauce to be quite lemony. The sauce is so rich it does need some acidity to balance it.

Clarify the butter by melting it over low heat, then skimming off any froth from the surface. Pour off the clear butter into another pan, leaving behind the white solids that will have collected at the bottom. Keep the clarified butter warm.

Put the water and egg yolks in a stainless steel or glass bowl set over a pan of simmering water, making sure the base of the bowl is not touching the water. Whisk until voluminous and creamy. Remove the bowl from the pan and gradually whisk in the warm clarified butter, building up an emulsion. Add the lemon juice, the cayenne pepper and salt. If the sauce splits, warm a clean pan, add 1 tablespoon of water and gradually whisk in the curdled sauce. Hollandaise is best used immediately, but you can hold it for up to 2 hours if you keep it covered in a warm place, such as over a pan of warm water.

Quick Hollandaise Sauce

Use the same ingredients for the recipe above, but put egg yolks, lemon juice and water into a blender. Turn on and pour in the hot clarified butter. Season with cayenne pepper and salt.

Green Curry Paste

Makes about 2/3 cup

2 to 4 green chilies
1 medium onion
2 lemongrass stalks
• 1-inch piece fresh
 galangal or ginger
1 cup fresh cilantro
3 garlic cloves
1 teaspoon ground
 coriander
1 teaspoon ground cumin
2 lime zest strips
 (optional)
1 teaspoon *blachan*
1 teaspoon salt
2 tablespoons water

This paste is made green with lots of fresh green chilies and fresh cilantro. As with the red curry paste below, although there are plenty of commercial pastes available now, freshly made curry pastes are much more fragrant and take me right back to those bustling streets in Bangkok.

Trim and roughly chop the chilies, onion, lemongrass and galangal or ginger. Put all the ingredients in a good processor and blend until smooth.

Olive Oil Dressing

Makes about 6 tablespoons

6 tablespoons extra-
    virgin olive oil
1/2 tablespoon white wine
    vinegar
1/2 teaspoon salt

Put all the ingredients in a bowl and whisk them together. Toss with salad just before serving.

Mustard Dressing

Makes about 1/2 cup

6 tablespoons sunflower
    oil
1 tablespoon white wine
    vinegar
1/2 teaspoon salt
1/2 shallot, finely chopped
1/2 small garlic clove, finely
    chopped
1 teaspoon English
    mustard

Either whisk all the ingredients together in a small bowl or put them in a screw-top jar and shake well to combine.

Mustard Mayonnaise

Makes about 1 1/4 cups

1 tablespoon English
    mustard
1 egg
1 tablespoon white wine
    vinegar
3/4 teaspoon salt
• A few turns of the white
    pepper mill
1 1/4 cups sunflower oil

This is good with dressed crab, cooked shrimp and boiled conch. See the recipe for Olive Oil Mayonnaise *(opposite) if you prefer to make your mayonnaise by hand.*

Put the mustard, egg, vinegar, salt and pepper into a blender. Turn on the machine and then gradually add the oil through the hole in the lid until you have a thick emulsion. The mayonnaise will keep for about a week in the refrigerator.

Olive Oil Mayonnaise

Makes about 1¼ cups

1   egg or 2 egg yolks
2   teaspoons white wine
    vinegar
½   teaspoon salt
1¼ cups olive oil

This recipe includes instructions for making mayonnaise in the blender and by hand. It is lighter made mechanically because the process uses a whole egg, and it's very quick, but I still prefer making it by hand since I like to do as much as possible in the kitchen by hand.

To make the mayonnaise in a machine, you need to use a whole egg. Put the egg, vinegar and salt into a blender. Turn on the machine and then gradually add the oil through the hole in the lid until you have a thick emulsion.

To make the mayonnaise by hand, use 2 egg yolks. Make sure all the ingredients are at room temperature before beginning. Put the egg yolks, vinegar and salt into a mixing bowl, then place the bowl on a tea towel to stop it slipping. Using a wire whisk, beat the oil into the egg mixture a few drops at a time until you have incorporated it all. Once you have carefully added about the same volume of oil as the original mixture of egg yolks and vinegar, you can add the oil more quickly.

The mayonnaise will keep for about a week in the refrigerator.

Lemon Mayonnaise

Makes about 1¼ cups

1   tablespoon lemon juice
1   egg
•   Finely grated zest of
    1 small lemon
½   teaspoon salt
⅔   cup sunflower oil
⅔   cup olive oil

See the recipe for Olive Oil Mayonnaise *(above) if you prefer to make your mayonnaise by hand.*

Put the lemon juice, egg, lemon zest and salt into a blender. Turn on the machine and then gradually add the oil through the hole in the lid until you have a thick emulsion. The mayonnaise will keep for about a week in the refrigerator.

Tapenade

Makes about ³⁄₄ cup

1	cup pitted black olives
8	anchovy fillets
2	tablespoons capers
1	lemon juice
2	tablespoons cognac
¹⁄₂	teaspoon mustard
•	Olive oil

Tapenade is a purée of black olives with anchovies and capers. It is available in all supermarkets, now but if you want to make your own, this is the recipe I use.

Mix all the ingredients together and purée.

Egg Pasta Dough

Makes about ¹⁄₄ pound

³⁄₄	cup all-purpose flour
•	A large pinch of salt
¹⁄₄	teaspoon olive oil
1	egg
2	egg yolks

This makes a rich, deep yellow pasta dough that is ideal for making ravioli, since the extra egg helps them hold together during poaching. If you want a general-purpose pasta dough that is not so rich, just use 1 egg in the recipe. It will provide enough liquid to produce a stiff dough suitable for rolling through a pasta machine. If rolling by hand, you may need to add a little extra water. The drier the dough is when you are making pasta, the less it will stick together when shaped.

Put all the ingredients into a bowl and mix together into a ball. Turn out onto a lightly floured surface and knead for about 10 minutes, or until smooth and elastic. Wrap in plastic wrap and leave to rest for 10 to 15 minutes before using. This dough will not keep for more than a couple of days wrapped in the refrigerator.

Baked Rice

Serves 4

1²⁄₃	cups long-grain rice, such as Thai jasmine or basmati
•	A small pat of butter
¹⁄₂	teaspoon salt
3	cups boiling water

This way of preparing rice prevents it becoming overcooked or waterlogged. Properly cooked rice is a good accompaniment to almost any fish dish in the Hot and Spicy chapter.

Preheat the oven to 400°F.

Wash the rice in cold water until the water runs clear. Melt the butter in a flameproof baking dish, add the rice, salt and water and bring to a boil. Cover with a tight-fitting lid or foil, and bake in the oven for 15 minutes.

Walnut Bread

Makes two 1-pound loaves

4⅓	cups whole-wheat flour
2	teaspoons salt
1	tablespoon light soft brown sugar
1	tablespoon active dry yeast
1⅞	cups hand-hot water
1½	tablespoons butter, melted
6	tablespoons walnut pieces
2	teaspoons sesame seeds

This is quick to make because it requires no bulk proofing.

Mix the flour, salt and sugar together in a large bowl. Put the yeast in a small bowl and gradually stir in ⅔ cup of the water. Add the yeast mixture to the remaining water and then gradually stir it into the flour with the melted butter to make a soft dough.

Turn the dough out onto a lightly floured surface and knead for 3 minutes, then knead in the walnuts. (The dough only has a short kneading time because the flour is low in gluten. Strong flours need longer to "develop" the gluten, i.e., to make it as elastic as possible to trap air.) Cut the dough in half and form into 2 fat sausage shapes. Put them in 2 buttered 1-pound (7½ by 3½ inches) loaf pans. Tie each pan into a large plastic bag and leave in a warm place for 45 minutes to 1 hour, or until doubled in size.

Preheat the oven to 450°F.

Sprinkle the sesame seeds over the loaves. Bake in the center of the oven for 25 to 30 minutes, then remove the loaves from the pans and return them to the oven for a further 5 minutes to crisp the crust. Leave to cool on a wire rack.

Red Curry Paste

Makes about ⅔ cup

5	large red finger chilies, roughly chopped
1	teaspoon salt
1	teaspoon chopped galangal or fresh ginger
1	tablespoon lemongrass
3	tablespoons chopped garlic
3	tablespoons roughly chopped shallots
1	teaspoon ground coriander
1	teaspoon ground cumin
1	teaspoon *blachan* (optional)
2	teaspoons paprika
½	teaspoon ground turmeric
1	tablespoon sunflower oil

This is a curry paste made red with lots of fresh red chilies and paprika. As well as being the base for the Thai Red Seafood on p. 70, it's also very good for using in meat and vegetable curries.

Blend all the ingredients in a food processor until smooth. If necessary, add a little water to help it purée more easily.

Basic Sweet Pastry

Sufficient to line an
8$\frac{1}{2}$–9-inch tart pan

$\frac{3}{4}$ cup all-purpose flour
5 tablespoons chilled
   butter, cut into pieces
2 tablespoons superfine
   sugar
$\frac{1}{2}$ tablespoon beaten egg
1 tablespoon cold water

Put the flour and butter in a food processor and blend until the mixture looks like fine bread crumbs. Add the sugar and blend for a few seconds. Mix the beaten egg with the cold water. Turn on the machine and pour the egg through the feed tube—after a couple of seconds the mixture will start to stick together in small lumps. Switch off the machine, tip the dough into a bowl and bring together gently into a ball. Wrap and chill for 30 minutes before use.

Stock Syrup

Makes 2$\frac{1}{2}$ cups

2$\frac{1}{2}$ cups water
1$\frac{1}{2}$ cups granulated sugar
•   Zest of 2 lemons
•   Zest of 2 small oranges
1   vanilla bean

This is useful for poaching fruit and can also be used in fruit salads and sorbets.

Put all the ingredients into a pan and leave over low heat until the sugar has completely dissolved. Bring to a boil, then remove from the heat and set aside for 30 minutes to allow the flavors to infuse. Lift out the zest and vanilla bean (you can rinse the vanilla bean, dry it and save it for later use). The syrup can be used immediately or stored in the refrigerator for up to 2 weeks.

Preserved Lemons

10 lemons
1$\frac{1}{4}$ cups salt
5   cups water

These can be used finely chopped in salads, dressings and sauces.

Cut the lemons almost into quarters, leaving them joined at one end. Sprinkle a little salt into the center of each, then arrange them, tightly packed, in a plastic or glass container. Bring the water and the rest of the salt to a boil in a large pan. Boil until the salt has dissolved, then remove from the heat and leave to cool. Pour the brine over the lemons, weigh them down with some sort of nonmetallic weight and leave for 3 to 4 weeks before using. They will keep indefinitely.

LISTING OF AMERICAN, AUSTRALIAN AND NEW ZEALAND FISH

The following list gives local names, where necessary, or suggests a similar fish as an alternative.

British Isles	USA	Australia and NZ
Anchovies	Anchovies	Anchovies
Brill	Petrale sole, brill sole	Sole, flounder, brill
Cod	Cod, Pacific cod	Blue cod
Coley	Haddock	Hoki
Conger eel	Conger eel	Blue grenadier, ribbon fish
Dover sole	English sole, gray sole	Sole, flounder
Flounder	Flounder	Flounder
Garfish	Skipper	Garfish
Grey mullet	Mullet, striped bass	Mullet
Gurnard	Searobin	Gurnard
Haddock	Haddock	Blue cod, hoki
Hake	Hake, silver hake	Hake, gemfish
Huss	Spurdog	Flake
John Dory	John Dory, Oreo Dory	John Dory
Lemon sole	English sole, flounder	Sole, flounder
Ling	Cusk, cobia	Ling
Mackerel	Atlantic mackerel	Mackerel, Spanish mackerel
Megrim sole	Flounder	Flounder
Monkfish	Monkfish, anglerfish	Monkfish, stargazer
Red bream	Red snapper	Snapper
Red mullet	Goatfish	Red mullet, barbounia
Salmon	Salmon	Atlantic salmon
Sardines	Sardines	Sardines, pilchards
Sea bass	Sea bass	Jewfish
Sea bream	Bream	Bream
Sea trout	Steelhead, sea trout	Ocean trout
Shark	Shark	Shark, flake
Skate	Skate	Skate
Snapper	Snapper	Snapper
Squid	Squid, calamari	Squid, calamari
Swordfish	Swordfish	Swordfish, broadbill
Tuna	Tuna	Tuna
Turbot	Turbot, flounder	Sole, John Dory, flounder

Shellfish		
Brown crab	Dungeness crab	Blue swimming crab
Clams	Hardshell clams	Clams
	Littleneck clams	Littleneck clams, pipi
	Cherrystone clams	Clams
Cockles	Cockles	Pipi, cockles
Crayfish, crawfish	Crayfish, spiny lobster	Yabbies, marron
Lobster	Lobster	Rock lobster
Mussels	Blue Mussels	Mussels
Oysters	Oysters	Oysters
Prawns	Shrimp	Prawn
Scallop	Sea scallop, bay scallop	Sea scallop, bay scallop
Spider crab	Snow crab	Blue swimming crab, salad crab
Spiny lobster	Spiny lobster, crawfish	Crayfish, spiny lobster

ALTERNATIVE FISH

This is a list of all the fish and shellfish in the book, giving an alternative to use if you can't get hold of the one in the recipe. The alternatives are not necessarily the most similar fish biologically but rather ones that work almost, if not equally, as well.

Conger eel: Shark, swordfish or tuna
Mackerel: Herring
Sardines: Smelt
Salmon: Large seatrout
Sea trout: Salmon or trout
John Dory: Turbot or brill
Ocean perch: Snapper
Sea bream: Bass or snapper
Mullet: Bass
Goatfish: Any of the bream family or sea bass
Sea bass: Goatfish
Cod: Haddock
Garfish: Searobin, English sole
Searobin: Sea bass
Monkfish: Grilled recipes – swordfish; others – turbot or John Dory
Haddock: Cod or hake
Hake: Haddock or cod

Ling: Monkfish
Shark: Tuna, swordfish or conger eel
Tuna: Swordfish or monkfish
English sole: Petrale sole, sand sole, lemon sole
Lemon sole: Flounder
Flounder: Lemon sole, sand dabs
Turbot: Brill, John Dory
Skate: Angel shark
Squid: Cuttlefish
Dungeness crab: Snow crab
Snow crab: Dungeness crab
Scallops: Slices of monkfish
Shrimp: Another species of shrimp
Clams: Cockles or mussels
Oysters: Mussels or clams
Lobster: Spiny lobster
Spiny lobster: Lobster

INDEX